PostgreSQL

Jeff Perkins

Premier
Press

Premier

Premier Press, is a regestered trademark of Premier Press, Press Inc., Indianapolis, Indiana 46204.

Linux is a registered trademark of Linus Torvalds. The Linux penguin, Tux, is used with permission from Larry Ewing (lewing@isc.tamu.edu). Ewing created this image using the GIMP (www.gimp.org). Modifications to Tux were made by Jim Thompson.

SQL and C are registered trademarks of Microsoft Corporation in the United States and other countries. The Open Source Initiative board has voted to certify the Python license as Open Source. Python was created by Guido van Rossum. PHPp was written by the PHP Development Team, and released under the GNU General Public License. Java is a trademark of Sun Microsystems, Inc.

All other trademarks are the property of their respective owners.

Important: Premier Press, Inc. cannot provide software support. Please contact the appropriate software manufacturer's technical support line or Web site for assistance.

Premier Press, Inc. and the author have attempted throughout this book to distinguish proprietary trademarks from descriptive terms by following the capitalization style used by the manufacturer.

Information contained in this book has been obtained by Premier Press, Inc. from sources believed to be reliable. However, because of the possibility of human or mechanical error by our sources, Premier Press, Inc., or others, the Publisher does not guarantee the accuracy, adequacy, or completeness of any information and is not responsible for any errors or omissions or the results obtained from use of such information. Readers should be particularly aware of the fact that the Internet is an ever-changing entity. Some facts may have changed since this book went to press.

ISBN: 1-931841-42-X

Library of Congress Catalog Card Number: 00-106668

Printed in the United States of America

01 02 03 04 RI 10 9 8 7 6 5 4 3 2 1

Publisher:
Stacy L. Hiquet

Associate Marketing Manager:
Heather Buzzingham

Managing Editor:
Sandy Doell

Acquisitions Editor:
Lynette Quinn

Project Editor:
Estelle Manticas

Technical Reviewer:
Dave Hannum

Copy Editor:
Kate Talbot

Interior Layout:
Scribe Tribe

Cover Design:
Mike Tanamachi

Indexer:
Sherry Massey

This book is dedicated to my father,
Chief Master Sergeant Alton Perkins,
United Stated Air Force, Retired.

Acknowledgments

Lynette Quinn has been my acquisitions editor for years; she is simply the best, combining high professional standards with an always-sunny personality. Thanks, Lynette. Thanks also to Julie Meloni for her excellent chapters on Perl and PHP for this book.

Jeff Perkins was born in Merced, California a long time ago. He graduated from the United States Air Force Academy and spent his first career as a B-52 bombardier, staff officer at Headquarters Strategic Air Command, project leader for a micro-computer based Mission Planning System, and finally, team leader for a B-52 planning team. His second career is as Senior Software Engineer at TYBRIN in Fort Walton Beach, Florida, where he works on projects for the Defense Department and the State of Florida.

He is married, has two wonderful children, and lives in the improbably named town of Niceville, Florida.

Contents

Chapter 3:
PostgreSQL Basic Security 41

Chapter 12:
Programming with C 205

Chapter 13:
Programming with Python 235

Part IV:
Advanced Topics

Chapter 17:
Advanced PostgreSQL Data Types

Chapter 18:
Inheritance and Advanced Arrays

The Open-Source movement has been one of the most interesting and potentially profitable evolutions of the computer world. Teams of volunteer programmers, building programs like the Apache Web server, the Linux operating system, and the PostgreSQL database have put world-class software into the hands of any developer with an Internet connection.

PostgreSQL is a client-server Relational Database Management System (RDBMS) based on the Structured Query Language (SQL) standard. Don't worry if you don't know what those terms mean—you will after reading this book. For those of you familiar with RDBMS and SQL, this book provides setup, administration, and coding examples to get you started building systems with PostgreSQL.

Who Should Read This Book?

This book is a basic look at PostgreSQL—its goal is just to get you up and running. This book doesn't dwell on theory—it takes you on an example-based trip through PostgreSQL.

This book is for you if

- you are a software developer and need a high-end relational database.
- you are new to databases and PostgreSQL is your first database.
- you are a student, and want to start learning about databases and database programming.
- you are a programmer looking for ways to use a relational database.

How This Book is Organized

Part I takes you step by step through the PostgreSQL installation process. Then Part II covers PostgreSQL administration—from security to administering PostgreSQL from a Microsoft Windows System. In Part III, Chapters 7 and 8 cover database design principles and the Structured Query Language (SQL). Chapter 9 describes the PostgreSQL data types and gives you your first taste of programming inside PostgreSQL, and Chapters 10 thru 16 cover different languages—including PL/PGSQL, Tcl, C, Python, Perl, Php, and Java—and their interfaces to PostgreSQL.

The final part, Part IV, covers PostgreSQL's advanced data types, including its library of graphic manipulation functions; PostgreSQL's use of the object oriented paradigm; and finally, some of the commercial aspects of PostgreSQL.

PART I
Installation

1 Setting Up PostgreSQL

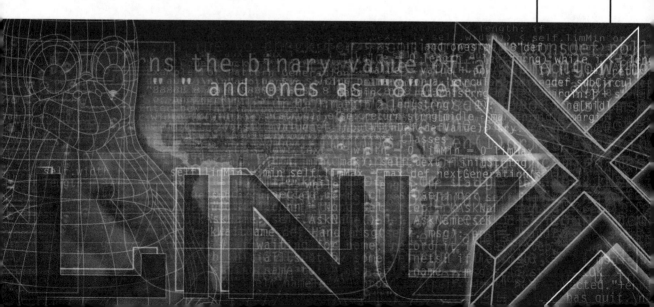

Chapter 1: Setting Up PostgreSQL

T he first step in setting up PostgreSQL is the most important. If you don't get the database set up or you lose data from a previous installation, you and those you work with will not be happy. In this chapter you'll learn how to install PostgreSQL on Red Hat from scratch, and how to use the Red Hat Package Manager. You'll also learn how to prepare your existing database for the transition to the latest version. Finally, you'll test your new installation.

Preparing Your Existing Database for Upgrade

The source for the most up-to-date PostgreSQL information is the PostgreSQL Web site at http://www.postgresql.org. This site contains the latest news, documentations, and links to software. Go to this site to find the most recent version of PostgreSQL.

To determine whether PostgreSQL is already loaded on your machine, type

```
ls - la /var/lib/postgresql
```

You have a version of PostgreSQL installed if your system returns the following:

```
drwxr-xr-x   3 postgres postgres    4096 Jul 16 22:50 ./
drwxr-xr-x  17 root     root        4096 Jun 29 04:02 ../
-rw------   1 postgres postgres       4 Jul 16 20:11 PG_VERSION
drwx------   4 postgres postgres    4096 Jul 16 23:38 base/
-rw-r--r--  1 postgres postgres     412 Jul 16 23:42 db.bak
-rw-r--r--  1 postgres postgres     228 Jul 16 22:58 db.out
-rw------   1 postgres postgres    8192 Jul 16 23:39 pg_database
-r--------  1 postgres postgres    3407 Jul 16 20:11 pg_geqo.sample
-rw------   1 postgres postgres       0 Jul 16 20:11 pg_group
-r--------  1 postgres postgres    5192 Jul 16 20:11 pg_hba.conf
-rw------   1 postgres postgres    8192 Jul 16 23:42 pg_log
-rw-rw-rw-  1 postgres postgres      52 Jul 16 20:11 pg_pwd
-rw------   1 postgres postgres    8192 Jul 16 20:11 pg_shadow
-rw------   1 postgres postgres    8192 Jul 16 23:42 pg_variable
```

If you don't have PostgreSQL installed, you do not have to prepare the database.

At this point in the chapter, I assume that you have a database installed or are reading this knowing that you might have to install a newer version of PostgreSQL at some point. To confirm the version of PostgreSQL you have installed, type

```
cat /usr/lib/pgsql/PG_VERSION
```

This will probably return something like the following:

```
6.5
```

Red Hat 6.x ships with the 6.5 database. As of this writing, the most current version of PostgreSQL is 7.x, and the examples in this book use this latest version, which has some fundamental changes from older versions.

One major change in version 7 is the directory structure. The directory structure you saw earlier is from a 6.x version of the database. The directory structure in 7.x looks like the following:

```
drwxr-xr-x    4 root     root          4096 Jul 17 12:16 .
drwxr-xr-x   11 root     root          4096 Jul 17 12:16 ..
drwx------    2 postgres postgres      4096 Jun 12 16:21 backups
drwx------    4 postgres postgres      4096 Jul 17 12:18 data
```

Notice that there is no PG_VERSION in the pgsql directory of version 7. The PG_VERSION in 7 is in the data directory. If you have version 7, there is no need to upgrade further to accomplish the examples in this book. You might want to keep reading, though, because you are about to learn how to back up your current database.

At the time of this writing, the most current rpm files install a file named README.rpm in the /usr/docs/postgresql7.x directory. README.rpm is not an rpm file but an ASCII text file containing, among other things, steps for using a script named Postgresql-dump to upgrade from previous versions. As the file notes, the script is still in a beta stage. The most straightforward way to upgrade is to back up your database, uninstall the present version, and then install the new version, as described in this section.

If you retain nothing else from this chapter, remember to back up your existing database before making changes. This is very important.

If you don't back up your data before upgrading your version of PostgreSQL and something goes wrong (who ever heard of something going wrong with a computer?) you will have lost your system's users, tables, functions, and data—in short, everything you have ever put in you PostgreSQL system.

I cover the backup utilities in detail in Chapter 4, "Interactive PostgreSQL Using PSQL," so don't worry about the details right now. Just log in or su to the postgres user prompt and type

```
pg_dumpall > PG6.5.bak
```

This creates a file named PG6.5.bak. Remember where you left it, because it is the key to re-creating your system on the new version. After you set up the database, you will use this file to re-create your database.

Uninstalling Previous Versions of PostgreSQL

Now uninstall your current version of PostgreSQL. Copy your backup file to some directory other than /var/lib/pgsql, because it can be erased in this process. I suggest that you put the file in your home directory.

From the command line, remove the packages one at a time. It will look like this:

```
[root@laura /root]# rpm -e postgresql-devel
[root@laura /root]# rpm -e postgresql-tk
[root@laura /root]# rpm -e postgresql-test
[root@laura /root]# rpm -e postgresql-tcl
[root@laura /root]# rpm -e postgresql-python
[root@laura /root]# rpm -e postgresql-perl
[root@laura /root]# rpm -e postgresql-odbc
[root@laura /root]# rpm -e postgresql-jdbc
[root@laura /root]# rpm -e postgresql-server
cannot remove /var/lib/pgsql/data - directory not empty
cannot remove /usr/lib/pgsql/backup - directory not empty
[root@laura /root]# rpm -e postgresql
```

Note that the rpm program tried to remove the /var/lib/pgsql/data and the /usr/lib/pgsql/backup directories. This is why you need to copy your backup file to a directory not involved with the PostgreSQL installation directories. You are now ready to install your version 7 database.

Setup in Red Hat Using the Red Hat Package

You can go to the PostgreSQL Web site, at www.postgresql.org, to find the latest version. Take a look at the files available for installation. The minor version numbers, such as .0.2, and the release number, such as -2, might change as bugs are worked out of the release.

The rpm files you can install are

- **Postgresql-7.0.2-2.i386.rpm**. This is the basic PostgreSQL database package. Installing this package provides all the programs and documentation required to run PostgreSQL as a stand-alone database.

- **Postgresql-server-7.0.2-2.i386.rpm**. This package includes the programs and documentation required to run PostgreSQL as a client server database.

- **Postgresql-test-7.0.2-2.i386.rpm**. The Test rpm installs programs for testing and benchmarking PostgreSQL after you have it installed.

- **Postgresql-tk-7.0.2-2.i386.rpm**. The TK rpm provides a graphic interface to PostgreSQL, named pgaccess. Pgaccess is discussed in Chapter 4.

- **Postgresql-perl-7.0.2-2.i386.rpm.** Hooks into the PostgreSQL database using the Practical Extraction and Report Language (*Perl*) are delivered by this rpm. Chapter 15, "Programming with Perl," covers using Perl to manipulate PostgreSQL.

- **Postgresql-tcl-7.0.2-2.i386.rpm.** This rpm contains libraries that enable the Tool Command Language (*TCL*) to access data in the PostgreSQL database. See Chapter 11, "Programming with PL/Tcl and Tcl," for details.

- **Postgresql-python-7.0.2-2.i386.rpm.** This rpm contains the files necessary to manipulate the PostgreSQL database from the Python programming language. Chapter 13, "Programming with Python," is where you can learn about Python's capabilities within PostgreSQL.

- **Postgresql-devel-7.0.2-2.i386.rpm.** This package holds the files necessary to connect C and C++ programs with data in PostgreSQL, discussed in detail in Chapter 12, "Programming with C."

- **Postgresql-jdbc-7.0.2-2.i386.rpm.** The Java Database Connectivity (*JDBC*) components are in this rpm. Using these components to connect PostgreSQL is covered in Chapter 16, "Programming with Java."

- **Postgresql-odbc-7.0.2-2.i386.rpm.** This rpm contains all the necessary files to allow an Open Database Connectivity–aware application, such as Applix, to use data in a PostgreSQL database.

You can either install or upgrade using these rpms. An install will put the rpm in the system separate from any previous installations, and an upgrade will replace any previous installations. Because you have deleted the existing database, you will perform an install, not an upgrade. (An upgrade will behave the same way as an install if there are no previous versions.) Run the following as root from the directory containing your rpm files:

```
rpm -ivh postgres*.rpm
```

Your system will return the following:

```
postgresql                    ################################################
postgresql-devel              ################################################
postgresql-jdbc               ################################################
postgresql-odbc               ################################################
postgresql-perl               ################################################
postgresql-python             ################################################
postgresql-server             ################################################
cannot remove /var/lib/pgsql - directory not empty
postgresql-tcl                ################################################
postgresql-test               ################################################
postgresql-tk                 ################################################
```

Note that the script again tried to delete /var/lib/pgsql. Now start up your new database. As root, type

```
[root@laura /root]# /etc/rc.d/init.d/postgresql start
```

The system will respond:

```
Checking postgresql installation: no database files found.
This database system will be initialized with username "postgres".
This user will own all the data files and must also own the server process.


Fixing permissions on pre-existing data directory /var/lib/pgsql/data
Creating database system directory /var/lib/pgsql/data/base
Creating database XLOG directory /var/lib/pgsql/data/pg_xlog
Creating template database in /var/lib/pgsql/data/base/template1
Creating global relations in /var/lib/pgsql/data/base
Adding template1 database to pg_database


Creating view pg_user.
Creating view pg_rules.
Creating view pg_views.
Creating view pg_tables.
Creating view pg_indexes.
Loading pg_description.
Vacuuming database.


Success. You can now start the database server using:
        /usr/bin/postmaster -D /var/lib/pgsql/data
```

or

```
        /usr/bin/pg_ctl -D /var/lib/pgsql/data start
Postmaster already running.
```

Congratulations! You have your PostgreSQL database running. Before going on to basic configuration and testing, you will see how to install PostgreSQL without using rpm.

Setup Using PostgreSQL Archive Files

The PostgreSQL database can also be installed using archive files. The following listing shows the files available via the http://www.postgresql.org site:

```
06/05/2000 12:17PM       2,338,356 postgresql-7.0.2.base.tar.92
06/05/2000 12:17PM              70 postgresql-7.0.2.base.tar.92
06/05/2000 12:16PM       2,545,529 postgresql-7.0.2.base.tar.92
06/05/2000 12:17PM              70 postgresql-7.0.2.base.tar.92
06/05/2000 12:17PM       1,322,640 postgresql-7.0.2.base.tar.92
06/05/2000 12:17PM              73 postgresql-7.0.2.base.tar.92
06/05/2000 12:16PM       7,211,311 postgresql-7.0.2.base.tar.92
06/05/2000 12:17PM              65 postgresql-7.0.2.base.tar.92
06/05/2000 12:17PM       1,006,213 postgresql-7.0.2.base.tar.92
06/05/2000 12:17PM              70 postgresql-7.0.2.base.tar.92
```

You are interested in the files that end in *gz*. These are gziped files. The files that end in *md5* are security and checksum files; you won't worry about them in this book. The postgresql-7.0.2.tar.gz file at about 7MB contains everything you need. For easier downloads, the PostgreSQL file is broken down into a docs file, a support file containing interfaces and libraries, a test file containing the regression test set, and a base file with everything else. If you have a slow or intermittent Internet connection, you might want to download the smaller chunks and reassemble them on your machine. Either way, your installation will go something like the following.

1. First, back up any existing data using the pg_dumpall program, and put that backup file somewhere safe. You will get back to it, I promise.

2. Second, uninstall any previous versions of PostgreSQL. This might involve using rpm files, as in the preceding section, or it might be more of a brute-force, delete kind of thing. Consult the documentation of the version you are running for de-installation. If there are no instructions, consider staying with the version you have, or back up your data and delete the /usr/lib/pgsql and /var/lib/pgsql directories after you have put your backup in another directory.

3. Now, cd as root to the directory where the gzip files are located. You will use the single large file, PostgreSQL, for this example. If you are using the smaller files, you will repeat the unzipping part of these directions for each file. Type

```
[root@rex postgresql]# gunzip postgresql-7.0.2.tar.gz
```

Follow this with

```
[root@rex postgresql]# tar -xf postgresql-7.0.2.tar
```

Finally, type

```
[root@rex postgresql]# mv postgresql-7.0.2 /usr/src
```

What you have done here is unpack all the source files and move them to the /usr/src directory. Next, check for the tools you need. Type

```
gmake --version
```

If you have the gmake tool, this will return

```
GNU Make version 3.77, by Richard Stallman and Roland McGrath.
Copyright (C) 1988, 89, 90, 91, 92, 93, 94, 95, 96, 97, 98
        Free Software Foundation, Inc.
This is free software; see the source for copying conditions.
There is NO warranty; not even for MERCHANTABILITY or FITNESS FOR A
PARTICULAR PURPOSE.


Report bugs to <bug-make@gnu.org>.
```

If you don't have gmake, get it from ftp://ftp.gnu.org. This is a site most developers bookmark as the source of industry standard, open-source tools and projects. Don't get me started on how good this site is! Just go there if you haven't already been.

Anyway, now that you have gmake, check whether you have enough disk space to install PostgreSQL. It has a small footprint—8MB of RAM and about 50MB of disk space—if you intend to do the regression tests (which you do).

Assuming that you have met these minimums, the next step is to create a postgres user account.

Creating a postgres User Account

PostgreSQL is set up not to run on root or other superuser accounts. The default owner for its administrative functions is postgres.

Create a postgres user account by typing

```
adduser postgres
```

Then add a password for postgres:

```
[root@rex postgresql]# passwd postgres
Changing password for user postgres
New UNIX password:
Retype new UNIX password:
passwd: all authentication tokens updated successfully
```

Change the directory to /usr/src/postgresql-7.0.2/src, and as root, type

```
./configure -help
```

This will return

```
[root@rex src]# ./configure --help
Usage: configure [options] [host]
Options: [defaults in brackets after descriptions]
Configuration:
  --cache-file=FILE       cache test results in FILE
  --help                  print this message
  --no-create             do not create output files
  --quiet, --silent       do not print 'checking...' messages
  --version               print the version of autoconf that created configure
...
  --with-pgport=PORTNUM   change default postmaster port
  --with-maxbackends=N    set default maximum number of server processes
  --with-tcl              build Tcl interfaces and pgtclsh
  --with-tclconfig=DIR    tclConfig.sh and tkConfig.sh are in DIR
  --with-tkconfig=DIR     tkConfig.sh is in DIR
  --with-perl             build Perl interface and plperl
  --with-odbc             build ODBC driver package
...
```

This listing is quite long. It has been edited to leave some of the more interesting bits.

Now you will configure by typing

```
./configure --with-tcl --with-perl
```

This script will create quite a few pages of data while it tests the system for various resources; this will take a couple of minutes. The script ends by creating and linking various make files. On my machine, the last lines look like this:

```
...
creating interfaces/odbc/Makefile.global
creating pl/plpgsql/src/Makefile
creating pl/plpgsql/src/mklang.sql
creating pl/tcl/mkMakefile.tcldefs.sh
creating test/regress/GNUmakefile
creating include/config.h
linking ./backend/port/dynloader/linux.c to backend/port/dynloader.c
linking ./backend/port/dynloader/linux.h to include/dynloader.h
linking ./include/port/linux.h to include/os.h
linking ./makefiles/Makefile.linux to Makefile.port
linking ./backend/port/tas/dummy.s to backend/port/tas.s
linking ./include/port to interfaces/odbc/port
linking ./makefiles to interfaces/odbc/makefiles
linking ./template to interfaces/odbc/template
linking ./include/config.h to interfaces/odbc/config.h
```

Now you create a make file by typing

```
gmake
```

You will see a seemingly endless stream of calls to the gcc compiler. Finally, after about 20 minutes of compiling, you will see this:

```
gmake[2]: Leaving directory '/usr/src/postgresql-7.0.2/src/pl/tcl'
gmake[1]: Leaving directory '/usr/src/postgresql-7.0.2/src/pl'
All of PostgreSQL is successfully made. Ready to install.
```

At Last, the Install

Okay, you're almost home. Install PostgreSQL by typing

```
gmake install
```

This ends with some contact information:

```
(2000-06-05)
PostgreSQL has a Web site at http://www.postgresql.org/ that carries details
on the latest release, upcoming features, and other information to make your
work or play with PostgreSQL more productive.
Please check the following URL for a listing of the current user-support
```

```
mailing lists:

        http://www.postgresql.org -> Info Central -> Mailing Lists
All of the mailing lists are currently archived and viewable at
        http://www.postgresql.org -> Info Central -> Mailing Lists
And, so that we have an idea of who is using what, please connect to the
following registration URL:
        http://www.postgresql.org -> Helping Us -> Survey/Register
Thank you for choosing PostgreSQL, the most advanced open source database
engine.
```

Take a look at what you have before starting it up. Remember that with the rpm install, most of the files went into two places: /var/lib/pgsql and usr/lib/pgsql. Also, while you weren't looking, the rpm install put the PostgreSQL administration and control programs into /usr/bin. This manual install put the files into /usr/local/pgsql. To change this, use the configuration options discussed at the beginning of this section.

Starting PostgreSQL and Creating a Database

The manual install doesn't provide /etc/rc.d/init.d/postgresql start, so I'll give you some alternatives. Here is a simple command line for starting up:

```
/usr/local/pgsql/bin/postmaster -D /usr/local/pgsql/data
```

The −D option is the data directory, which you haven't defined yet. Because creating an initial database requires a directory for files, create one by typing the following as the root user:

```
mkdir /usr/local/pgsql/data
```

Then, hand over ownership to your postgres account:

```
chown postgres /usr/local/pgsql/data
```

Now, change into postgres, and create the default database:

```
su - postgres
/usr/local/pgsql/bin/initdb -D /usr/local/pgsql/data
```

This returns the following segment, which is similar to what you saw at this same stage with the rpm files. In the case of the rpm's, the initdb process was kicked off automatically by the /etc/rc.d/init.d/postgresql start command.

```
This database system will be initialized with username "postgres".
This user will own all the data files and must also own the server process.
```

```
Fixing permissions on pre-existing data directory /usr/local/pgsql/data
Creating database system directory /usr/local/pgsql/data/base
Creating database XLOG directory /usr/local/pgsql/data/pg_xlog
Creating template database in /usr/local/pgsql/data/base/template1
Creating global relations in /usr/local/pgsql/data/base
Adding template1 database to pg_database
Creating view pg_user.
Creating view pg_rules.
Creating view pg_views.
Creating view pg_tables.
Creating view pg_indexes.
Loading pg_description.
Vacuuming database.
Success. You can now start the database server using
        /usr/local/pgsql/bin/postmaster -D /usr/local/pgsql/data
or
        /usr/local/pgsql/bin/pg_ctl -D /usr/local/pgsql/data start
```

Now that you have a database, start the server:

```
/usr/local/pgsql/bin/postmaster -D /usr/local/pgsql/data&
```

As it starts running PostgreSQL as a background process, this returns

```
[1] 19979
[postgres@rex pgsql]$ DEBUG:  Data Base System is starting up at Mon Jul 17 12:4
7:11 2000
DEBUG:  Data Base System was shut down at Mon Jul 17 12:47:07 2000
DEBUG:  Data Base System is in production state at Mon Jul 17 12:47:11 2000
```

There are just a few more tasks in this manual process before you can rejoin the rpm readers. cd into the /home/postgres directory and modify the .bash profile_user to look something like the following:

```
# .bash_profile

# Get the aliases and functions
if [ -f ~/.bashrc ]; then
        . ~/.bashrc
fi
# User-specific environment and startup programs
PATH=$PATH:$HOME/bin/:/usr/local/pgsql/bin
BASH_ENV=$HOME/.bashrc
```

```
USERNAME=""
LD_LIBRARY_PATH=/usr/local/pgsql/lib
export USERNAME BASH_ENV PATH LD_LIBRARY_PATH

#start up the postgres database
/usr/local/pgsql/bin/postmaster -D /usr/local/pgsql/data &
```

This was modified from the original in four places. The path /usr/local/pgsql/bin was added to `PATH`. The line `LD_LIBRARY_PATH=/usr/local/pgsql/lib` was added. `LD_LIBRARY_PATH` was added to the exports. And the line `/usr/local/pgsql/bin/post-master...` was added to the end of the file. The net result is that whenever you log in as postgres, the database will start. Some improvements, depending on your needs, would be to grep the stream from ps on entry and to bring up the server only if it is not already up. I would suggest looking at the PostgreSQL file that the rpm file puts in the /etc/rc.d/init.d/ directory and building something like that for your unique requirements.

> As more users are added to this configuration using the createuser program described in Chapter 2, their `.bash_profiles` (or whatever file controls their shell) will have to be changed to add the `PATH` and `LD_LIBRARY_PATH` data.

Loading the Data from the Old Version of PostgreSQL

At this point, both the rpm and the manual install groups are at the same point. Now is the time to remember where you put that backup file you made at the beginning of the chapter. (You know, the one you named PG6.5.bak.)

Okay, before you bring in the old data, it would be prudent to dump your current configuration. As postgres, type

```
pg_dumpall > todays.bak
```

Now, given that I saved my backup in my home directory,

```
psql -d template1 -f ~/PG6.5.bak
```

This results in the following:

```
You are now connected to database template1.
SELECT
DELETE 1
DROP
```

```
You are now connected to database template1 as user postgres.
CREATE DATABASE
You are now connected to database postgres as user postgres.
You are now connected as new user postgres.
CREATE
You are now connected to database template1 as user perkins.
CREATE DATABASE
You are now connected to database perkins as user perkins.
You are now connected as new user perkins.
CREATE
```

And the data is restored! You have already seen that your installations are running. PostgreSQL comes with a set of regression tests that give the system a real workout.

Testing the Setup

PostgreSQL comes with its own suite of test programs. To run them, start the database and su in as postgres. Run this command:

```
cd /usr/lib/pgsql/test/regress (for rpm)
```

Then type this line:

```
time ./regress.sh linux | tee regress.out
```

Here are the results for my Red Hat 6.2 setup using PostgreSQL 7.02:

```
[postgres@alton postgres]$ cd /usr/lib/pgsql/test/regress
[postgres@alton regress]$ time ./regress.sh linux | tee regress.out
=============== Notes...                     ==================
postmaster must already be running for the regression tests to succeed.
The time zone is set to PST8PDT for these tests by the client frontend.
Please report any apparent problems to ports@postgresql.org
See regress/README for more information.


=============== dropping old regression database...   ==================
ERROR:  DROP DATABASE: Database "regression" does not exist
dropdb: database removal failed
=============== creating new regression database...   ==================
CREATE DATABASE
=============== installing languages...       ==================
installing PL/pgSQL .. ok
=============== running regression queries...         ==================
```

```
boolean .. ok
char .. ok
name .. ok
varchar .. ok
text .. ok
int2 .. ok
int4 .. ok
…
4.03user 3.51system 4:41.66elapsed 2%CPU (0avgtext+0avgdata 0maxresident)k
0inputs+0outputs (46065major+22276minor)pagefaults 0swaps
```

This listing is an abbreviated version of the result file. Don't worry about those tests now—it is not likely that the functions they cover will affect your daily operations. The important thing to remember is that after an installation you can run tests that show with some precision how PostgreSQL interfaces with a particular hardware setup.

If you have manually installed PostgreSQL and want to test it, you can run the same tests out of the /usr/src/postgresql-7.0.2/src/test/regress directory

---

Creating Your First Database

Before wrapping up this chapter, you must create the account you will use for the rest of the examples in this book. To create a new user, go in as postgres and type

```
[postgres@alton sql]$ createuser perkins
```

This will return

```
Shall the new user be allowed to create databases? (y/n) y
Shall the new user be allowed to create more new users? (y/n) y
CREATE USER
```

Then su to your new user, and create a new database by typing

```
su - perkins
createdb
```

This returns

```
CREATE DATABASE
```

You are now ready for the rest of the examples in the book.

Summary

You have covered a lot of ground in this chapter— where to get the installation files, which files to install, how to install them, and, finally, how to test the installation after it is running. It is important that you understand the basics of setting up and running a database. Knowing these basics will make you a better developer.

As the chapter demonstrates, much more effort and expertise are required in a manual setup. If you are new to Linux and/or PostgreSQL, I recommend using an rpm-based version of Linux, such as Red Hat or Mandrake. By using rpm files, you can focus on learning the new stuff, such as finding your way around the system or interacting with the database. If you are an experienced Linux system operator, you will manually configure the system the way you want it and focus on the database. In the next chapter you will learn how to secure your database.

PART II

Administration

Chapter 2: PostgreSQL Administrative Programs

Administering PostgreSQL

In this chapter, I'll cover the administrative programs native to PostgreSQL. These programs enable you to create and destroy users and databases, back up and restore data, and clean up.

Using createdb to Create a Database

The fundamental function of any database system is creation. PostgreSQL uses the program createdb to create databases. All of PostgreSQL's administrative programs use the -help flag to print out an overview.

Type **createdb -help**. You should see

```
[perkins@laura perkins]$ createdb --help
createdb creates a PostgreSQL database.


Usage:
  createdb [options] dbname [description]


Options:
  -D, --location=PATH          Alternative place to store the database
  -E, --encoding=ENCODING      Multibyte encoding for the database
  -h, --host=HOSTNAME          Database server host
  -p, --port=PORT              Database server port
  -U, --username=USERNAME      Username to connect as
  -W, --password               Prompt for password
  -e, --echo                   Show the query being sent to the backend
  -q, --quiet                  Don't write any messages
```

Frequently Used Options

If you are like me and try things before reading about them, go ahead and type in **createdb**. You will get something like this:

```
[perkins@laura perkins]$ createdb
ERROR:  CREATE DATABASE: database "perkins" already exists
createdb: database creation failed
```

Used without any arguments, createdb tries to create a database with the user's name on the local machine, if the user who invoked createdb has create database privileges. (See "createuser," later in this chapter for user creation details, or go there now if you want to). To create a database on the local machine with the database name *newbie01*, type `createdb newbie01`. You will get

```
[perkins@laura perkins]$ createdb newbie01
CREATE DATABASE
```

Not a very exciting response, but effective. To create a database on a different machine, use the -h and -p switches, the -h to set the host name and -p for the port, as in

```
[perkins@laura perkins]$ createdb -h laura.perkinsfamily -p 5432 newbie03
CREATE DATABASE
```

The default port for PostgreSQL is 5432 (which you can find in the /etc/services file). If PostgreSQL is using the default port, you can write

```
[perkins@laura perkins]$ createdb -h laura.perkinsfamily -p 5432 newbie03
CREATE DATABASE
```

If PostgreSQL has been set up to require a password, you will see

```
[perkins@laura perkins]$ createdb -h laura.perkinsfamily  newbie05
Password:
CREATE DATABASE
```

Should you ever feel the need to be prompted for your password, use the -W option, which looks like this:

```
[perkins@laura perkins]$ createdb -h laura.perkinsfamily  -W newbie06
Password:
CREATE DATABASE
```

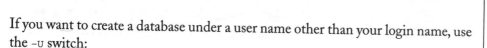

The IP address from which you are calling and any required passwords must be mentioned in the pg_hba.conf file, usually found in the /var/lib/pgsql/data/ directory. See Chapter 3, "PostgreSQL Basic Security," for details. The default security settings do not allow you to create a database from an external IP address.

If you want to create a database under a user name other than your login name, use the -U switch:

```
[perkins@laura perkins]$ createdb -U otheruser newbie07
CREATE DATABASE
```

Infrequently Used Options

The -e switch echoes the command sent to the database, but doesn't provide much new information, as is shown by typing `createdb -e newbie02`:

```
[perkins@laura perkins]$ createdb -e newbie02
CREATE DATABASE "newbie02"
CREATE DATABASE
```

Conversely, the -q switch causes output to be suppressed

```
[perkins@laura perkins]$ createdb -q newbie08
```

The -D switch specifies where this instance of PostgreSQL keeps the tables used to create a database, not where data for the created database will be stored. If the data directory was not set up to use the default location, you will need to know that location and use it behind the -D switch to create a database. This is a good argument for using the default location during PostgreSQL setup.

The -E switch, used for encoding the database, is used when ASCII text, the default encoding method, won't handle the language you need to put in your database. Valid values for -E appear in Table 2.1.

Table 2.1   Valid Values for the -E Switch

Abbreviation	Encoding Types
SQL_ASCII	ASCII
EUC_JP	Japanese EUC
EUC_CN	Chinese EUC
EUC_KR	Korean EUC
EUC_TW	Taiwan EUC
UNICODE	Unicode(UTF-8)
MULE_INTERNAL	Mule internal
LATIN1	ISO 8859-1 English and some European languages
LATIN2	ISO 8859-2 English and some European languages
LATIN3	ISO 8859-3 English and some European languages
LATIN4	ISO 8859-4 English and some European languages
LATIN5	ISO 8859-5 English and some European languages
KOI8	KOI8-R
WIN	Windows CP1251
ALT	Windows CP866

Encoding is an advanced topic, and is beyond the scope of a book concerned with building a foundation for the use of PostgreSQL. If you must use encoding or just want to know more about it, a starting point is the README.mb file, authored by Pavel Behal and edited by Tatsuo Ishii, in the /usr/doc/postgresql-7.x.x directory.

createlang

The createlang program enables you to add languages to the database. These languages are used to program database functions and triggers. Being able to use a language other than SQL for programming functions and triggers allows you to use the strengths of that language to solve your problems. Use the -help switch to see what createlang has to offer.

```
[perkins@laura perkins]$ createlang --help
createlang installs a procedural language into a PostgreSQL database.


Usage:
  createlang [options] [langname [dbname]]


Options:
  -h, --host=HOSTNAME          Database server host
  -p, --port=PORT              Database server port
  -U, --username=USERNAME      Username to connect as
  -W, --password               Prompt for password
  -d, --dbname=DBNAME          Database to install language in
  -L, --pglib=PGLIB            Find language interpreter in directory PGLIB
  -l, --list                   Show a list of currently installed languages
```

Frequently Used Options

The -h, -p, -U, and -W switches operate exactly the same way as their counterparts in createdb. The -l function shows you which languages have been installed by createlang in your database.

```
[perkins@laura perkins]$ createlang -l perkins
    Procedural languages
 Name | Trusted? | Compiler
------+----------+----------
(0 rows)
```

This is a little misleading because your database is created with both the SQL and C languages installed. These show up in a table named `pg_languages`. Type the following:

```
[perkins@laura perkins]$ psql -c "select * from pg_language";
 lanname | lanispl | lanpltrusted | lanplcallfoid | lancompiler
---------+---------+--------------+---------------+------------
 internal | f       | f            |             0 | n/a
 C        | f       | f            |             0 | /bin/cc
 sql      | f       | f            |             0 | postgres
(3 rows)
```

Here you see an internal language (which you cannot use and will thus ignore), SQL (covered in Chapter 8, "Basic SQL"), and C (covered in Chapter 12, "Programming with C"). The normal PostgreSQL installation sets up but does not install two other languages: PL/PGSQL (covered in Chapter 10, "Programming with PL/PGSQL") and Tk/Tcl (Chapter 11, "Programming with PL/Tcl and Tcl"). The directory /usr/lib/pgsql contains two shared objects, `pltcl.so` and `plpgsql.so`, that are used to install these languages. Other languages can be installed, but the process of creating shared objects to implement different languages, as outlined on the PostgreSQL Web site, is very involved and beyond the scope of this book. You will install the following two languages:

```
[perkins@laura perkins]$ createlang -L /usr/lib/pgsql plpgsql perkins
[perkins@laura perkins]$ createlang -L /usr/lib/pgsql pltcl perkins
```

Notice how the `-L` switch is used to specify the location of the shared objects. Now, check your work:

```
[perkins@laura perkins]$ createlang -l perkins
    Procedural languages
 Name    | Trusted? | Compiler
---------+----------+----------
 plpgsql | t        | PL/pgSQL
 pltcl   | t        | PL/Tcl
(2 rows)
```

Infrequently Used Options

None.

createuser

After the database is set up, the next thing you need to do is create some users. Type **createuser -help** to see the options for createuser:

```
[perkins@laura perkins]$ createuser --help
createuser creates a new PostgreSQL user.


Usage:
  createuser [options] [username]


Options:
  -d, --createdb                User can create new databases
  -D, --no-createdb             User cannot create databases
  -a, --adduser                 User can add new users
  -A, --no-adduser              User cannot add new users
  -i, --sysid=SYSID             Select sysid for new user
  -P, --pwprompt                Assign a password to new user
  -h, --host=HOSTNAME           Database server host
  -p, --port=PORT               Database server port
  -U, --username=USERNAME       Username to connect as (not the one to create)
  -W, --password                Prompt for password to connect
  -e, --echo                    Show the query being sent to the backend
  -q, --quiet                   Don't write any messages
```

Frequently Used Options

The switches -h, -p, -w, and -u (host, port, prompt for password, and connect as user) work the same as the corresponding switches described in createdb. The basic form of createuser is

```
[perkins@laura perkins]$ createuser
Enter name of user to add: newuser01
Shall the new user be allowed to create databases? (y/n) n
Shall the new user be allowed to create more new users? (y/n) n
CREATE USER
```

After naming the user, you are given the options of allowing the user to create databases and to create more users. To create a user from the command line with both create user and create database capabilities, use the -a (add user) and -d (create database) switches:

```
[perkins@laura perkins]$ createuser -a -d newuser02
CREATE USER
```

The -A (no add user) and -D (no create database) switches have the opposite effect:

```
[perkins@laura perkins]$ createuser -A -D newuser03
CREATE USER
```

To create a user with a password, use the -P switch:

```
 [perkins@laura perkins]$ createuser -P newuser04
Enter password for user "newuser04":
Enter it again:
Shall the new user be allowed to create databases? (y/n) y
Shall the new user be allowed to create more new users? (y/n) n
CREATE USER
```

Infrequently Used Options

The -e switch shows you the query sent to the database and is the default setting. The -q option turns off the messages.

If your passion is system administration, you can use the -I option to specify the system id for the new user instead of having the system pick one for you.

dropdb

That's it for the create functions. Each create function has a corresponding delete function. To see the options for deleting a database, type **dropdb -help**. You should see:

```
[perkins@laura perkins]$ dropdb --help
dropdb removes a PostgreSQL database.

Usage:
  dropdb [options] dbname

Options:
  -h, --host=HOSTNAME          Database server host
  -p, --port=PORT              Database server port
  -U, --username=USERNAME      Username to connect as
  -W, --password               Prompt for password
  -i, --interactive            Prompt before deleting anything
  -e, --echo                   Show the query being sent to the backend
  -q, --quiet                  Don't write any messages
```

Frequently Used Options

The switches -h, -p, -W, and -U (host, port, prompt for password, and connect as user) work the same as the corresponding switches described in createdb.

To drop a database, type

```
[perkins@laura perkins]$ dropdb newbie08
DROP DATABASE
```

And the database will be gone—nifty if you intended to delete the database, but if you accidentally typed in the wrong database name you may experience feelings of unhappiness or even abject terror when you realize that it is gone for good. But of course you recently ran one of the dump commands (discussed later in this chapter) to back up your data, right?

To get a final chance to consider your actions before deleting, use the -i switch:

```
[perkins@laura perkins]$ dropdb -i newbie07
Database "newbie07" will be permanently deleted.
Are you sure? (y/n) y
DROP DATABASE
```

Without the -i switch all deletions are final.

Infrequently Used Options

The -e switch shows you the query sent to the database and is the default setting. The -q option turns off the messages.

droplang

If you need to drop a language from your PostgreSQL system, use the droplang program.

```
Usage:
  droplang [options] [langname [dbname]]


Options:
  -h, --host=HOSTNAME          Database server host
  -p, --port=PORT              Database server port
  -U, --username=USERNAME      Username to connect as
  -W, --password               Prompt for password
  -d, --dbname=DBNAME          Database to remove language from
  -l, --list                   Show a list of currently installed languages
```

Frequently Used Options

The switches -h, -p, -W, and -U (host, port, prompt for password, and connect as user) work the same as the corresponding switches described in createdb.

One switch not seen in the other delete, -l, allows you to see a list of the currently installed languages:

```
[perkins@laura perkins]$ droplang -l
     Procedural languages
  Name   | Trusted? | Compiler
--------+----------+----------
 plpgsql | t        | PL/pgSQL
 pltcl   | t        | PL/Tcl
(2 rows)
```

To delete the pltcl languages, type

```
[perkins@laura perkins]$ droplang -l
     Procedural languages
  Name   | Trusted? | Compiler
--------+----------+----------
 plpgsql | t        | PL/pgSQL
 pltcl   | t        | PL/Tcl
(2 rows)
```

Notice that the database name is specified. The droplang function doesn't assume the default database, unlike the most of the other administrative functions.

Infrequently Used Options

None.

dropuser

Tired of a user? Drop him or her using the dropuser command with the options shown by the dropuser -help command:

```
[perkins@laura perkins]$ dropuser --help
dropuser removes a PostgreSQL user.

Usage:
  dropuser [options] [username]

Options:
```

```
-h, --host=HOSTNAME              Database server host
-p, --port=PORT                 Database server port
-U, --username=USERNAME         Username to connect as (not the one to drop)
-W, --password                  Prompt for password to connect
-i, --interactive               Prompt before deleting anything
-e, --echo                      Show the query being sent to the backend
-q, --quiet                     Don't write any messages
```

Frequently Used Options

The switches -h, -p, -W, and -U (host, port, prompt for password, and connect as user) work the same as the corresponding switches described in createdb.

To drop a user, type

```
[perkins@laura perkins]$ dropuser newuser04
DROP USER
```

Like with deletedb, there is a -I switch to give you some time to consider your decision:

```
[perkins@laura perkins]$ dropuser -i newuser03
User "newuser03" will be permanently deleted.
Are you sure? (y/n) y
DROP USER
```

Infrequently Used Options

The -e switch shows you the query sent to the database and is the default setting. The -q option turns off the messages.

pg_ctl

The pg_ctl program controls the PostgreSQL database. If you installed PostgreSQL using the Red Hat Package Manager as described in Chapter 1, you might never use this command directly. To see the options for pg_ctl, use the -help switch:

```
[perkins@laura perkins]$ pg_ctl --help
Usage: pg_ctl [-w][-D database_dir][-p path_to_postmaster][-o "postmaster_opts"]
 start
        pg_ctl [-w][-D database_dir][-m s[mart]|f[ast]|i[mmediate]] stop
        pg_ctl [-w][-D database_dir][-m s[mart]|f[ast]|i[mmediate]][-o "postmaste
r_opts"] restart
        pg_ctl [-D database_dir] status
```

Frequently Used Options

The reason you might never use this program if you installed using Red Hat Package Manager(RPM) is the PostgreSQL script install in /etc/rc.d/init.d by the rpm. As discussed in Chapter 1, you can launch the PostgreSQL database using the /etc/rc.d/init.d/postgresql start command. The PostgreSQL script contains the pg_ctl program. Here is an excerpt from the start case of the script:

```
echo -n "Starting postgresql service: "
            su -l postgres -c "/usr/bin/pg_ctl  -D $PGDATA -p /usr/bin/postmaster
start >/dev/null 2>&1"
```

Notice how the `pg_ctl` command is run by the postgres user and how the –D switch is used to designate the PGDATA directory (PGDATA is defined earlier in the script). The –p option is the path and name of the postmaster program. Finally, the `start` option is used to start the database.

The PostgreSQL script collects the `pid` of the postmaster when it comes up, and it uses the `pid` to shut down the postmaster, as shown in the following excerpt from the stop case:

```
stop)
        echo -n "Stopping postgresql service: "
        killproc postmaster
        sleep 2
        rm -f /var/run/postmaster.pid
        rm -f /var/lock/subsys/postgresql
        echo
        ;;
```

This is an okay way to stop if you want to disconnect all your users. The pg_ctl program has a `stop` command, which has the –m switch. The –m switch will have one of three values: s (smart), f (fast), and I (immediate). The default value, s (smart), won't shut down the database until all the users have logged out. The f (fast) value will cause all the active database transitions to be rolled back, meaning that any work users haven't committed will be lost. The last value, I, causes an immediate shutdown and will cause the database to rebuild itself when it is restarted. The `stop` command works only if you have started the database using the following:

```
[postgres@laura postgres]$ pg_ctl start -D /var/lib/pgsql/data -p /usr/bin/
postmaster
postmaster successfully started up.
[postgres@laura postgres]$ 000912.02:01:10.076  [1869] DEBUG:  Data Base System
```

```
is starting up at Tue Sep 12 02:01:10 2000
000912.02:01:10.077  [1869] DEBUG:   Data Base System was shut down at Tue Sep 12
 02:01:07 2000
000912.02:01:10.083  [1869] DEBUG:   Data Base System is in production state at
 Tue Sep 12 02:01:10 2000
```

Notice all of the debug lines. I will discuss how to control the quantity of debug lines in a moment. To stop the server, type

```
[postgres@laura postgres]$ pg_ctl stop -D /var/lib/pgsql/data -p /usr/bin/postma
ster
Smart Shutdown request at Tue Sep 12 02:04:20 2000
000912.02:04:20.806  [1905] DEBUG:   Data Base System shutting down at Tue Sep 12
 02:04:20 2000
000912.02:04:20.812  [1905] DEBUG:   Data Base System shut down at Tue Sep 12
 02:04:20 2000
postmaster successfully shut down.
```

While the server is running, you can check on its status by typing

```
[postgres@laura postgres]$ pg_ctl status -D /var/lib/pgsql/data -p /usr/bin/post
master
pg_ctl: postmaster is running (pid: 1931)
options are:
/usr/bin/postmaster
-p 5432
-D /var/lib/pgsql/data
-B 64
-b /usr/bin/postgres
-i
-N 32
```

From the postmaster man page (type **man postmaster** at any command line), you'll find that p is the port, -D the data directory, and -B the number of 8K buffers, which must be twice -N, the number of backend processes. The -I indicates that this database accepts connections via TCP/IP, and the -b shows the location of the postgres binary program. This is where the debugging information comes in. In the PGDATA directory is a file, postmaster.opts.default, in which you can pass variables to the postmaster. For an increase in the number of debug lines, add -d with a number from 1 to 5 to the postmaster.opts. default file, like this:

```
[postgres@laura postgres]$ cat /var/lib/pgsql/data/postmaster.opts.default
-i -d 5
```

This will make your output more verbose:

```
[postgres@laura postgres]$ FindExec: found "/usr/bin/postgres" using argv[0]
binding ShmemCreate(key=52e2c1, size=1104896)
000912.02:29:52.018  [2329] DEBUG:  Data Base System is starting up at Tue Sep 1
 2 02:29:52 2000
000912.02:29:52.019  [2329] DEBUG:  Data Base System was shut down at Tue Sep 12
 02:29:42 2000
000912.02:29:52.026  [2329] DEBUG:  Data Base System is in production state at
 Tue Sep 12 02:29:52 2000
000912.02:29:52.026  [2329] proc_exit(0)
000912.02:29:52.028  [2329] shmem_exit(0)
000912.02:29:52.028  [2329] exit(0)
/usr/bin/postmaster: reaping dead processes...
```

As my daughters said at the end of one of my life-lesson stories, "That's way too much information!" PostgreSQL lets you decide which kind of information you want to see, just as pg_ctl enables you to fine-tune how your database comes up and shuts down.

Infrequently Used Options

None.

pg_dump and pg_dumpall

One current backup of your database can save you from coming up with a hundred excuses as to why your data was lost. Take a look at pg_dump first:

```
[perkins@laura perkins]$ pg_dump --help
pg_dump dumps a database as a text file.

Usage:
  pg_dump [options] dbname

Options:
  -a, --data-only          dump out only the data, not the schema
  -c, --clean              clean (drop) schema prior to create
  -d, --inserts            dump data as INSERT, rather than COPY, commands
  -D, --attribute-inserts  dump data as INSERT commands with attribute names
  -h, --host <hostname>    server host name
  -i, --ignore-version     proceed when database version != pg_dump version
```

```
-n, --no-quotes          suppress most quotes around identifiers
-N, --quotes             enable most quotes around identifiers
-o, --oids               dump object ids (oids)
-p, --port <port>        server port number
-s, --schema-only        dump out only the schema, no data
-t, --table <table>      dump for this table only
-u, --password           use password authentication
-v, --verbose            verbose
-x, --no-acl             do not dump ACL's (grant/revoke)
```

If no database name is supplied, then the PGDATABASE environment variable value is used.

Frequently Used Options

The switches -h, -p, -W, and -U (host, port, prompt for password, and connect as user) work the same way as the corresponding switches described in createdb.

The common use of pg_dump is

```
[postgres@laura postgres]$ pg_dump perkins >db.out
```

This produces a script named db.out. When this script is run in the psql program (described in Chapter 4, "Interactive PostgreSQL Using PSQL") it uses SQL to describe both the structure (*schema* in database speak) and the data to the database.

Here is db.out:

```
[postgres@laura postgres]$ cat db.out
\connect - perkins
CREATE TABLE "customersnotnull" (
        "firstname" character varying(15) NOT NULL,
        "lastname" character varying(20) NOT NULL,
        "age" int4,
        "jobdescription" character varying(15),
        "employeeid" int4
);
CREATE TABLE "customersdrone" (
        "firstname" character varying(15) NOT NULL,
        "lastname" character varying(20) NOT NULL,
        "age" int4,
        "jobdescription" character varying(15) DEFAULT 'Drone',
        "employeeid" int4
```

```
);
CREATE TABLE "customerscheck" (
        "firstname" character varying(15) NOT NULL,
        "lastname" character varying(20) NOT NULL,
        "age" int4,
        "jobdescription" character varying(15) DEFAULT 'Drone',
        "employeeid" int4,
        CONSTRAINT "customerscheck_age" CHECK ((age > 0))
);
CREATE TABLE "customersunique" (
        "firstname" character varying(15) NOT NULL,
        "lastname" character varying(20) NOT NULL,
        "age" int4,
        "jobdescription" character varying(15) DEFAULT 'Drone',
        "employeeid" int4,
        CONSTRAINT "customersunique_age" CHECK ((age > 0))
);
CREATE TABLE "customersprimarykey" (
        "firstname" character varying(15) NOT NULL,
        "lastname" character varying(20) NOT NULL,
            "age" int4,
        "jobdescription" character varying(15) DEFAULT 'Drone',
        "employeeid" int4 NOT NULL,
        CONSTRAINT "customersprimarykey_age" CHECK ((age > 0)),
        PRIMARY KEY ("employeeid")
);
CREATE TABLE "customersmultikey" (
        "firstname" character varying(15) NOT NULL,
        "lastname" character varying(20) NOT NULL,
        "age" int4,
        "jobdescription" character varying(15) DEFAULT 'Drone',
        "employeeid" int4,
        CONSTRAINT "customersmultikey_age" CHECK ((age > 0)),
        PRIMARY KEY ("lastname", "firstname")
);
CREATE TABLE "address" (
        "nickname" character varying(10),
        "street" character varying(15),
        "state" character varying(2)
```

```
  );
  CREATE TABLE "opps" (
          "firstname" character varying(15),
          "lastname" character varying(20),
          "age" int4
  );
  CREATE TABLE "family" (
          "firstname" character varying(15),
          "lastname" character varying(20),
          "age" int4
  );
  CREATE FUNCTION "plpgsql_call_handler" ( ) RETURNS opaque AS '/usr/lib/pgsql/plp
  gsql.so' LANGUAGE 'C';
  CREATE TRUSTED PROCEDURAL LANGUAGE 'plpgsql' HANDLER "plpgsql_call_handler" LANC
  OMPILER 'PL/pgSQL';
  COPY "customersnotnull" FROM stdin;
  \.
  COPY "customersdrone" FROM stdin;
  Tyler   Perkins \N      Drone  \N
  \.
  COPY "customerscheck" FROM stdin;
  Tyler    Perkins \N      Drone  \N
  \.
  COPY "customersunique" FROM stdin;
  \.
  COPY "customersprimarykey" FROM stdin;
  \.
  COPY "customersmultikey" FROM stdin;
  \.
  COPY "address" FROM stdin;
  Leslie  1313 MBird Lane CA
  Laura   Rt 66    AZ
  Kelly   1010 Pudder Ln  FL
  \.
  COPY "opps" FROM stdin;
  \.
  COPY "family" FROM stdin;
  Alton   Perkins 22
  Leslie  Perkins 27
```

```
Laura    Perkins 22
Kelly    Perkins 19
Ruth     Perkins 17
Jeff     Perkins 47
\.
CREATE UNIQUE INDEX "customersunique_employeeid_key" on "customersunique" using
btree ( "employeeid" "int4_ops" );
```

That's a lot of data, but very handy to have around when you have to rebuild lost data. The program pg_dump allows a more selective output. To save the design of the tables in the database, use the -s (schema only) switch:

```
[postgres@laura postgres]$ pg_dump -s perkins >db.out.schema
```

This produces a smaller file that doesn't include the data, just as the -a switch creates a file with just the data. Alternatively, you can use the -t switch, followed by a table name, to save a script to rebuild one table:

```
[postgres@laura postgres]$ pg_dump -t family perkins >db.out.familytable
[postgres@laura postgres]$ cat db.out.familytable
\connect - perkins
CREATE TABLE "family" (
        "firstname" character varying(15),
        "lastname" character varying(20),
        "age" int4
);
COPY "family" FROM stdin;
Alton    Perkins 22
Leslie   Perkins 27
Laura    Perkins 22
Kelly    Perkins 19
Ruth     Perkins 17
Jeff     Perkins 47
\.
```

What pg_dump does for one database, pg_dumpall does for all of the databases in the PostgreSQL system. Just don't try to use a table or database name; otherwise, all of the pg_dump options apply. Type

```
[postgres@laura postgres]$ pg_dumpall >db.all
```

This creates a really big file that contains everything needed to reconstitute this database system, including users.

Infrequently Used Options

None.

vacuumdb

The program vacuumdb is a tuning tool for your database. Running vacuumdb cleans up internal PostgreSQL elements and creates internal data used to speed up database operations. Here is the syntax:

```
[perkins@laura perkins]$ vacuumdb --help
vacuumdb cleans and analyzes a PostgreSQL database.


Usage:
  vacuumdb [options] [dbname]


Options:
  -h, --host=HOSTNAME         Database server host
  -p, --port=PORT             Database server port
  -U, --username=USERNAME     Username to connect as
  -W, --password              Prompt for password
  -d, --dbname=DBNAME         Database to vacuum
  -a, --all                   Vacuum all databases
  -z, --analyze               Update optimizer hints
  -t, --table='TABLE[(columns)]'  Vacuum specific table only
  -v, --verbose               Write a lot of output
  -e, --echo                  Show the command being sent to the backend
  -q, --quiet                 Don't write any output
```

Frequently Used Options

The switches -h, -p, -w, and -U (host, port, prompt for password, and connect as user) work the same as the corresponding switches described in createdb.

The basic usage is

```
[postgres@laura postgres]$ vacuumdb perkins
VACUUM
```

This vacuums the database and analyzes the structure for tuning. To analyze the data, type

```
[postgres@laura postgres]$ vacuumdb -z perkins
VACUUM
```

Use -v if you don't think vacuumdb is doing anything, and you will be presented with several pages of reports regarding the internal restructuring caused by vacuumdb.

Infrequently Used Options

The -e switch shows you the query sent to the database and is the default setting. The -q option turns off the messages.

Summary

Administering your database is the next block to database setup in your foundation. These programs enable you to start up, add to, delete from, fine-tune, and shut down the PostgreSQL system. Two more building blocks remain in your basic knowledge: security and psql.

Chapter 3: PostgreSQL Basic Security

In this chapter, I'll cover basic security concepts in a PostgreSQL database. Your data, especially if you share it across the Web, is vulnerable to two hazards. One hazard is inadvertent changes. These are the "oops" kind of problems, like when you accidentally wipe out your programming team's database, for example. The other hazard is intentional misuse of your database—when someone intentionally logs into your database to misuse your data. By the end of this chapter, you'll be able to guard against both threats to your data.

Preventing Inadvertent Changes to Data

Accidentally erasing a critical PostgreSQL file or dropping all the tables in the database are two examples of inadvertent changes. Unfortunately, inadvertent changes happen all the time. Your first line of defense against inadvertent changes is backup. Use the administrative program dump_all, described in Chapter 2, "PostgreSQL Administrative Programs," to back up your data on a regular basis. What constitutes a regular basis? The rule I use is: How much data can you afford to lose? If you have an application that collects data, and your income depends on that data, you should probably back up at least once a day. If you have a database containing your family genealogy, and your family is producing fewer than one new entry a week, you might consider backing up every week or so. A convenient way to do this is to put a script in /etc/cron.daily, /etc/cron.weekly, or etc/cron.monthly. To back up every month, the script you put in /etc/cron.monthly should look something like this:

```
#!/bin/sh
#Save the whole PostgreSQL database
pg_dumpall > /backups/pgsql/$(date +%b-Backup)
```

This saves a file named Sep-Backup (or whatever month your system thinks is current) to the directory /backups/pgsql/. If you want a weekly rotation, use something like this:

```
#!/bin/sh
#Save the whole PostgreSQL database
pg_dumpall > /backups/pgsql/$(date +%A-Backup)
```

This script, if you put it in the /etc/cron.daily/ directory, creates a new backup every day in the /backups/pgsql/ directory. The name of the file is *Mon-Backup* (or whichever day your system thinks is current).

If you have disk space limitations or just want to be more precise, you can write the script using the administrative program pg_dump, also described in detail in Chapter 2. pg_dump allows you to write specific tables. I personally prefer the shotgun approach taken by pg_dumpall because I can never seem to anticipate which data I will need to recover.

Also, you can and should use a system wide file backup system, such as BRU, to back up the files that constitute your PostgreSQL system. Alternatively, you can use the RAID (*Redundant Array of Inexpensive Disks*) capabilities in Linux to mirror your data. When I started in computers 20 years ago there were no "inexpensive disks," but this is a strange industry. My father called me during the writing of this book to say that he had just bought a 20GB disk for under 100 dollars! I personally recommend using hard drives as backup devices because they are cheaper and faster than tape drives. However, backing up your system and setting up RAID are not subjects a database book should describe in detail. A good start is *Red Hat Linux Administrator's Guide* by Kerry Cox (Prima Tech).

PostgreSQL also has some built-in features that work to keep your data safe from inadvertent changes. You cannot, for example, read, change, or add data to a database object you did not create. Therefore, if user perkins logged into user other's database, perkins would be able to read data but not change or add data, as shown by the following example.

First, using psql (described in detail in Chapter 4), log in to PostgreSQL, and use the \dt switch to show the available tables:

```
 [perkins@laura perkins]$ psql
Welcome to psql, the PostgreSQL interactive terminal.

Type:  \copyright for distribution terms
       \h for help with SQL commands
       \? for help on internal slash commands
       \g or terminate with semicolon to execute query
       \q to quit


perkins=# \dt
        List of relations
     Name         | Type  | Owner
--------------------+------+--------
```

```
address              | table | perkins
customerscheck       | table | perkins
customersdrone       | table | perkins
customersmultikey    | table | perkins
customersnotnull     | table | perkins
customersprimarykey  | table | perkins
customersunique      | table | perkins
family               | table | perkins
opps                 | table | perkins
pga_forms            | table | perkins
pga_layout           | table | perkins
pga_queries          | table | perkins
pga_reports          | table | perkins
pga_schema           | table | perkins
pga_scripts          | table | perkins
(15 rows)
```

The pga tables are discussed in Chapter 5, "Getting Graphical with PostgreSQL: The pgacess Program" which covers pgaccess, a graphical interface to postgres. Note that all the tables are owned by perkins. Now, log in, using psql as a user named otherusr:

```
[perkins@laura perkins]$ psql -U otherusr -d perkins
Welcome to psql, the PostgreSQL interactive terminal.


Type:  \copyright for distribution terms
       \h for help with SQL commands
       \? for help on internal slash commands
       \g or terminate with semicolon to execute query
       \q to quit


perkins=>
```

Try to see the rows stored in the address table by using Structured Query Language (*SQL*), which is covered in Chapter 8:

```
perkins=> select * from family;
ERROR:  family: Permission denied.
```

Otherusr can't even look at the table unless perkins specifically grants permission.

```
perkins=# GRANT SELECT ON ADDRESS TO otherusr;
CHANGE
```

The GRANT was done by the user perkins. Try to select the data as otherusr:

```
perkins=> select * from address;
 nickname |     street     | state
----------+----------------+------
 Leslie   | 1313 MBird Lane | CA
 Laura    | Rt 66          | AZ
 Kelly    | 1010 Pudder Ln | FL
(3 rows)
```

> For GRANT to take effect, otherusr has to log out of psql (\q) and then log back
> in. In other words, your privileges are read when you log in to psql and are not
> affected by any changes made by other users.

The GRANT command makes your data safe from other users, giving you precise control over what other users are allowed to do.

Granting privileges on a user-by-user basis is fine for an environment in which you have only a few users, but when you get more than a couple users, this can become tedious. Fortunately, PostgreSQL allows you to create groups of users that share permissions on database objects (if, for example, otherusr were one of a group of users that need to add data to the address table). First, you (as the owner of the table, in this case perkins) create a GROUP named UPDATERS:

```
perkins=# CREATE GROUP UPDATERS WITH USER otherusr, newuser01, newuser02;
CREATE GROUP
```

Then, grant the ability to update the table to the group UPDATERS:

```
perkins=# GRANT INSERT ON ADDRESS TO GROUP UPDATERS;
CHANGE
```

Finally, log back in as otherusr, and insert the data:

```
perkins=# INSERT INTO ADDRESS VALUES('Ruth', '4624 Minn', 'CA');
INSERT 409568 1
perkins=# select * from address;
 nickname |     street     | state
----------+----------------+------
 Leslie   | 1313 MBird Lane | CA
 Laura    | Rt 66          | AZ
 Kelly    | 1010 Pudder Ln | FL
```

```
Ruth      | 4624 Minn      | CA
(4 rows)
```

Note that otherusr can now add data. Well, what's to keep some disgruntled employee from logging in as otherusr and putting in bad address data? It's time to learn how to prevent deliberate misuse of data.

Preventing Deliberate Misuse of Data

The only way to be absolutely sure that your data is safe is to lock your computer in a room with no connections to the outside world, a solution my system administrator has advocated on several occasions. Why have a database, though, if no one can get to your data? Well, then, how can your database be protected? Start by limiting your audience.

When it starts, PostgreSQL must be told to listen for connections from other machines. This is done with the -i option in pg_ctl (covered in Chapter 2), which tells PostgreSQL to listen to the network for connections. If you want to limit PostgreSQL to conversations from its home computer, take the -i option out of whatever script you use to start PostgreSQL. This secures your data but kind of takes the *client* out of client/server. The next best thing is to limit the database's contact with the outside world. PostgreSQL has a file in which you can make this happen.

The pg_hba.conf file in the $PGDATA directory, normally the /var/lib/pgsql/data directory, is where PostgreSQL gets instructions about how to handle contacts with the outside world. The hba.conf file is full of good information and is a must-read for your understanding of PostgreSQL. In the next couple paragraphs, you'll learn the basics. Look at the end of the file, and find the section that looks like this:

```
# By default, allow anything over UNIX domain sockets and localhost.
local      all                                      trust
host       all       127.0.0.1     255.255.255.255  trust
```

These two records allow the admin programs, such as pg_dump and psql, running on the same machine to talk to the PostgreSQL database. I don't suggest modifying these lines, but take a look at the details so that you can learn how to restrict your connections.

The first column can contain either local or host. Local applies to the local machine. I will discuss the local record first; it covers everything in the host record except IP addresses and IP masks.

In a local record, you can specify a database name in the second column, or `all`, to apply the line to every database on the system. A local record doesn't contain any IP address or IP mask information, which leaves only the last column. The last column can be either `trust`, `password`, `crypt`, `ident`, `krb4`, `krb5`, or `reject`.

`trust` is the default setup for the local record. Using `trust` allows users to connect without an authentication or a password. For those less trusting, there is the `password` option. In the section discussing createuser in Chapter 2, I covered the option of adding a password to the user. If you use the `password` option where the `trust` option is used, the passwords you put in with your usernames will be used. The `reject` keyword is used to reject connections. If you put this on the local record, nobody could run any of the administrative programs on the local machine—not a normal configuration, but possible. I will come back to the more common use of `reject` in a moment, when I cover the host records. The `crypt`, `krb4`, and `krb5` options deal with encryption and are beyond the scope of this book. If you need encryption, you can glean the details from the security sections of the PostgreSQL documentation in the /usr/docs/postgresql-7.0.2/ directory. I will cover the `ident` option after a discussion of the host record.

The host record deals with how the outside world is allowed to connect to the database. The host record you originally looked at says to trust all connections that come from the 127.0.0.1 IP address. This is a special IP address, called a *loopback* address. It isn't especially useful to the current discussion. On my network, which is behind a firewall, the line I use to allow IP addresses to access this database is

```
host    all    192.168.0.0      255.255.0.0      trust
```

This allows all machines with addresses that start with 192.168. to run as a client against my PostgreSQL server. If I wanted to require passwords, I would replace the word *trust* with the word *password*. To shut out a range of IP addresses, I would use the `reject` keyword. My suggestion is to allow only the connections you need. For example, in a Web-based application, you would allow the application to connect solely to the Web server's machine. Allowing more connections than necessary will only break your heart in the long run.

That leaves the `ident` function. The `ident` function uses the pg_ident.conf file in the $PGDATA directory to map system usernames to PostgreSQL usernames. Looking in your newly installed $PGDATA directory, you notice that there isn't a pg_ident.conf file! There is a sample file you can copy in the /usr/lib/pgsql directory. At this point, it's enough to know that you can use `ident` and the pg_ident.conf file to map system users to PostgreSQL users. You will find this useful in your future dealings with PostgreSQL.

Summary

This chapter gave you the basic security skills necessary to prevent both inadvertent and deliberate corruption of your data. Remember, start with a backup, use GRANT to assign needed permissions on data, and allow contact with the minimum number of IP addresses. These three concepts will prevent about 90 percent of the horrible things that can happen to your database.

Chapter 4: Interactive PostgreSQL Using psql

O f all the administrative programs that come with the PostgreSQL database, psql is the one where the database user spends the most time. The most basic function of the psql program is to provide a workspace where SQL (*Structured Query Language*), can be implemented. However, like a Swiss Army knife, psql has many other uses as well. This chapter first covers the command-line usage of psql. Then you will log in to psql and learn about the slash commands, which, oddly enough, all begin with a backward slash (\).

Command-Line Options

You can use psql from the command line to do some very useful work, such as generate HTML files filled with data from your tables. As in the other administrative programs, psql has a `help` option. Exercise the help function by typing **psql -help**.

```
[perkins@laura perkins]$ psql --help
This is psql, the PostgreSQL interactive terminal.


Usage:
  psql [options] [dbname [username]]
```

Table 4.1 shows the other options available with psql.

Frequently Used Options

Start your tour of the remaining command-line options with a list of the available databases. Type **psql -l**. You should see something like the following:

```
[perkins@laura perkins]$ psql -l
        List of databases
  Database   |  Owner   | Encoding
------------+----------+----------
 newbie01    | perkins  | SQL_ASCII
 newbie02    | perkins  | SQL_ASCII
 newbie03    | perkins  | SQL_ASCII
 newbie04    | perkins  | SQL_ASCII
 newbie05    | perkins  | SQL_ASCII
 newbie06    | perkins  | SQL_ASCII
 perkins     | perkins  | SQL_ASCII
 regression  | postgres | SQL_ASCII
 template1   | postgres | SQL_ASCII
(9 rows)
```

Table 4.1   Options for psql

Option	Description
`-a`	Echo all input from script
`-A`	Unaligned table output mode (`-P` format=unaligned)
`-c <query>`	Run only single query (or slash command) and exit
`-d <dbname>`	Specify database name to connect to (default: perkins)
`-e`	Echo queries sent to backend
`-E`	Display queries that internal commands generate
`-f <filename>`	Execute queries from file, and exit
`-F <string>`	Set field separator (default: "|") (`-P` fieldsep=)
`-h <host>`	Specify database server host (default: domain socket)
`-H`	HTML table output mode (`-P` format=html)
`-l`	List available databases, and exit
`-n`	Disable readline
`-o <filename>`	Send query output to filename (or |pipe)
`-p <port>`	Specify database server port (default: hardwired)
`-P var[=arg]`	Set printing option 'var' to 'arg' (see `\pset` command)
`-q`	Run quietly (no messages, only query output)
`-R <string>`	Set record separator (default: newline) (`-P` recordsep=)
`-s`	Single step mode (confirm each query)
`-S`	Single line mode (newline terminates query)
`-t`	Print rows only (`-P` tuples_only)
`-T text`	Set HTML table tag options (width, border) (`-P` tableattr=)
`-U <username>`	Specify database username (default: perkins)
`-v name=val`	Set psql variable 'name' to 'value'
`-V`	Show version information, and exit
`-W`	Prompt for password (should happen automatically)
`-x`	Turn on expanded table output (`-P` expanded)
`-X`	Do not read startup file (~/.psqlrc)

The pgsql -1 command shows all databases on the PostgreSQL system, along with their owners and their encoding. (See Chapter 3, "PostgreSQL Basic Security," for a discussion of encoding.)

The most commonly used command line switch is -c. The -c option allows the execution of a SQL statement (discussed in Chapter 8, "Basic SQL") or one of the slash (\) commands covered in the next section. For example, to get data from the address table to the command line, type

```
[perkins@laura perkins]$ psql -c 'select * from address';
 nickname |     street      | state
----------+-----------------+------
 Leslie   | 1313 MBird Lane | CA
 Laura    | Rt 66           | AZ
 Kelly    | 1010 Pudder Ln  | FL
 Ruth     | 4624 Minn       | CA
(4 rows)
```

You can also use sets of double quotes (" "). Double quotes allow embedded variables. Consider the following example:

```
[perkins@laura perkins]$ export TABLENAME=address
[perkins@laura perkins]$ psql -c "select * from $TABLENAME";
 nickname |     street      | state
----------+-----------------+------
 Leslie   | 1313 MBird Lane | CA
 Laura    | Rt 66           | AZ
 Kelly    | 1010 Pudder Ln  | FL
 Ruth     | 4624 Minn       | CA
(4 rows)
```

The use of system variables opens up a galaxy of options in the area of command-line scripts. However, an in-depth discussion of command-line scripting is beyond the scope of this book.

Another commonly used option is -f. The option -f reads in a file and executes it. The contents of the file are treated as if they were typed in at the psql prompt. This option is frequently used to restore backup data created by the pg_dump and pg_dumpall programs, covered in Chapter 2, "PostgreSQL Administrative Programs." Following is an example that illustrates this common use. First, make a backup of the address table:

```
[perkins@laura perkins]$ pg_dump -t address perkins > address.bu
```

Now, for curiosity's sake, let's see what the pg_dump made:

```
[perkins@laura perkins]$ cat address.bu
\connect - perkins
CREATE TABLE "address" (
        "nickname" character varying(10),
        "street" character varying(15),
        "state" character varying(2)
);
REVOKE ALL on "address" from PUBLIC;
GRANT SELECT on "address" to "otherusr";
GRANT INSERT,UPDATE,DELETE on "address" to GROUP "updaters";
COPY "address" FROM stdin;
Leslie   1313 MBird Lane CA
Laura    Rt 66     AZ
Kelly    1010 Pudder Ln  FL
Ruth     4624 Minn       CA
\.
```

Taking a leap of faith that this backup will work, delete the address table.

```
[perkins@laura perkins]$ psql -c 'DROP TABLE address'
DROP
```

Use the -c switch to see whether the table was eliminated.

```
[perkins@laura perkins]$ psql -c "select * from address"
ERROR:  Relation 'address' does not exist
```

Now, read in the backup file with the -f switch.

```
[perkins@laura perkins]$ psql -f address.bu
You are now connected as new user perkins.
CREATE
CHANGE
CHANGE
CHANGE
```

Finally, check your work.

```
[perkins@laura perkins]$ psql -c "select * from address"
 nickname |     street      | state
----------+-----------------+------
 Leslie   | 1313 MBird Lane | CA
 Laura    | Rt 66           | AZ
```

```
Kelly    | 1010 Pudder Ln | FL
Ruth     | 4624 Minn      | CA
(4 rows)
```

If you want to use a database on a different machine, use the -h and -p switches—
-h to set the host name and -p for the port. Reworking the example used to bring
the items in the address table to the command line, you get this:

```
[perkins@laura perkins]$ psql -h laura.perkinsfamily -p 5432 -c 'select * from a
ddress'
Password:
 nickname |     street     | state
----------+----------------+------
 Leslie   | 1313 MBird Lane | CA
 Laura    | Rt 66          | AZ
 Kelly    | 1010 Pudder Ln | FL
 Ruth     | 4624 Minn      | CA
(4 rows)
```

The default port for PostgreSQL is 5432 (which you can find in the /etc/services
file). Notice the Password: prompt on the second line. This means that PostgreSQL
has been set up to require a password for user perkins, as described in Chapter 3,
"PostgreSQL Basic Security."

> The IP address from which you are calling and any required passwords should be
> mentioned in the pg_hba.conf file, usually found in the /var/lib/pgsql/data/ di-
> rectory. See Chapter 3, "PostgreSQL Basic Security," for details.

Should you ever want to be prompted for your password or log in as a different
user, use the -w and -u options, which look like this:

```
[perkins@laura perkins]$ psql -h laura.perkinsfamily -p 5432 -W -d perkins -U ne
wbie01 -c 'select * from address'
Password:
 nickname |     street     | state
----------+----------------+------
 Leslie   | 1313 MBird Lane | CA
 Laura    | Rt 66          | AZ
 Kelly    | 1010 Pudder Ln | FL
 Ruth     | 4624 Minn      | CA
(4 rows)
```

Notice how the -d switch is for specifying the perkins database. Otherwise, PostgreSQL would default to the newbie01 database, if one existed.

> When connecting with a username different from the desired database name, be sure to specify the desired database. Without a specified database, the results of your actions will be put in the database with the same name as the user.

Another very useful switch is -H. The -H switch changes the output to HTML. If you wanted to create an HTML page named myaddress.html with data from the address table, you would type

```
[perkins@laura perkins]$ psql -H -c 'select * from address' > myaddress.html
[perkins@laura perkins]$ cat myaddress.html
<table border=1>
  <tr>
    <th align=center>nickname</th>
    <th align=center>street</th>
    <th align=center>state</th>
  </tr>
  <tr valign=top>
    <td align=left>Leslie</td>
    <td align=left>1313 MBird Lane</td>
    <td align=left>CA</td>
  </tr>
  <tr valign=top>
    <td align=left>Laura</td>
    <td align=left>Rt 66</td>
    <td align=left>AZ</td>
  </tr>
  <tr valign=top>
    <td align=left>Kelly</td>
    <td align=left>1010 Pudder Ln</td>
    <td align=left>FL</td>
  </tr>
  <tr valign=top>
    <td align=left>Ruth</td>
    <td align=left>4624 Minn</td>
    <td align=left>CA</td>
  </tr>
```

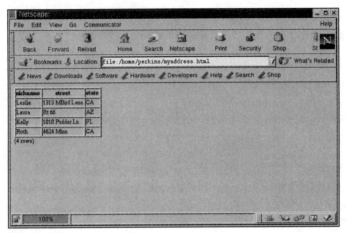

Figure 4.1 *Myaddress.html in Netscape*

```
</table>
(4 rows)<br>
```

When it is called in Netscape, this looks like Figure 4.1.

Less Frequently Used Options

The -a option echoes all the input from the script, so if you run an SQL query, the query will be echoed. For example:

```
[perkins@laura perkins]$ psql -a -c 'select * from address'
select * from address
 nickname  |     street      | state
-----------+-----------------+------
 Leslie    | 1313 MBird Lane | CA
 Laura     | Rt 66           | AZ
 Kelly     | 1010 Pudder Ln  | FL
 Ruth      | 4624 Minn       | CA
(4 rows)
```

Notice that select * from address is printed out before the results of the query. The -e switch also echoes queries. Here is the same example, using -e.

```
  -e            Echo queries sent to backend
[perkins@laura perkins]$ psql -e -c 'select * from address'
select * from address
 nickname  |     street      | state
```

```
-----------+-----------------+------
 Leslie    | 1313 MBird Lane | CA
 Laura     | Rt 66           | AZ
 Kelly     | 1010 Pudder Ln  | FL
 Ruth      | 4624 Minn       | CA
(4 rows)
```

If you need the output without any formatting, use the -A switch. This switch causes psql to print the data and the separator characters.

```
[perkins@laura perkins]$ psql -A -c 'select * from address'
nickname|street|state
Leslie|1313 MBird Lane|CA
Laura|Rt 66|AZ
Kelly|1010 Pudder Ln|FL
Ruth|4624 Minn|CA
```

This format is suitable for input into another program, such as a spreadsheet. Another use is to simplify the input to any parsing programs, such as grep, thereby minimizing the logic needed to deal with all the formatted white space.

To find out which actions are being done behind the scenes to generate the data you request, use the -E switch. Here is an example that passes in the slash command \dt, described in the next section. Using -E shows you how the system gets a listing of the tables.

```
[perkins@laura perkins]$ psql -E -c '\dt'
********* QUERY *********
SELECT c.relname as "Name", 'table'::text as "Type", u.usename as "Owner"
FROM pg_class c, pg_user u
WHERE c.relowner = u.usesysid AND c.relkind = 'r'
  AND not exists (select 1 from pg_views where viewname = c.relname)
  AND c.relname !~ '^pg_'
UNION
SELECT c.relname as "Name", 'table'::text as "Type", NULL as "Owner"
FROM pg_class c
WHERE c.relkind = 'r'
  AND not exists (select 1 from pg_views where viewname = c.relname)
  AND not exists (select 1 from pg_user where usesysid = c.relowner)
  AND c.relname !~ '^pg_'

ORDER BY "Name"
```

```
*************************


            List of relations
        Name         |  Type  |  Owner
---------------------+--------+--------
  address            | table  | perkins
  customerscheck     | table  | perkins
  customersdrone     | table  | perkins
  customersmultikey  | table  | perkins
  customersnotnull   | table  | perkins
  customersprimarykey| table  | perkins
  customersunique    | table  | perkins
  family             | table  | perkins
  opps               | table  | perkins
  pga_forms          | table  | perkins
  pga_layout         | table  | perkins
  pga_queries        | table  | perkins
  pga_reports        | table  | perkins
  pga_schema         | table  | perkins
  pga_scripts        | table  | perkins
(15 rows)
```

The -E command is a good way to learn in which tables the PostgreSQL system stores certain data. It is also a good way to see advanced queries at work and should give you ideas for your own queries. (SQL queries are discussed in detail in Chapter 8, "Basic SQL.")

If you use the -A switch to remove the formatting from your output, and you want something other than the pipe (|) character to separate the data, use the -F switch.

```
[perkins@laura perkins]$ psql -F "#" -A -c 'select * from address'
nickname#street#state
Leslie#1313 MBird Lane#CA
Laura#Rt 66#AZ
Kelly#1010 Pudder Ln#FL
Ruth#4624 Minn#CA
(4 rows)
```

If you want comma-delimited format (for example, for a spreadsheet), use a comma (,) instead of the pound sign (#).

The -o sends the output from your other switches to a file. To make an HTML page and save it to the file hyaddress.html, type the following and then cat myaddress.html to check your work, as shown here.

```
[perkins@laura perkins]$ psql -H -o myaddress.html -c 'select * from address'
[perkins@laura perkins]$ cat myaddress.html
<table border=1>
  <tr>
    <th align=center>nickname</th>
    <th align=center>street</th>
    <th align=center>state</th>
  </tr>
  <tr valign=top>
    <td align=left>Leslie</td>
    <td align=left>1313 MBird Lane</td>
    <td align=left>CA</td>
  </tr>
  <tr valign=top>
    <td align=left>Laura</td>
    <td align=left>Rt 66</td>
    <td align=left>AZ</td>
  </tr>
  <tr valign=top>
    <td align=left>Kelly</td>
    <td align=left>1010 Pudder Ln</td>
    <td align=left>FL</td>
  </tr>
  <tr valign=top>
    <td align=left>Ruth</td>
    <td align=left>4624 Minn</td>
    <td align=left>CA</td>
  </tr>
</table>
(4 rows)<br>
```

PostgreSQL has a number of internal variables that you can set with the -P switch. (See the coverage of the \pset command in the next section for a listing of these internal variables.) For now, set the field separator to #, as you did in the example for the -F switch. This time, type

```
[perkins@laura perkins]$ psql -P fieldsep="#" -A -c 'select * from address'
nickname#street#state
```

```
Leslie#1313 MBird Lane#CA

Laura#Rt 66#AZ

Kelly#1010 Pudder Ln#FL

Ruth#4624 Minn#CA

(4 rows)
```

Note that this is exactly the same as the output using the -F switch.

To suspend all messages and get the results of your query, use the -q switch. To achieve quiet operation, type

```
[perkins@laura perkins]$ psql -q -c 'select * from address'
 nickname |      street     | state
----------+-----------------+------
 Leslie   | 1313 MBird Lane | CA
 Laura    | Rt 66           | AZ
 Kelly    | 1010 Pudder Ln  | FL
 Ruth     | 4624 Minn       | CA
(4 rows)
```

You'll notice that this is exactly the same as using the -c by itself.

If you need your example to be one continuous line, not broken up by newlines and carriage returns, use the -R switch. In the version of PostgreSQL used in this book (7.02), this switch is broken. Good thing there's a backup! Until this switch is fixed, use the -P with an argument of recordsep.

```
[perkins@laura perkins]$ psql -A -F "#" -P recordsep="$" -c 'select * from address'
nickname#street#state$Leslie#1313 MBird Lane#CA$Laura#Rt 66#AZ$Kelly#1010 Pudder
 Ln#FL$Ruth#4624 Minn#CA$(4 rows)
```

Say that you want to read in a script from a file using the -f switch, but you want to control which queries are run. PostgreSQL has just the switch: -c. Try the same line you did with -f, but add -c.

```
[perkins@laura perkins]$ psql -s -f address.bu
You are now connected as new user perkins.
***(Single step mode: Verify query)**********************************************
CREATE TABLE "address" (
        "nickname" character varying(10),
        "street" character varying(15),
        "state" character varying(2)
);
```

```
***(press return to proceed or enter x and return to cancel)*******************

psql:address.bu:6: ERROR:  Relation 'address' already exists
***(Single step mode: Verify query)*********************************************
REVOKE ALL on "address" from PUBLIC;
***(press return to proceed or enter x and return to cancel)*******************
x
***(Single step mode: Verify query)*********************************************
GRANT SELECT on "address" to "otherusr";
***(press return to proceed or enter x and return to cancel)*******************
...
```

You get the idea—every query is presented for your approval. Note that I let the first query run, which threw an error because the table already existed.

To see which version of psql you are working with, use the -v switch. This produces the following:

```
psql (PostgreSQL) 7.0.2
contains readline, history, multibyte support
Portions Copyright (c) 1996-2000, PostgreSQL, Inc
Portions Copyright (c) 1996 Regents of the University of California
Read the file COPYRIGHT or use the command \copyright to see the
usage and distribution terms.
```

If the normal table format is not enough for you, try the extended format caused by the -x switch. Type

```
[perkins@laura perkins]$ psql -x -c 'select * from address'
-[ RECORD 1 ]------------
nickname | Leslie
street   | 1313 MBird Lane
state    | CA
-[ RECORD 2 ]------------
nickname | Laura
street   | Rt 66
state    | AZ
-[ RECORD 3 ]------------
nickname | Kelly
street   | 1010 Pudder Ln
state    | FL
-[ RECORD 4 ]------------
nickname | Ruth
```

```
street  | 4624 Minn
state   | CA
```

If less information is what you want, use the -t switch. It loses the column names.

```
[perkins@laura perkins]$ psql -t -c 'select * from address'
 Leslie | 1313 MBird Lane | CA
 Laura  | Rt 66           | AZ
 Kelly  | 1010 Pudder Ln  | FL
 Ruth   | 4624 Minn       | CA
```

Finally, if you have created a .psqlrc file and placed it in your home directory, the lines in the file will be executed as you enter psql—which you will do in a few lines when I start the discussion of the slash commands available from inside the psql program. To avoid running this file, use the -x switch. Say, for example, that your .psqlrc file is set up to talk to a database on a different machine (see the -h, -p, and -d switches), but you want to open up a file on the local machine. You would type **psql -x** to avoid running the .psqlrc file.

Slash Commands

Inside the psql program there are dozens of commands to help you get exactly the data you need. Some of the commands covered have counterparts in the list of command-line functions. For example, where you used -help to list the command-line switches when inside psql, you use your first slash command, \?, to return a list of the available slash commands.

```
perkins=# \?
```

Table 4.2 lists the available slash commands.

Frequently Used Options

To connect to a different database, use the \c command. When logged in to the perkins database, you can reach the template1 database and log in a user perkins by typing

```
perkins=# \c template1 perkins
You are now connected to database template1 as user perkins.
```

To give your data outputs a title, use the \c switch. If your title has spaces in it, surround it with quotes.

```
perkins=# \C "My Address Data"
Title is ""My Address Data"".
perkins=# select * from address;
```

```
          "My Address Data"
 nickname |     street     | state
----------+----------------+------
 Leslie   | 1313 MBird Lane | CA
 Laura    | Rt 66          | AZ
 Kelly    | 1010 Pudder Ln | FL
 Ruth     | 4624 Minn      | CA
(4 rows)
```

To make sure that the next table you build doesn't use this inspired title, type the \c command again to unset the title.

```
perkins=# \C
Title is unset.
```

To copy data to a file, use the \copy command. For example, to get address information to a file named address.dat, type

```
perkins=# \copy address to address.dat using delimiters ','
perkins=# \q
[perkins@laura perkins]$ cat address.dat
Leslie,1313 MBird Lane,CA
Laura,Rt 66,AZ
Kelly,1010 Pudder Ln,FL
Ruth,4624 Minn,CA
```

The using delimiters clause allows you to insert the desired delimiter (in this case, a comma) between the data of each record.

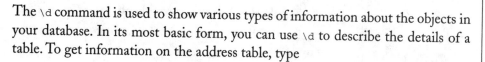

Don't use the ; at the end of a / command. Here, it would result in an output file named address.dat;—not what you want!

CAUTION

The \d command is used to show various types of information about the objects in your database. In its most basic form, you can use \d to describe the details of a table. To get information on the address table, type

```
perkins=# \d address
        Table "address"
 Attribute |    Type     | Modifier
-----------+-------------+----------
 nickname  | varchar(10) |
 street    | varchar(15) |
 state     | varchar(2)  |
```

Table 4.2   Slash Commands in psql

Command	Description
`\a`	Toggle between unaligned and aligned mode
`\c[onnect] [dbname| - [user]]`	Connect to new database (currently 'perkins')
`\C <title>`	Table title
`\copy ...`	Perform SQL COPY with data stream to the client machine
`\copyright`	Show PostgreSQL usage and distribution terms
`\d <table>`	Describe table (or view, index, or sequence)
`\d{t|i|s|v}`	List tables/indices/sequences/views
`\d{p|S|l}`	List permissions/system tables/lobjects
`\da`	List aggregates
`\dd [object]`	List comment for table, type, function, or operator
`\df`	List functions
`\do`	List operators
`\dT`	List data types
`\e [file]`	Edit the current query buffer or [file] with external editor
`\echo <text>`	Write text to stdout
`\encoding <encoding>`	Set client encoding
`\f <sep>`	Change field separator
`\g [file]`	Send query to backend (and results in [file] or |pipe)
`\h [cmd]`	Help on syntax of sql commands, * for all commands
`\H`	Toggle HTML mode (currently off)
`\i <file>`	Read and execute queries from <file>
`\l`	List all databases
`\lo_export, \lo_import, \lo_list, \lo_unlink`	Large object operations
`\o [file]`	Send all query results to [file], or |pipe
`\p`	Show the content of the current query buffer

Table 4.2   (continued)

Command	Description
\pset <opt>	Set table output <opt> = {format|border|expanded|fieldsep|null|recordsep|tuples_only|title|tableattr|pager}
\q	Quit psql
\qecho <text>	Write text to query output stream (see \o)
\r	Reset (clear) the query buffer
\s [file]	Print history or save it in [file]
\set <var> <value>	Set internal variable
\t	Show only rows (currently off)
\T <tags>	HTML table tags
\unset <var>	Unset (delete) internal variable
\w <file>	Write current query buffer to a <file>
\x	Toggle expanded output (currently off)
\z	List table access permissions
\! [cmd]	Shell escape or command

This shows the name and type of each column of data. Data types are covered in Chapter 9, "Basic PostgreSQL Data Types and SQL Functions."

Another variation of \d is \dt. The \dt command shows all the tables that users have created on a particular database. Type

```
perkins=# \dt
          List of relations
        Name        | Type  | Owner
--------------------+-------+--------
 address            | table | perkins
 customerscheck     | table | perkins
 customersdrone     | table | perkins
 customersmultikey  | table | perkins
 customersnotnull   | table | perkins
 customersprimarykey| table | perkins
 customersunique    | table | perkins
 family             | table | perkins
```

```
opps                  | table | perkins
pga_forms             | table | perkins
pga_layout            | table | perkins
pga_queries           | table | perkins
pga_reports           | table | perkins
pga_schema            | table | perkins
pga_scripts           | table | perkins
(15 rows)
```

To see who has permissions for what options, use the \dp command. For example:

```
perkins=# \dp
                    Access permissions for database "perkins"
        Relation        |                Access permissions
------------------------+---------------------------------------------------
  address               | {"=arwR","otherusr=r","newbie01=r","group updaters=aw"}
  customerscheck        |
  customersdrone        |
  customersmultikey     |
  customersnotnull      |
  customersprimarykey   |
  customersunique       |
  family                |
  opps                  |
  pga_forms             | {"=arwR"}
  pga_layout            | {"=arwR"}
  pga_queries           | {"=arwR"}
  pga_reports           | {"=arwR"}
  pga_schema            | {"=arwR"}
  pga_scripts           | {"=arwR"}
(15 rows)
```

This shows that, on the address table, the users newbie01 and otheruser have read permissions (newbie01=r), which means that they can run selects on the data. Anyone belonging to the group updaters can delete or update (w) data and append (a) data to the table. The R permission covers the ability to create rules about the data.

The SQL specification allows four built-in functions, called *aggregate functions*. To see the aggregate functions implemented in your database, use the \da command.

```
perkins=# \da
        List of aggregates
  Name  |    Type    | Description
```

```
------+-----------+------------
 avg  | float4    |
 avg  | float8    |
 avg  | int2      |
 avg  | int4      |
 avg  | int8      |
 avg  | interval  |
 avg  | money     |
 avg  | numeric   |
count | (all types) |
 max  | abstime   |
 max  | date      |
 max  | float4    |
 max  | float8    |
 max  | int2      |
 max  | int4      |
 max  | int8      |
 max  | interval  |
 max  | money     |
 max  | numeric   |
--More--
```

There are more functions, but because of the space limitations of this book, I won't list them all.

Obtaining the exact data you want sometimes requires that you compare or add two or more pieces of data. PostgreSQL provides a host of operators for this purpose. Typing \dd lists the available operators.

```
perkins=# \dd
                              Object descriptions
         Name            | Object |                         Description

-----------------------+----------+--------------------------------------------
---------------------------
 !                       | operator | factorial
 !!                      | operator | factorial
 !!=                     | operator | not in
 !~                      | operator | does not match regex., case-sensitive
 !~*                     | operator | does not match regex., case-insensitive
 !~~                     | operator | does not match LIKE expression
 #                       | operator | box intersection (another box)
```

```
      #                        | operator | intersection point
      #                        | operator | number of points in polygon
      #                        | operator | # points in path
      ##                       | operator | closest point on box
      ##                       | operator | closest point on line
      ##                       | operator | closest point on line segment
      ##                       | operator | closest point to line on box
      ##                       | operator | closest point to line on line segment
      ##                       | operator | closest point to line segment on box
      ##                       | operator | closest point to line segment on line
--More--
```

There are pages and pages of operators—too many to list here. You will use many of these operators in Part III, "Programming."

Chapter 9, "Basic PostgreSQL Data Types and SQL Functions," covers the data types available in PostgreSQL in detail. These data types are displayed when you type \dT.

```
perkins=# \dT
                          List of types
      Type    |                     Description
------------+---------------------------------------------------------------
  SET         | set of tuples
  abstime     | absolute, limited-range date and time (UNIX system time)
  aclitem     | access control list
  bit         | fixed-length bit string
  bool        | boolean, 'true'/'false'
  box         | geometric box '(lower left,upper right)'
  bpchar      | char(length), blank-padded string, fixed storage length
  bytea       | variable-length string, binary values escaped
  char        | single character
  cid         | command identifier type, sequence in transaction id
  cidr        | network IP address/netmask, network address
  circle      | geometric circle '(center,radius)'
  date        | ANSI SQL date
  filename    | filename used in system tables
  float4      | single-precision floating point number, 4-byte storage
  float8      | double-precision floating point number, 8-byte storage
  inet        | IP address/netmask, host address, netmask optional
  int2        | -32 thousand to 32 thousand, 2-byte storage
  int2vector  | array of 16 int2 integers, used in system tables
--More--
```

Again, there are more types than I need to list here. They are all covered in Chapter 9.

The psql program puts the queries you type into a buffer. To edit the queries in the buffer, use the \e command.

```
perkins=# \e
select * from address;
~
~
~
~
"/tmp/psql.edit.500.7763" 1L, 23C
```

If you don't like VIM, the "improved" VI editor, set the environmental variable EDITOR, PSQL_EDITOR, or VISUAL to the name of the editor you want before you enter the psql program.

The -g command runs whatever is in the query buffer. The \p command shows what is in the buffer, which you could have just edited with the \e command. The following exchange uses the \p command to show what is in the query buffer and then \g to execute the command in the buffer.

```
perkins=# \p
select * from address;
perkins=# \g
 nickname  |     street      | state
-----------+-----------------+------
 Leslie    | 1313 MBird Lane | CA
 Laura     | Rt 66           | AZ
 Kelly     | 1010 Pudder Ln  | FL perkins=# \H
 Ruth      | 4624 Minn       | CA
(4 rows)
```

\H toggles the output to HTML, which is one of the most interesting options. It works like the -H switch discussed earlier. To make an HTML page from your address table, type

```
perkins=# \H
Output format is html.
perkins=# select * from address;
<table border=1>
  <tr>
    <th align=center>nickname</th>
    <th align=center>street</th>
```

```
          <th align=center>state</th>
      </tr>
      <tr valign=top>
        <td align=left>Leslie</td>
        <td align=left>1313 MBird Lane</td>
        <td align=left>CA</td>
      </tr>
      <tr valign=top>
        <td align=left>Laura</td>
        <td align=left>Rt 66</td>
        <td align=left>AZ</td>
      </tr>
      <tr valign=top>
        <td align=left>Kelly</td>
        <td align=left>1010 Pudder Ln</td>
        <td align=left>FL</td>
      </tr>
      <tr valign=top>
        <td align=left>Ruth</td>
        <td align=left>4624 Minn</td>
        <td align=left>CA</td>
      </tr>
    </table>
    (4 rows)<br>
```

If you used the \o switch to send this output to a file named myaddress.html, it would look like this:

```
perkins=# \o myaddress.html
perkins=# select * from address;
perkins=# \o
```

Notice the second \o. This resets the output to the standard output path—in this case, the terminal. If you want to look at this file using Lynx, a text-based HTML browser, but you don't want to leave psql, use the \! command to run Lynx, and then return to psql. It would look like this:

```
perkins=# \! lynx myaddress.html
```

This would result in the following:

```
   nickname      street        state
   Leslie    1313 MBird Lane CA
```

```
Laura     Rt 66          AZ
Kelly     1010 Pudder Ln FL
Ruth      4624 Minn      CA


(4 rows)
```

```
Commands: Use arrow keys to move, '?' for help, 'q' to quit, '<-' to go back.
  Arrow keys: Up and Down to move.  Right to follow a link; Left to go back.
 H)elp O)ptions P)rint G)o M)ain screen Q)uit /=search [delete]=history list
```

Typing Q will end the Lynx session and return to the psql prompt.

To read in files and run their contents, PostgreSQL provides the /i command. Using the backup address table you made when you did the command-line equivalent (-f), delete the address table and then restore it by typing

```
perkins=# DROP TABLE address;
DROP
perkins=# \i address.bu
You are now connected as new user perkins.
CREATE
CHANGE
CHANGE
CHANGE
```

Now, verify that the address is back.

```
perkins=# select * from address;
 nickname |     street      | state
----------+-----------------+------
 Leslie   | 1313 MBird Lane | CA
 Laura    | Rt 66           | AZ
 Kelly    | 1010 Pudder Ln  | FL
 Ruth     | 4624 Minn       | CA
(4 rows)
```

As you do more and more complex tasks with PostgreSQL, you will start putting your work in scripts and reading them in, using the \i command.

To quit psql, use the \q command.

Infrequently Used Options

To put output from a query into an unformatted form, use the \a command. If the \a command has already been used and you want to go back to a formatted alignment, use the \a command again. Here is an example.

```
perkins=# \a
Output format is unaligned.
perkins=# select * from address;
nickname|street|state
Leslie|1313 MBird Lane|CA
Laura|Rt 66|AZ
Kelly|1010 Pudder Ln|FL
Ruth|4624 Minn|CA
(4 rows)
perkins=# \a
Output format is aligned.
perkins=# select * from address;
 nickname |     street      | state
----------+----------------+------
 Leslie   | 1313 MBird Lane | CA
 Laura    | Rt 66          | AZ
 Kelly    | 1010 Pudder Ln  | FL
 Ruth     | 4624 Minn      | CA
(4 rows)
```

Notice how psql tells you the current alignment status after each \a command.

Should you have copyright questions, use the /copyright command to answer them. Here is the /copyright command at work.

```
perkins=# \copyright
PostgreSQL Data Base Management System


Portions Copyright (c) 1996-2000, PostgreSQL, Inc


This software is based on Postgres95, formerly known as Postgres, which
contains the following notice:


Portions Copyright(c) 1994 - 7 Regents of the University of California


Permission to use, copy, modify, and distribute this software and its
```

Should you feel the need to send text to the standard output, which is normally the screen, use the /echo command. Here is an example:

```
perkins=# \echo "HELLO!"
"HELLO!"
```

The encoding switch will show the encoding and the language and character set used in your database. The subject of encoding and the various types of encoding are covered in Chapter 2, "PostgreSQL Administrative Programs," in the section on create_db. The following example uses \encoding to show which encoding scheme is being used.

```
perkins=# \encoding
SQL_ASCII
```

The \f command allows you to insert your own delimiter into unaligned data. If you wanted to use the percent (%) symbol, you would type

```
perkins=# \a
Output format is unaligned.
perkins=# \f '%'
Field separator is '%'.
perkins=# select * from address;
nickname%street%state
Leslie%1313 MBird Lane%CA
Laura%Rt 66%AZ
Kelly%1010 Pudder Ln%FL
```

```
Ruth%4624 Minn%CA

(4 rows)
```

To get a list of all the SQL commands use the \h command.

```
perkins=# \h
Available help:
  ABORT                 CREATE TRIGGER        FETCH
  ALTER GROUP           CREATE TYPE           GRANT
  ALTER TABLE           CREATE USER           INSERT
  ALTER USER            CREATE VIEW           LISTEN
  BEGIN                 DECLARE               LOAD
  CLOSE                 DELETE                LOCK
  CLUSTER               DROP AGGREGATE        MOVE
  COMMENT               DROP DATABASE         NOTIFY
  COMMIT                DROP FUNCTION         REINDEX
  ...
```

Using the \h command with a given SQL statement produces the syntax for
that statement.

```
perkins=# \h DELETE
Command:     DELETE
Description: Removes rows from a table
Syntax:
DELETE FROM table [ WHERE condition ]
```

A convenient way to list the databases on a system is by using the \l command.
This command is like the -l command-line function. It looks like this:

```
perkins=# \l
          List of databases
  Database   |  Owner   | Encoding
-------------+----------+----------
 newbie01    | perkins  | SQL_ASCII
 newbie02    | perkins  | SQL_ASCII
 newbie03    | perkins  | SQL_ASCII
 newbie04    | perkins  | SQL_ASCII
 newbie05    | perkins  | SQL_ASCII
 newbie06    | perkins  | SQL_ASCII
 perkins     | perkins  | SQL_ASCII
 regression  | postgres | SQL_ASCII
```

```
template1 | postgres | SQL_ASCII
(9 rows)
```

If you have a large file you need to store in the database, PostgreSQL provides the `lo_` commands to add, query, and delete it. Usually, this is done with pictures. To add a picture to the database, use this command:

```
perkins-# \lo_import '/usr/share/wallpapers/cosmic_gears.jpg' 'some picture I fo
und'
lo_import 409729
```

Then, use `\lo_list` to see the items you have imported.

```
perkins-# \lo_list
            Large objects
  Owner  |   ID   |     Description
--------+--------+---------------------
 perkins | 409729 | some picture I found
(1 row)
```

Notice the ID column. This is the number you use to delete the object from the database.

```
perkins-# \lo_unlink 409729
NOTICE:  Caution: DROP TABLE cannot be rolled back, so don't abort now
NOTICE:  Caution: DROP INDEX cannot be rolled back, so don't abort now
lo_unlink 409729
```

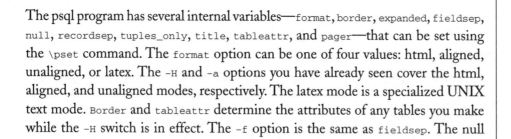

I do not recommend putting binary objects, such as pictures, into a database. Instead, store the path and file name. It seems that whenever I put something into the database, I end up needing to run it through another program, which requires extracting, operating on, and then reinserting the file. If you store just the path and name of the file, modifications don't become a database operation.

NOTE

The psql program has several internal variables—`format`, `border`, `expanded`, `fieldsep`, `null`, `recordsep`, `tuples_only`, `title`, `tableattr`, and `pager`—that can be set using the `\pset` command. The `format` option can be one of four values: html, aligned, unaligned, or latex. The `-H` and `-a` options you have already seen cover the html, aligned, and unaligned modes, respectively. The latex mode is a specialized UNIX text mode. `Border` and `tableattr` determine the attributes of any tables you make while the `-H` switch is in effect. The `-f` option is the same as `fieldsep`. The null option allows you to set what is printed if a field in the database is empty. PostgreSQL normally does not print anything in a `null` field. If you would rather have the word *null*, set this value. `Tuples_only` eliminates the header and footer information in a table, leaving you with just the data—which can also be done using the `\t` option. The `\c` option works the same as `title`. Finally, `pager` sets the program that psql uses to show large amounts of data, normally the more program.

Summary

As you can see, the psql program is like a Swiss Army knife—it has dozens of uses. As a command-line program, it can be used to move data in and out of your scripts, or you can use it in a CGI program to manufacture parts of an HTML page. Inside psql, you can manipulate your system and your data. Programmers need to know psql basics. Those destined to become database administrators will spend most of their time in psql and will learn all of its capabilities.

Chapter 5: Getting Graphical with PostgreSQL: The pgaccess Program

The pgaccess program is a GUI-based supplement to the psql program. Constantin Teodorescu is the author, and the Web site is http://www.flex.ro/pgaccess/index.html. The pgaccess program offers a large subset of the functions available in psql, including manipulating tables, queries, views, and users.

The Basic Screen

From a command-line window, type **pgaccess&**. The ampersand (&) is not required, but it starts pgaccess as a separate process and allows you to use the command box to launch other programs. Figure 5.1 shows the result.

This screen is very straightforward. The first thing you need to do is connect to a database.

Connecting to a Database

To connect to a database, click the Open button on the basic screen. The database menu and the connection details screen appear in Figure 5.2. Notice that you can also run the vacuum function and import and export files.

The connection details screen contains the name or IP address of the machine running PostgreSQL, the port to connect to (remember, this defaults to 5432), the

Figure 5.1   *The basic pgaccess screen*

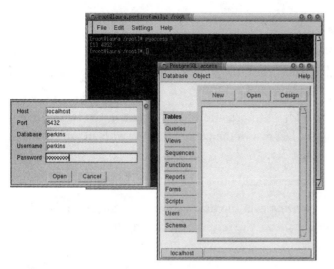

Figure 5.2 *The database menu and the connection details screen*

desired database, the user, and a password. Remember from Chapter 3, "PostgreSQL Basic Security," that a password is optional. Not specifying the user name is a common error. For example, if you log in to your system as *root* and then run pgaccess and try to log in to the perkins database without specifying a user name, the PostgreSQL system will tell you that *root* is not a valid user.

Click the Open button, and you will be connected to your database, as shown in Figure 5.3.

Figure 5.3 *Connected to the database*

Working with Tables

The pgaccess program allows you to edit existing tables or make new ones. To edit the data in an existing table, select the table and click the Open button. Figure 5.4 shows the selection of the Address table.

This window allows you to add, edit, sort, and filter the data in the table. To add data, write the new data in the last row of the table—the row with an asterisk (*) in each field—as shown in Figure 5.5.

After the data is added, click the Reload button or select a different row.

Editing data is as simple as writing over the field you want to change and clicking the Reload button. Figure 5.6 shows the results of changing the Street and State values for the last row of data.

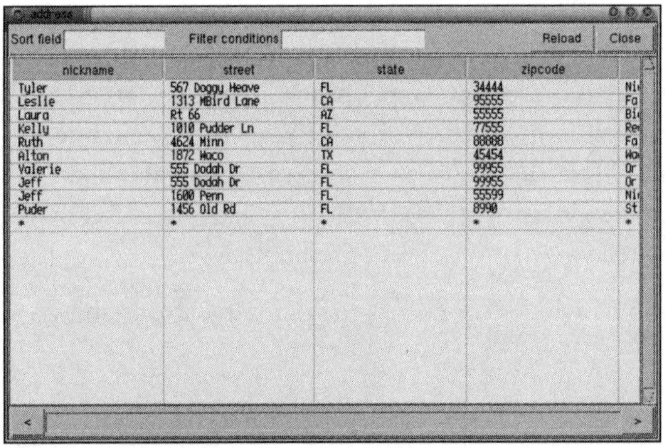

Figure 5.4   *Selecting the Address table*

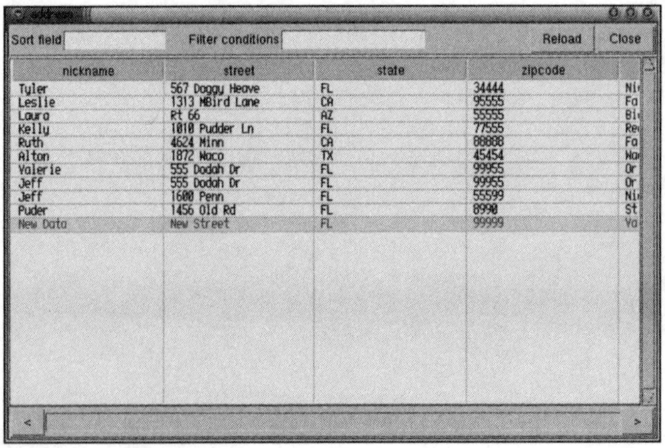

Figure 5.5   *Adding data to a table*

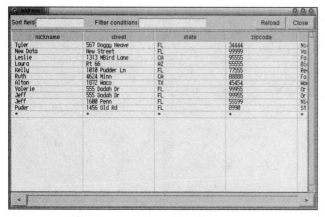

Figure 5.6   *Editing a value in a table*

To sort a table by one of its values, place the column name in the Sort Field text box and click the Reload button. Figure 5.7 illustrates sorting the Address table by the Nickname field.

To apply a filter to the values in the table, use the Filter Conditions text box. To find everyone in the state of California, type `state = 'CA'` in the Filter Conditions text box and click the Reload button, as shown in Figure 5.8.

The sort and filter functions can be used together. Try adding a few more people from your favorite state to the Address table. Then order them by nickname and filter them by state.

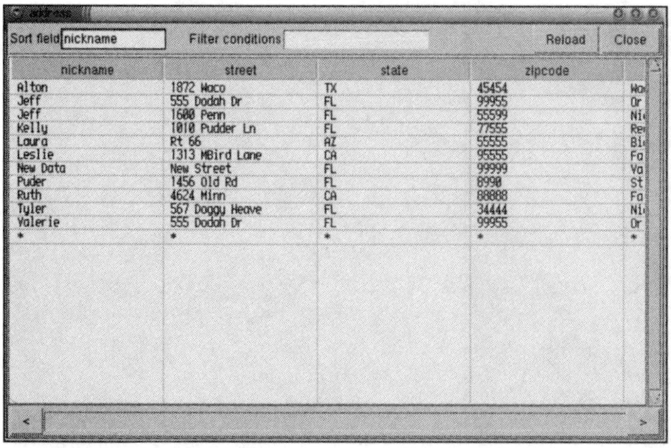

Figure 5.7   *Sorting by the Nickname column*

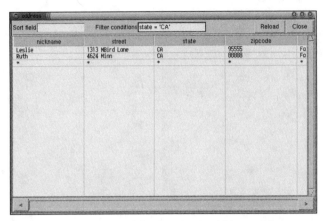

Figure 5.8   *Finding the Californians in the Address table*

What if you want to change the structure of a table? Using pgaccess, you select the table to restructure and then click the Design button. This displays the design screen, shown in Figure 5.9.

At the top of the design screen are four tabs. The first tab, General, displays non-editable information about the table. The other three tabs are more interesting from a design standpoint. Use the Columns tab to add and rename columns and to add a new index. Figure 5.10 shows the addition of a zip code column and a city column.

Adding an index to a table increases PostgreSQL's capability to search for data. To add an index in the zip code field, highlight the field and click the Add New Index button. This displays the screen shown in Figure 5.11.

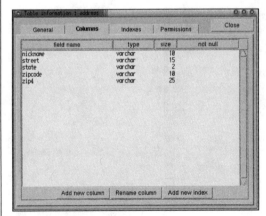

Figure 5.9   *The design screen*

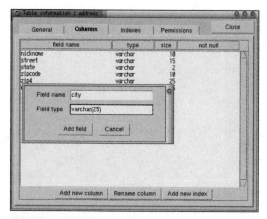

Figure 5.10   *Adding a city column*

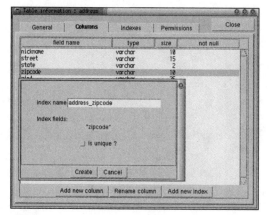

Figure 5.11   *Adding an index in the zipcode column*

If you had an index with unique values, such as social security numbers, you would check the Is Unique? button. Because a zip code is not unique, you click the Create button and move to the Indexes tab, shown in Figure 5.12.

From this screen, you can delete or cluster the index. Deleting is straightforward and probably needs no explanation. *Clustering* an index creates one index out of many. Clustering is an advanced topic that is beyond the scope of this book.

If you end up administering a PostgreSQL database, you will spend a lot of time in the Permissions screen, shown in Figure 5.13. This screen lets you graphically assign permissions for this table to groups and users. This Process is equivalent to the command-line methods discussed in Chapter 3, "PostgreSQL Basic Security." Figure 5.14 shows the user newbie01 being assigned select, update, insert, and rule privileges on this table. To change permissions, you use the same screen.

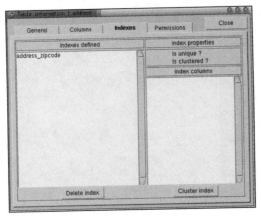

Figure 5.12   *The Indexes tab*

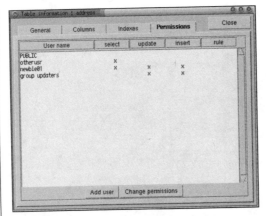

Figure 5.13   *The Permissions tab*

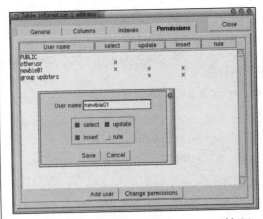

Figure 5.14   *Assigning permissions to user newbie01*

Do not try to use the Permissions tab to *create* users. There is a separate function for that; it will be covered later. If you do put a new name in here, pgaccess will complain. Click the Users tab on the main pgaccess screen to see which users are available.

Sometimes what you need is a brand new table. Figure 5.15 shows a new table named *friends*, with the fields *nickname*, *birthday*, and *ssn*.

Before you click the Create button, go back to the database menu (refer to Figure 5.2), and click the SQL Window menu item. Then click the Create button on the Create New Table screen. You should get something like the screen in Figure 5.16.

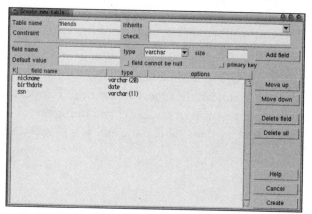

Figure 5.15 *A new way to "make" friends*

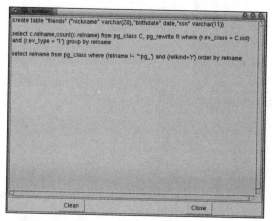

Figure 5.16 *The SQL window*

The SQL window echoes all the SQL commands used by pgaccess. You can use this window to teach or learn SQL and also to snoop around the system tables in PostgreSQL.

If you ever use PostgreSQL's object-oriented side (covered in Chapter 18, "Advanced Topics in PostgreSQL") you will discover that the Inherits list box (refer to Figure 5.15) allows you to base your new table on an existing table. When you need to put in a constraint to check the data going into your table, use the Constraint field to name your constraint and the Check field to describe it. You will see constraints covered in detail in Part III, "Programming."

Working with Queries

Chapter 8, "Basic SQL," is full of psql-based, command-line SQL query examples. When you reach that chapter, you might want to fire up pgaccess and go to the Queries tab. From there you can create a new query, open an already created query, or design a query.

Clicking the New button displays the Query Builder screen. Type in your SQL query in the center text area, giving it a name in the Query Name field. Then click the Execute Query button. As you can see on your computer and in Figure 5.17, pgaccess displays the same screen used to show table data, and fills it with the results of your query.

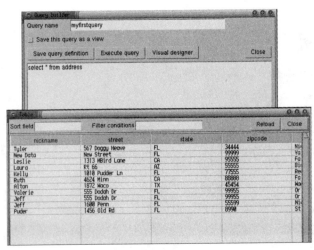

Figure 5.17   *A query and its result set*

If you don't want to concentrate on SQL syntax for your query, you can click the Visual Designer button. The Visual Designer, shown in Figure 5.18, allows you to pick tables and values from those tables to create a query graphically.

After the query is designed, you can save it for later use. (You will see how queries can be used in forms later in this chapter.) You can also check the Save This Query as a View check box (refer to Figure 5.17) before saving the query, which, as you probably guessed, saves the query as a view.

Selecting an existing query and clicking the Open button displays a table view of the query results, shown in Figure 5.19.

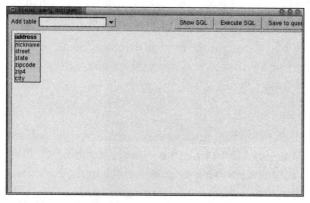

Figure 5.18   *Visually designing a query*

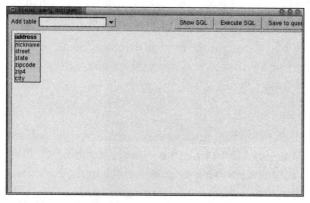

Figure 5.19   *Opening an existing query*

Data with a View

A *view*, in database terms, is like a table you can see but can't update. Database designers use views to create objects that satisfy a user's need for data but make it impossible for the user to enter any data.

As with the Queries tab, choosing an existing view and clicking the Open button displays a table view of the query results (refer to Figure 5.19). The New and Design buttons also display the same screens as the Queries tab, except that the Save This Query as a View check box is selected.

Sequences

When working with a database, you will find that occasionally you need a sequence of numbers to act as a unique identifier for a row of data. A *sequence* is a database function you can call to get such a number. To create a sequence named *addone*, select the Sequences tab and fill out the screen as is done in Figure 5.20.

Now click Define Sequence to add the sequence to your database. Sequences are an advanced database topic and aren't covered in detail in this book.

Functions

PostgreSQL allows you to add your own functions to the database. As you will see in Part III, you have various languages from which to choose, including C, Perl, and SQL. To learn how to build a function using pgaccess, switch to the Functions tab and, using SQL as your language, create a function named addnumbers that adds two numbers and returns the result. Figure 5.21 shows this in action.

Figure 5.20   *Creating a sequence*

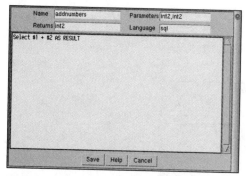

Figure 5.21   *Creating a function to add two numbers*

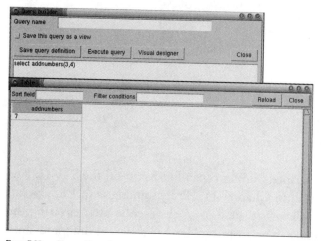

Figure 5.22   *Running the* addnumbers *function*

Test your work after you save your new function by going back to the Queries tab, making a new query (select addnumbers(3,4)), and executing the query. Your screen should look something like Figure 5.22.

Creating Reports

The pgaccess program has a graphic report generator that allows you to create reports using table objects. To create a new report, select New, and then add a report name. Next, choose a table; in Figure 5.23, the Address table is used. Then, drag and drop the report fields to the lines on the form. If you make a mistake and need to delete a field, select the field and press Delete. A sample report and its preview appear in Figure 5.23. Opening an existing report and pressing the Design button invokes the same screen.

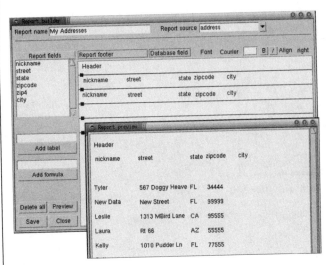

Figure 5.23   *A basic report*

Forms and Scripts

pgaccess has a form- and script-building capability based on the Tcl/Tk language, which I cover in detail in Chapter 11, "Programming with PL/Tcl and Tcl." In Chapter 11, you will revisit these parts of pgaccess after covering the basics of the Tcl/Tk language. The form builder has a typical drag-and-drop IDE, shown in Figure 5.24.

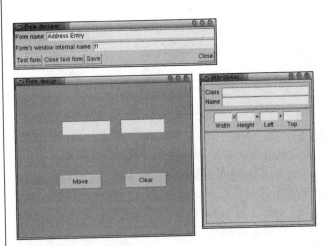

Figure 5.24   *The Form Designer*

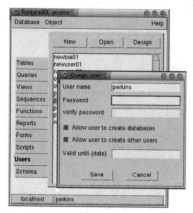

Figure 5.25   *The Users screen*

Working with Users

In Chapter 2, you learned how to create users with the createuser program. The pgaccess Users tab gives you a graphical tool for creating new users and editing existing users. Both the New and Design buttons use the same form, with the Design button filling in the current information for the selected user, as shown in Figure 5.25.

Schemas

A database schema shows the relationships between tables. For example, earlier you saw a Friends table containing a Nickname column. Suppose that you want to relate the information in the Friends table to the information in the Address table, which also has a Nicknames column (see Chapter 7, "Basic Relational Database Design," for more information on relationships between tables). Using the Schema tab, you click the New button, add the Friends and Address tables, and drag the nickname from the Friends table to the Address table. The result would look like Figure 5.26.

Summary

The pgaccess program is a valuable tool for maintaining your PostgreSQL database. It greatly simplifies creating and editing the basic building blocks of your database—tables and users. pgaccess also has excellent support for more advanced activities, such as writing functions, views, and queries. You should also keep an eye on the rapidly developing report, form, and scripting support in future versions.

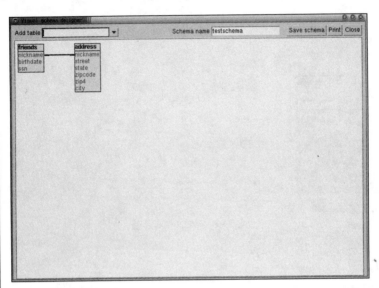

Figure 5.26   *The Schema screen*

Chapter 6: Running PostgreSQL from Windows

ostgreSQL doesn't run under Microsoft Windows, but there are a couple ways to administer PostgreSQL from a computer running one of the Microsoft operating systems. In this chapter, you will learn about two programs, the Zeos Database Explorer and a Microsoft Windows version of the pgaccess program. Both programs are free, and both allow you to manipulate your PostgreSQL from the comfort of your Microsoft Windows computer.

The Zeos Database Explorer

The Zeos Database Explorer, which originated in Russia, is built from Borland's Delphi, which, for those of you who have never used it, is an object-oriented flavor of Pascal.

> Linux programmers in the audience might want to keep an eye on the Borland Web page (http://www.borland.com/). Some time in the near future, Borland will release Kylix (http://www.borland.com/kylix/), which produces executable programs for Linux from object-oriented Pascal, implemented in a component-based, drag-and-drop, integrated development environment. As Linux becomes more popular as a client platform, programs like Kylix will become the tool of choice for building database front ends and middle-ware for multi-tier applications on the Linux platform.

To get started with Database Explorer, head to the Zeos Web site, http://www.marms.com/zeos/eng/zeos_home.html, shown in Figure 6.1.

Click the Products button on the left navigation bar, and choose the link to Interactive PostgreSQL in the center of the page. You will move to the page shown in Figure 6.2.

Choose the latest version of the Database Explorer. It will be in a zde archive, which contains the components required to connect to several databases, including PostgreSQL. Depending on the version, the file you download will look something like this: zde-1.1.2.zip.

After you download the file, extract the contents to a directory on your Microsoft Windows machine. Figure 6.3 shows the files extracted to the zde directory on my C: drive.

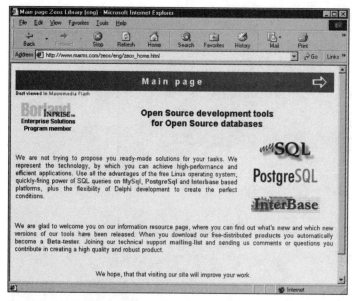

Figure 6.1   *Zeos's Web home*

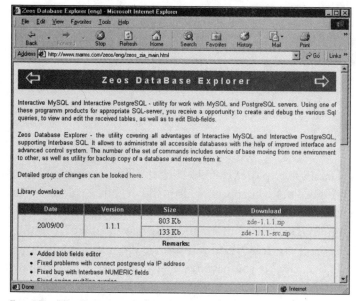

Figure 6.2   *The Zeos download page*

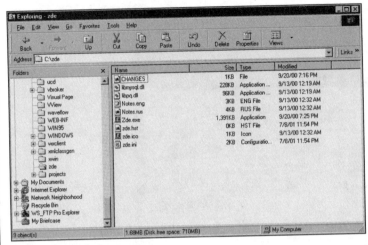

Figure 6.3 *The Zeos directory*

Figure 6.4 *The Zeos Database Explorer Logon*

To start using the Zeos Database Explorer, double-click the Zde.exe icon. A login screen similar to that in Figure 6.4 will appear. This is the default Explorer login screen. It defaults to Borland's Interbase database. Select PostgreSQL as the database, and fill in your PostgreSQL database information. Review Chapter 1, "Setting Up PostgreSQL," Chapter 2, "PostgreSQL Administrative Programs," and Chapter 3, "PostgreSQL Basic Security," if you haven't already installed your database and set it up to receive outside connections. I connect to the database that serves as an example in other chapters using the screen shown in Figure 6.5.

The main Database Explorer screen shows the user and system tables. Figure 6.6 shows the Address table selected in the left pane and the data in the Address table in the right pane. You can navigate through and edit the data in the table by using the navigation bar above the table data (the one that looks like cassette controls). You can add records using the plus (+) sign and then type values directly into the table. When you are done editing, commit your changes using the check mark.

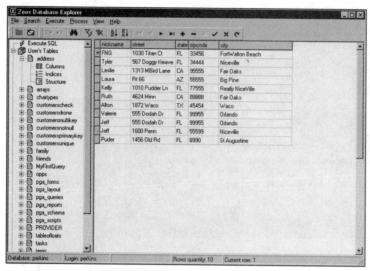

Figure 6.5   *The Zeos Database Explorer logon for the perkins database*

You can enter SQL statements, as shown in Figure 6.6 (see Chapter 8, "Basic SQL," for SQL specifics), by clicking the Execute SQL entry at the top of the left pane, next to the lightening bolt. Clicking Execute SQL displays two panes on the right. Type in `select * from address` in the top-right pane, and click the Execute SQL button on the toolbar (again, the lightening bolt), or press Control+R. Your screen will look similar to that in Figure 6.6.

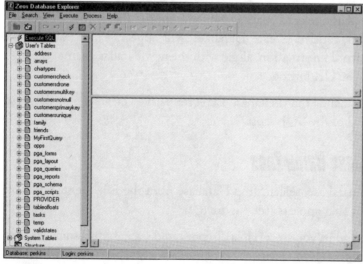

Figure 6.6   *Query results*

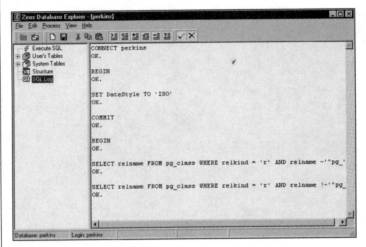

Figure 6.7   *The SQL Log*

Notice that the query in the top pane disappears and you are left with the results of the query in the lower pane.

Selecting the last item in the left pane, SQL Log, displays a record of your conversation with the PostgreSQL server, as shown in Figure 6.7.

You can use this log to help you learn some of the details behind the PostgreSQL server and to sharpen your SQL skills.

Creating a New Database Using Zeos

To create a new database, select Create Database from the File menu. The Database Explorer screen, retitled Create Database, will appear. Enter your server, username, and password information, along with the new database name (see Figure 6.8), then click the OK button.

You can see the commands that Database Explorer used to create a new database by looking at the end of the SQL Log.

Deleting a Database Using Zeos

To dispense with a database, select Drop Database from the File menu. Click on yes in the dialog box that appears (see Figure 6.9).

After the database is gone, you are left in a disconnected state. In this state, you can quit (File, Exit), connect (File, Connect Database), or create a new database (File, Create Database).

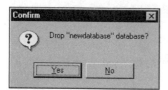

Figure 6.8 *The Create Database screen*

Figure 6.9 *Deleting a database*

There is no explicit control for creating other database objects, such as users or tables. As you will learn in Chapter 8, though, you can use the Execute SQL function to manipulate your data and its structure.

> Those who do your database front-end programming for the Microsoft Windows operating system using Borland's Delphi might want to try out the Zeos PostgreSQL components for Delphi. These components are also available on the Zeos site.

pgaccess via Windows

In Chapter 5 I covered pgaccess, an important contribution to the PostgreSQL effort. There is no need to rehash the pgaccess functionality. Instead, in this section, you will focus on how to set up the pgaccess program on a Microsoft Windows computer.

The pgaccess program is built out of the Tcl/Tk language. This is the key to making pgaccess work on Microsoft Windows. The first thing you need is a Tcl/Tk version that runs on the Microsoft operating system. You can find this version at http://dev.scriptics.com/software/tcltk/. At the time of this writing, the 8.3 version of Tcl/Tk doesn't work with pgaccess, so download the 8.2 version at http://dev.scriptics.com/software/tcltk/download82.html, shown in Figure 6.10.

When the file is downloaded, install it by double-clicking tcl823.exe. Use the installation program defaults.

Now, return to the pgaccess site, http://www.flex.ro/pgaccess/, and download using the Windows.zip link, which turns out to be the pgaccess-0.98.6.zip file. Unzip the file, and change to the \pgaccess\win32\dll directory, shown in Figure 6.11.

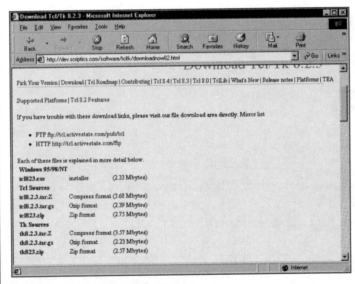

Figure 6.10   *The Tcl/Tk download site*

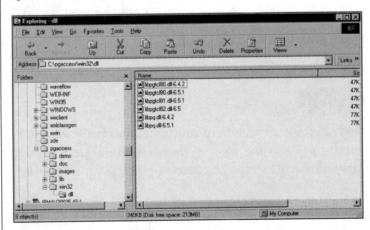

Figure 6.11   *The pgAacess dll directory*

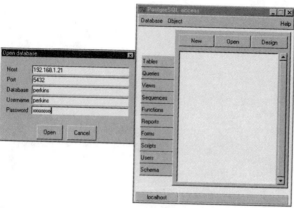

Figure 6.12   *pgaccess on a Microsoft Windows computer*

Change the name of the libpgtcl82.dll-6.5 file to *libpgtcl.dll*, and move it to the \Windows\System directory. This will provide the links between the Tcl/Tk language and the database. Notice that two other dlls in this directory begin with *libpq*. I don't recommend using either library. Instead, copy the file libpq.dll from the \zde directory to the Windows\System directory. As of this writing, the file that comes with the Zeos Database Explorer is newer than the files that come with pgaccess. After you have the dll's in place, go to the pgaccess directory and double-click the main.tcl file. This produces the PostgreSQL Access screens, shown in Figure 6.12.

Now that your system is configured to run pgaccess in Microsoft Windows, you might want to revisit Chapter 5 to review the details on pgaccess.

Summary

There are tens of millions of Microsoft Windows platforms in the computer world. Odds are, you will need to administer your PostgreSQL system from a Microsoft Windows platform. In this chapter, you learned how to install two Windows-based programs, Zeos Database Explorer and pgaccess. In addition, you were introduced to the functions available with the Database Explorer. This chapter ends the setup and administration portions of the book. Now it's time to study database programming and design.

PART III

Programming

Chapter 7: Basic Relational Database Design

This chapter is Relational Database 101: everything you need to get started using a relational database. I'll begin by reviewing the defining points of a relational database, then I'll discuss the primary building block of a relational database, the table. Finally, I'll explain basic database design principles.

A Brief History

Long, long ago, like about 30 years, data was stored on physically large and proprietary computers. Each of these computers had its own way of storing and retrieving data. Teams of programmers, schooled in the workings of one particular data system, labored to write special programs for each request for data, and no two systems were alike. Then, in 1970, someone had a better idea.

In 1970, Dr. E. F. Codd wrote a paper entitled "A Relational Model of Data for Large Shared Data Banks." This paper defined a new kind of database called a *relational* database. The definition of a relational database is contained in what are called *Codd's 12 Rules*. The unexplained mystery is that there are actually 13 rules! You don't need to memorize these, but they will contribute to your knowledge of how database systems are built, which, in turn, will make you smarter when designing database programs based on these systems. Following are Dr. Codd's rules:

- **Rule 0: Foundation.** A relational Database Management System (DBMS) must be able to manage databases entirely through its relational capabilities.

- **Rule 1: Information.** All information in a relational database (including table and column names) is represented explicitly as values in tables.

- **Rule 2: Guaranteed Access.** Every value in a relational database is guaranteed to be accessible by consisting of a combination of the table name, primary key value, and column name.

- **Rule 3: Systematic Null Value Support.** The DBMS provides systematic support for the treatment of *null values* (unknown or inapplicable data), distinct from default values and independent of any domain.

- **Rule 4: Active, On-Line Relational Catalog.** The description of the database and its contents is represented at the logical level by tables and can therefore be queried using the database language.

- **Rule 5: Comprehensive Data Sublanguage.** At least one language must be supported, have a well-defined syntax, and be comprehensive in that it supports data definition, manipulation, integrity rules, authorization, and transactions.

- **Rule 6: The View Updating Rule.** All views that are theoretically possible can be updated through the system.
- **Rule 7: Set-Level Insertions, Updates, and Deletions.** The DBMS supports not only set-level retrievals but also set-level inserts, updates, and deletes.
- **Rule 8: Physical Data Independence.** Application programs and ad hoc programs are logically unaffected when physical access methods of storage structures are altered.
- **Rule 9: Logical Data Independence.** Application programs and ad hoc programs are logically unaffected when changes are made to the table structures.
- **Rule 10: Integrity Independence.** The database language must be capable of defining integrity rules. They must be stored in the on-line catalog, and they cannot be bypassed.
- **Rule 11: Distribution Independence.** Application programs and ad hoc requests are logically unaffected when data is first distributed or when it is redistributed.
- **Rule 12: Nonsubversion.** It must not be possible to bypass the integrity rules defined through the database language by using lower-level languages.

Most of these rules are a reaction to the way the first data systems operated. Rule 8, for example, which talks about physical data independence, gives you, as a programmer, an assurance that your database programs won't have to be rewritten if the hardware on which the database is hosted changes.

All these rules are enforced by the relational databases available today. Oracle, Microsoft SQL PostgreSQL, and Microsoft Access enforce them for you. Rules 4 and 5 reference a database language; this need for a common database language is what caused SQL to be created. Without SQL, we programmers would have to learn a proprietary language for every database we need to access. A basic knowledge of SQL gives us a tool we can use across a whole industry of relational databases. SQL is covered in Chapter 8, "Basic SQL."

Database Structure

How do you go about building a database based on Codd's rules? You start with the basics. The following sections examine the database building blocks.

Database Building Blocks

Relational databases contain tables, triggers, stored procedures, and views.

Tables

The sets of data contained in a database are organized into tables. A table contains a collection of objects, such as the objects that make up an address: street name, city, and zip code, as shown in Figure 7.1

Each item of data, called a *value* in database speak, is in its own column. One entire set of data—address, street name, city, and zip code, for example—is called a *record*. Looking at Figure 7.1, you can also see why records are also called *rows*, because a record represented in table format is a row.

Triggers

Triggers are pieces of code executed when certain events, such the addition of a record, occur in the database. Triggers are primarily used to enforce data integrity as stated in Dr. Codd's Rule 10. For example, if you wanted to ensure that the zip codes entered into your table are exactly five characters long, you would put in a trigger for your Address table that checks the length of the zip code. If the zip code were too long or too short, the record would not be entered into the database.

Basic Table

StreetAddress	City	ZipCode	State
123 W 23 St	VictorVille	55555	NV
123 West 23rd St	victorVille	55555-4544	Nevada
123 W 23rd Street	V'Ville	5555	Nev

Figure 7.1   *Data in a table*

Stored Procedures

In Rule 5, Dr. Codd gives database manufacturers a way to include their own database manipulation languages ("at least one language"). Every major database has taken advantage of it by including database manipulation languages that make up the database building block known as a *stored procedure*. Stored procedures enable a database programmer to put a database operation inside the database but still allow it to be accessed by programmers using SQL. For example, say your database contains sensitive information, such as salaries, that you don't want everyone in your organization to know. You can grant read and write privileges (see Chapter 2 for examples) for the Salary table to only a few users. Then you can write a stored procedure, accessible to many users, that sanitizes the actual salaries. When the normal programmer uses the stored procedure for salaries, he or she can access average salaries but not the salaries associated with names. Stored procedures are covered in Chapter 5, "Getting Graphical with PostgreSQL: The pgaccess Program."

Views

A *view*, in database terms, is a set of data that doesn't come from just one table. The section "What Is Normalization?" in this chapter describes the reasons why related data might be in more than one table. For example, user information—such as name, address, and phone number—can be in one table, and the order the user makes for pencils can be in another. With a view internally stated using the query syntax covered in Chapter 8, you can get a data set from the database that contains the user's name, address, and what the user ordered.

Building a Better Database

Codd's rules apply only to the programmers who build relational databases. As a user of a relational database product, you still need to follow certain design rules that make your database usable and reusable. The question now is: How do you design your database?

The Normalization Rule

There is one rule that will more than pay for the time you spend implementing it: *Normalize your data.* If you normalize your data, your database will be easier to understand and use. If you don't normalize your data, bad things can happen. For example, you could build a table of orders, each with a ship-to address, and wind up 10 different address for one customer, each one spelled a different way. Not only would you have spent more time entering address data, but the more time you spent, the more likely your data would contain mistakes, and, if a customer moved, you would have to correct address data in several places.

What Is Normalization?

Normalizing your data means organizing it efficiently. There are several different layers of normalization, each one adding a higher degree of organization. In database speak each layers of organization is called an *Orders Normal*. Following are the technical different Orders of Normal:

- **First Order Normal.** Each value in a table must contain a single value, and the table must not contain repeating groups of data.

- **Second Order Normal.** Data not directly dependent on the table's primary key is moved into another table.

- **Third Order Normal.** Remove all fields that can be derived from data contained in other columns in the table or other tables in the database.

For all practical purposes, this can be boiled down to ensuring that your data is stored in only one place. For example, you put a form on a Web site where your users request some service you perform, such as installing telephone lines. On this form, your user lists the kind of service he or she wants, where he or she wants it, and the telephone and e-mail address of the point of contact for this installation. At first glance, you might want to put all this data into one table, which might look okay, especially to someone new to databases. However, what you'd have is a potential mess. For example, if the same location put in a request, it could type its address a different way every time, or the contact name could have several spellings for the same person. *Alton Perkins*, *A. E. Perkins*, or *Perk* could all refer to the same person. Over time, if you asked your database for A. E. Perkins' address, you could get several answers. If you wanted to correct an address, you would have to correct it on several lines.

This leads to the most basic rule of database design: *Data should appear in the database only once.* Take a look at the information from your form, organized using the first normal form (see Figure 7.2).

From what you just learned about normalization, the first order form calls for each column to contain a single value. There was no problem with this in the original data because there was only one piece of data in each column. Had I collected the city and zip code into the same column, the first order normalization would have

User Table

UserID	LastName	FirstName	StreetAddress	City	ZipCode	State	ContactPhone	ContactEmail
1	Perkins	Alton	123 W 23 St	VictorVille	55555	NV	555-5555	perkins@dodah.com

Request Table

ServiceType	RequiredByDate	PriceforService	Surcharge	TotalCharge	UserID
New Phone Line	15-May-01	$500.00	$50	$550.00	1
Install Fax Line	5/15/01	$600.00	$60	$660.00	1
Install T1	15/5/2001	$700.00	$70	$770.00	1

Figure 7.2   *Data in the first normal form*

dictated the creation of a zip code column. The first order normal also calls for the elimination of repeating pieces of data. In Figure 7.2, you see two tables.

The first table contains user data, repeated several times in the original table. Now if you want to change or correct a zip code, you only have to do it in one place. The second table is the Request table. The new column on the Request table is UserID, which corresponds to the user ID number in the User table. What you can see from these two tables is that there are three service requests from a single individual; this was not apparent in the original data.

Now let's apply the second normal form (see Figure 7.3).

State Table

StateID	State
1	Nevada
2	California
3	Texas
...	...

Services Table

ServiceID	Service
1	Install a Phone Line
2	Install a Fax Line
3	Install a T1

Figure 7.3   *Data in the second normal form*

Revised Service Table

ServiceID	RequiredByDate	PriceforService	Surcharge	UserID
1	15-May-01	$500.00	$50	1
2	5/15/01	$600.00	$60	1
3	15/5/2001	$700.00	$70	1

Figure 7.4 *The Services Data table in the third normal form*

The second normal form charges you to move data not directly dependent on the table's primary key into another table. This results in the creation of two new tables, Services and States. The type of service provided is not dependent on the user's request. The user selects a service from an existing list. Note that each service has a ServiceID that is placed into the Request table. States are handled in a similar way, broken down into a separate table, with StateID as the key to the data. This design allows you to change the names of the states in one place. For example, you can change the name *Nevada* to the abbreviation *NV* in the States table.

You have one more form to apply: the third order normal. It changes only one table, as shown in Figure 7.4.

The second normal form of the Services table has data that can be computed from other data in the table. Specifically, the Total field is computed from the Price and Surcharge field. The third normal form dictates that you remove any data that can be created from other values contained in this table or other tables in the database. Without this change, your data would be dependent on an external program to add and save the numbers correctly. The key to an easily maintainable database is to make it as independent as possible. One key to this independence is normalization the other is Data Integrity.

Data Integrity

In the preceding example, where the states are broken out into a separate table, it would be bad if somehow a StateID 51 wound up in the table. Because there are only 50 states, as of this writing, a StateID of 51 would not point to any meaningful data. This is where you use the concept of data integrity to tell the database not to accept any StateIDs on new user records that aren't in the State table. There are a couple ways to do this, using database items called *triggers* and *constraints*, which are covered in detail in Chapters 9 - 16. Data integrity is an important consideration, not always accounted for by programmers who design databases. Programmers tend to protect the database with the program rather than use the database's own data integrity. Work to protect your data at the database level.

Summary

If you don't start your database on a good foundation it can become a real pain to maintain. A little planning using the three orders of normal for laying out your data will make the database easy to understand and modify. Programming triggers and constraints, which you will learn in the programming chapters, will protect you from your users' ceaseless attempts to cram bad data into your database.

Chapter 8: Basic SQL

n this chapter, you will review a brief history of SQL, then you'll learn how to use SQL to create database objects, delete database objects, insert data, update data, and select data. Finally, you will learn about aggregate functions and built-in functions. You will be doing more than just reading about SQL. Every topic I discuss includes examples using PostgreSQL. To run these examples, you need to have installed PostgreSQL and created a database, as explained in Chapter 1, "Setting Up PostgreSQL." You will use the psql program, described in detail in Chapter 4, "Interactive PostgreSQL Using psql," to enter in the SQL commands and observe the results. For those of you new to databases, this will be your first practical application of database theory. For those of you new to PostgreSQL, it will be your first step toward using PostgreSQL to solve your database problems.

An Overview of SQL

To run the examples in this chapter, you will use the database you created at the end of Chapter 1. The user name and database name in Chapter 1 is perkins, something I can remember. First, check whether PostgreSQL is running. Enter this command:

```
/etc/rc.d/init.d/postgresql status
```

If you get this response:

```
postmaster (pid 13458) is running...
```

the postmaster is running, and you can proceed to the next step. If you get this response:

```
postmaster is stopped
```

you need to change to the postgres user (su - postgres) and enter this command:

```
/etc/rc.d/init.d/postgresql start
```

Then change to the user you created in Chapter 1—in my case that would be perkins, again using su - perkins. Then type **psql**. Typing psql brings up the database with the same name as the user. After typing psql, your screen should look like this:

```
[perkins@laura perkins]$ psql
Welcome to psql, the PostgreSQL interactive terminal.

Type:  \copyright for distribution terms
       \h for help with SQL commands
       \? for help on internal slash commands
```

```
    \g or terminate with semicolon to execute query
    \q to quit
```

```
perkins=#
```

Don't worry about the specifics of the psql program now. Chapter 4 covers these in detail. For the rest of this chapter, you will use psql to enter SQL statements and view their results.

Start your tour of SQL by creating some common database objects.

Creating Database Objects

The one database object you will create again and again is the table. I discussed the table as the basic building block for database design in Chapter 7, "Basic Relational Database Design." Now you will see how you can build a table in PostgreSQL using SQL.

The SQL command to build a table is CREATE TABLE. This is the complete syntax for CREATE TABLE, which you can get by typing \h **CREATE TABLE**.

```
CREATE [ TEMPORARY | TEMP ] TABLE table (
    column type
    [ NULL | NOT NULL ] [ UNIQUE ] [ DEFAULT value ]
    [column_constraint_clause | PRIMARY KEY } [ ... ] ]
    [, ... ]
    [, PRIMARY KEY ( column [, ...] ) ]
    [, CHECK ( condition ) ]
    [, table_constraint_clause ]
    ) [ INHERITS ( inherited_table [, ...] ) ]
```

Start with an example. At your psql prompt, type

```
CREATE TABLE Customers00(
LastName varchar(20),
FirstName varchar(15),
Age Int
);
```

If all goes well, your session will look like this:

```
perkins=# CREATE TABLE Customers00
perkins-# (
perkins(# FirstName varchar(15),
perkins(# LastName varchar(20),
```

```
perkins(# Age int
perkins(# );
CREATE
```

Take a look at a couple basic rules that apply to all SQL statements. First, case doesn't matter. You can type the CREATE TABLE statement as:

```
Create Table CUSTOMERS00
(
FirstName varchar(15),
LastName varchar(20),
Age int
);
```

or

```
create table customers00
(
FirstName varchar(15),
LastName varchar(20),
Age int
);
```

This produces the same table as the first example.

The second general rule is that all SQL statements in PostgreSQL end with a semicolon (;). This allows you to type your statement over several lines. The psql program looks for the semicolon to determine when to execute the statement. If you don't type in this terminator, psql will wait patiently until you do before executing your query.

You could type in the query on one line, like this:

```
Create Table CUSTOMERS00(FirstName varchar(15),LastName varchar(20),Age int);
```

Again, as long as the terminator is at the end of the statement, psql will create the table.

Now, take a look at the CREATE TABLE specifics. The first line up to the open parenthesis, Create Table CUSTOMERS00, tells the database to create a table named Customers00. The table isn't very useful unless it has some structure. The lines inside the parentheses describe the structure in the table. This table has three elements: FirstName, LastName, and Age. FirstName and LastName are character strings with lengths of 15 and 20, respectively. The last element, Age, is an integer. Don't worry about the syntax of the items inside the parentheses yet; I will go over their syntax very soon.

To confirm that the table was created, type \dt and press Enter. You should see this:

```
perkins=# \dt
        List of relations
    Name     | Type  |  Owner
-------------+-------+--------
 customers00 | table | perkins
(1 row)
```

The details of the command \dt are covered in the Chapter 4, "Interactive PostgreSQL Using PSQL." This command is useful for showing you the tables you have built.

You can also use the CREATE TABLE statement to make what is called a *temporary* table. Try this:

```
perkins=# CREATE TEMP TABLE CustomersTEMP
perkins-# (
perkins(# FirstName varchar(15),
perkins(# LastName varchar(20),
perkins(# Age int
perkins(# );
```

This creates a table to which you can write data and from which you can get data, but it doesn't show up on the \dt you used to verify the creation of the last table. Entering \dt still shows the Customers00 table you created, as demonstrated by the following:

```
perkins=# \dt
        List of relations
    Name     | Type  |  Owner
-------------+-------+--------
 customers00 | table | perkins
(1 row)
```

You don't see the temporary table. Another attribute of temporary tables is that they are not saved between sessions. When you exit from psql, the temporary table and the data in it are destroyed. This is not a feature you will use often, but it is good to know that you can "hide" a table, or create a table you don't have to clean up after the session. For example, suppose that you are computing sensitive data, such as payroll information, that comes from combining hours from a timesheet with an hourly wage and applying various (normally very large) deductions to compute a biweekly wage. You probably don't want to leave the resulting table around for other people in your organization to discover accidentally. A temporary table disappears after your session is over.

Moving to the syntax inside the parentheses, the first thing you see is this:

```
column type
```

When I first saw this, I read it as one item called *column type*. I was wrong. This is really two things—the column, which for you programmer types is the same as a variable, and the type, which corresponds to the variable type. Therefore, this value:

```
FirstName varchar(15)
```

means that a column named FirstName will exist in every row of this database and will be of the type varchar, which stands for a *variable character* type with a specified length. In this case, the varchar would be 15 characters long. You can absorb all the nuances of varchar and all the other data types available in PostgreSQL in Chapter 9, "Basic PostgreSQL Data Types and SQL Functions." For now, I will stick to the syntax.

Most programmers who have to design database tables normally stop here. They create simple tables and then control the kinds of data that flow into the table with the programming code that calls the table. For example, in the Customers00 table, none of the variables (`FirstName`, `LastName`, or `Age`) would be very valuable if they were blank. The normal programmer response to this would be to put checks in the code to make sure that blank data or null data doesn't creep into the database.

> If you have programmed using databases before, you know that there is a difference between blank data and null data. If you are new to databases, this can be a confusing distinction. A *null value* is the absence of any value for the column in the table. A *blank value*, such as " ", even though it has zero length, is not null. Watch the next couple of examples.

Over the years, I have noticed that the database you design rarely stays exclusively connected to the application you wrote for it. George, in Accounting, needs to use data from your table for his report, and Valerie, from Personnel, wants to use her application to put data in your tables without going through your application. This means that you either have to trust your brother and sister programmers not to put "bad" data in your database, or you have to find a way for the database to protect itself—not that other people can't be trusted. However, their code might be written between the hours of 10 p.m. and 4 a.m. the night before the project or demo is due—unlike your code, which is written only during normal working hours, months ahead of schedule. In any case, here is how to protect your data.

The way the Customer00 is written, any data, including NULL, can be put into any of the columns. If you have data you can't allow to be null, you use the NOT NULL directive after the Column Type declaration, as shown in the following example.

```
perkins=# CREATE TABLE CustomersNOTNULL
perkins-# (
perkins(# FirstName       varchar(15)  NOT NULL,
perkins(# LastName        varchar(20)  NOT NULL,
perkins(# Age             int,
perkins(# JobDescription varchar(15),
perkins(# EmployeeID      int
perkins(# );
```

Note that two new columns, JobDescription and EmployeeID, have been added. The construction of this table guards against anyone entering null data into FirstName and LastName. That's a good start.

Say that the organization is mostly made up of people with the position Drone, and the company wants to save money by not paying someone to type *Drone* thousands of times. You can solve your company's problems by using the DEFAULT clause, defaulting the value of JobDescription to Drone by typing

```
perkins=# CREATE TABLE CustomersDRONE
perkins-# (
perkins(# FirstName       varchar(15)  NOT NULL,
perkins(# LastName        varchar(20)  NOT NULL,
perkins(# Age             int,
perkins(# JobDescription varchar(15)  DEFAULT 'Drone',
perkins(# EmployeeID      int
perkins(# );
```

Next, you notice that Valerie's program is putting negative values in the Age column. You don't like direct confrontation but you want to protect your database, so you use the CHECK clause to make sure that the ages are right.

```
perkins=# CREATE TABLE CustomersCheck
perkins-# (
perkins(# FirstName       varchar(15)  NOT NULL,
perkins(# LastName        varchar(20)  NOT NULL,
perkins(# Age             int          CHECK(Age > 0),
perkins(# JobDescription varchar(15)  DEFAULT 'Drone',
```

```
perkins(# EmployeeID    int
perkins(# );
```

Now, when Valerie tries to stuff a negative number into the Age column, the database will throw an error—which will be her problem. When she asks you whether you changed the database, you can feign innocence.

It is common practice for companies to tattoo barcode on their employees for easy identification (well, it could be someday). This mark translates to a unique number for each employee. To ensure that a column will always hold a unique number, use the UNIQUE keyword.

```
perkins=# CREATE TABLE CustomersUNIQUE
perkins-# (
perkins(# FirstName      varchar(15)   NOT NULL,
perkins(# LastName       varchar(20)   NOT NULL,
perkins(# Age            int           CHECK(Age > 0),
perkins(# JobDescription varchar(15)   DEFAULT 'Drone',
perkins(# EmployeeID     int           UNIQUE
perkins(# );
NOTICE:  CREATE TABLE/UNIQUE will create implicit index
    'customersunique_employe eid_key' for table 'customersunique'
```

Notice this last bit about creating an index. Databases use indexes to increase search speed. When you use the UNIQUE keyword, PostgreSQL automatically creates an index for your column. You can also use PRIMARY KEY to specify a unique value.

```
perkins=# CREATE TABLE CustomersPRIMARYKEY
perkins-# (
perkins(# FirstName      varchar(15)   NOT NULL,
perkins(# LastName       varchar(20)   NOT NULL,
perkins(# Age            int           CHECK(Age > 0),
perkins(# JobDescription varchar(15)   DEFAULT 'Drone',
perkins(# EmployeeID     int           PRIMARY KEY
perkins(# );
NOTICE:  CREATE TABLE/PRIMARY KEY will create implicit index
    'customersprimaryke y_pkey' for table 'customersprimarykey'
```

Again, notice that the system created an index. You can have only one PRIMARY KEY in a table, but it can consist of multiple columns, like this:

```
perkins=# CREATE TABLE CustomersMULTIKEY
perkins-# (
perkins(# FirstName      varchar(15)   NOT NULL,
```

```
perkins(# LastName        varchar(20)   NOT NULL,
perkins(# Age             int           CHECK(Age > 0),
perkins(# JobDescription  varchar(15)   DEFAULT 'Drone',
perkins(# EmployeeID      int,
perkins(# PRIMARY KEY(LastName, FirstName)
perkins(# );
NOTICE:  CREATE TABLE/PRIMARY KEY will create implicit index 'customersmultikey_
pkey' for table 'customersmultikey'
```

When the revolution comes and the barcodes are removed, you can key your files on FirstName and LastName. Of course, your new masters will dictate that employees with the same first and last names must add unique vowels to the end of each name, but hey, no system is perfect.

So far, you have learned how to create a total of seven tables.

```
perkins=# \dt
          List of relations
        Name          | Type  | Owner
----------------------+-------+--------
 customers00          | table | perkins
 customerscheck       | table | perkins
 customersdrone       | table | perkins
 customersmultikey    | table | perkins
 customersnotnull     | table | perkins
 customersprimarykey  | table | perkins
 customersunique      | table | perkins
(7 rows)
```

Not only have you created seven tables, but you have also learned how to protect the data inside the tables—except that the tables contain no data! How can data be inserted into a table? Time to take the next step.

Inserting Data

The SQL implemented in PostgreSQL uses the standard SQL insert statement to insert data into tables. The syntax for the insert statement is

```
INSERT INTO table [ ( column [, ...] ) ]
    { VALUES ( expression [, ...] ) | SELECT query }
```

You start by putting some data into your Customer00 table. Type

```
perkins=# INSERT INTO Customers00 VALUES('Alton', 'Perkins', 21);
INSERT 407409 1
```

The system returns INSERT, followed by an internally generated number, followed by the number of rows inserted. You will peek into the future to check that the data got into the table by using a basic select statement. Don't worry about the syntax. In your database career or database programming career, you will type more select statements than you can count (select is covered in the next section), so type

```
perkins=# Select * from Customers00;
```

which returns

```
firstname | lastname | age
----------+----------+----
 Alton    | Perkins  | 21
(1 row)
```

This shows you that one row in the table contains the data in the INSERT INTO statement. Check out some of the data protection stuff covered in Part III. Remember, this basic table has no protection, so you can do something like this:

```
INSERT INTO Customers00 VALUE('', '', -999);
```

Then, to check the data in the table, type the select statement again.

```
perkins=# Select * from Customers00;
```

This now returns

```
perkins=# Select * from Customers00;
 firstname | lastname | age
-----------+----------+------
 Alton     | Perkins  |   21
           |          | -999
(2 rows)
```

This shows the two blanks and the really bad age. Now stick in a NULL. To do that, you put in only one value and let the other two default to NULL. Type

```
perkins=# INSERT INTO Customers00 (Age) VALUES( -999);
INSERT 407521 1
```

Then, to see the data, type

```
perkins=# Select * from Customers00;
```

which shows you this:

```
firstname | lastname | age
-----------+----------+------
 Alton     | Perkins  |   21
```

```
           |          |  -999
           |          |  -999
(3 rows)
```

Try this same INSERT INTO statement with your CustomersNOTNULL table.

```
perkins=# INSERT INTO CustomersNOTNULL (Age) VALUES( -999);
ERROR:  ExecAppend: Fail to add null value in not null attribute firstname
```

Your first error! But it is a good error because you didn't want any null data in your table. Now see whether the Drone default you put in the CustomersDrone table works. The whole transaction looks like this:

```
perkins=# INSERT INTO CustomersDRONE(FirstName,LastName)
perkins-# VALUES('Tyler','Perkins');
INSERT 407522 1
perkins=# select * from CustomersDRONE;
 firstname | lastname | age | jobdescription | employeeid
-----------+----------+-----+----------------+------------
 Tyler     | Perkins  |     | Drone          |
(1 row)
```

The default worked! You didn't type Drone, but there it is. Also, notice that the Age and EmployeeID columns have no values. Now try this query with the CustomersCHECK table.

```
perkins=# INSERT INTO CustomersCHECK(FirstName,LastName)
perkins-# VALUES('Tyler','Perkins');
```

You would think that this would produce an error because you told it that Age has to be greater than zero. However, PostgreSQL accepted the row because you didn't tell it that Age couldn't be null. Now try to enter a negative number.

```
perkins=# INSERT INTO CustomersCHECK(FirstName,LastName,Age)
perkins-# VALUES('Tyler','Perkins', -999);
ERROR:  ExecAppend: rejected due to CHECK constraint customerscheck_age
```

There is the expected error! No one will ever put negative ages into your data again!

You have two of the required skills under your belt. You can create and populate a table. Now you will learn to query the table.

Selecting Data

The select statement is the payoff for all the time and effort you spend building and populating a database. With select, your wish is the database's command. Want to find all the people in your database with the last name *Perkins* who are older than 40? Use the select statement. Here is the syntax:

```
SELECT [ ALL | DISTINCT [ ON ( expression [, ...] ) ] ]
    expression [ AS name ] [, ...]
    [ INTO [ TEMPORARY | TEMP ] [ TABLE ] new_table ]
    [ FROM table [ alias ] [, ...] ]
    [ WHERE condition ]
    [ GROUP BY column [, ...] ]
    [ HAVING condition [, ...] ]
    [ { UNION [ ALL ] | INTERSECT | EXCEPT } select ]
    [ ORDER BY column [ ASC | DESC | USING operator ] [, ...] ]
    [ FOR UPDATE [ OF class_name [, ...] ] ]
    LIMIT { count | ALL } [ { OFFSET | , } start ]
```

Put some data in the Customer00 table created in the preceding section by typing the following insert statements:

```
perkins=# INSERT INTO Customers00 VALUES('Leslie', 'Perkins', 26);
INSERT 407552 1
perkins=# INSERT INTO Customers00 VALUES('Laura', 'Perkins', 21);
INSERT 407553 1
perkins=# INSERT INTO Customers00 VALUES('Kelly', 'Perkins', 18);
INSERT 407554 1
perkins=# INSERT INTO Customers00 VALUES('Jeff', 'Perkins', 45);
INSERT 407555 1
perkins=# INSERT INTO Customers00 VALUES('Ruth', 'Perkins', 16);
INSERT 407557 1
```

Here is the mother of all select statements:

```
Select * from Customers00;
```

Go ahead and type it in. If you've been playing along at home, your session should look like this:

```
perkins=# SELECT * FROM Customers00;
 firstname | lastname | age
-----------+----------+------
 Alton     | Perkins  |   21
           |          | -999
           |          | -999
 Leslie    | Perkins  |   26
```

```
Laura      | Perkins  |  21
Kelly      | Perkins  |  18
Jeff       | Perkins  |  45
Ruth       | Perkins  |  16
(8 rows)
```

The asterisk (∗) in this query tells PostgreSQL to get all the columns in the row from the table Customer00. You could do the same thing with the following query.

```
SELECT Firstname, Lastname, Age FROM Customers00;
```

This results in

```
perkins=# SELECT Firstname, Lastname, Age FROM Customers00;
 firstname | lastname | age
-----------+----------+------
 Alton     | Perkins  |  21
           |          | -999
           |          | -999
 Leslie    | Perkins  |  26
 Laura     | Perkins  |  21
 Kelly     | Perkins  |  18
 Jeff      | Perkins  |  45
 Ruth      | Perkins  |  16
(8 rows)
```

This is the same as the result using ∗. To change the column headings, you type an **as** and the desired column name next to the actual column name, like this:

```
SELECT Firstname as "First Name", Lastname as "Last Name",
  Age as "Age in Years" FROM Customers00;
```

Here is what the session looks like.

```
perkins=# SELECT Firstname as "First Name", Lastname as "Last Name", Age as "Age
 in Years" FROM Customers00;
 First Name | Last Name | Age in Years
------------+-----------+--------------
 Alton      | Perkins   |           21
            |           |         -999
            |           |         -999
 Leslie     | Perkins   |           26
 Laura      | Perkins   |           21
 Kelly      | Perkins   |           18
```

```
Jeff        | Perkins  |          45
Ruth        | Perkins  |          16
(8 rows)
```

Say that you want to see who in this group can legally gamble. You want everybody who is 21 or older. Type this:

```
Select * from Customers00
Where Age >= 21;
```

and you end up with this:

```
perkins=# Select * from Customers00
perkins-# Where Age >= 21;
 firstname | lastname | age
-----------+----------+----
 Alton     | Perkins  | 21
 Leslie    | Perkins  | 26
 Laura     | Perkins  | 21
 Jeff      | Perkins  | 45
(4 rows)
```

Standard Structured Query Language contains several useful comparison operators. Here they are:

> Greater than

< Less than

>= Greater than or equal to

<= Less than or equal to

= Equal to

There are also several key words that serve as comparison operators.

- **AND** joins two or more statements and returns true if *all* statements are true. Otherwise, it returns false.

- **OR** joins two or more statements and returns true if *any* statements are true. Otherwise, it returns false.

- **LIKE** is used to find partial matches. For example, the code to find everyone in the Customer00 table whose name starts will *L* would look like this:

  ```
  perkins=# Select * from Customers00
  perkins-# Where FirstName Like 'L%';
   firstname | lastname | age
  ```

```
      ----------+----------+----
    Leslie   | Perkins |  26
    Laura    | Perkins |  21
    (2 rows)
```

- **SELECT** can retrieve data from more than one table. Create and populate a new table named Address, as shown here.

```
perkins=# CREATE TABLE ADDRESS
perkins-# (NickName varchar(10),
perkins(#  Street   varchar(15),
perkins(#  State    varchar(2)
perkins(# );
CREATE
perkins=# INSERT INTO ADDRESS VALUES('Leslie', '1313 MBird Lane','CA');
INSERT 407569 1
perkins=# INSERT INTO ADDRESS VALUES('Laura', 'Rt 66','AZ');
INSERT 407570 1
perkins=# INSERT INTO ADDRESS VALUES('Kelly', '1010 Pudder Ln','FL');
INSERT 407571 1
```

Now you get the first name, last name, and address for anyone whose first name in the Customer00 table matches a nickname in the Address table.

```
Select c.FirstName as "First Name",
c.LastName as "Last Name",
a.Street,
a.State
FROM Customers00 c, Address a
WHERE c.FirstName = a.NickName;
```

which produces this:

```
First Name | Last Name |     street      | state
-----------+-----------+-----------------+------
  Kelly    | Perkins   | 1010 Pudder Ln  | FL
  Laura    | Perkins   | Rt 66           | AZ
  Leslie   | Perkins   | 1313 MBird Lane | CA
(3 rows)
```

That covers basic uses of the select statement. Those two blanks in the Customer00 table that were put in to demonstrate why you need protection for your data are bothersome. Read on to see how you can get rid of them.

Deleting Data from Tables

The DELETE clause is like a circular saw. It is a very powerful tool that makes your job easier, but if it is not used carefully, it can wreak havoc. Here is the syntax:

```
DELETE FROM table [ WHERE condition ]
```

Note how the WHERE clause is optional. First, look at the dangerous part.

Copy your Customer00 table into a table called *Opps*. What's that? You say I haven't covered how to copy from one table to another? Well, it's time to learn how! Use the SELECT statement like this:

```
SELECT * INTO TABLE OPPS FROM Customers00;
```

To prove that this statement worked, check it with a SELECT *.

```
perkins=# SELECT * FROM OPPS;
 firstname | lastname | age
-----------+----------+------
 Alton     | Perkins  |   21
           |          | -999
           |          | -999
 Leslie    | Perkins  |   26
 Laura     | Perkins  |   21
 Kelly     | Perkins  |   18
 Jeff      | Perkins  |   45
 Ruth      | Perkins  |   16
(8 rows)
```

Now, where were we? Oh yes, why is the delete dangerous? Say that you have spent most of your day putting data into the Opps table. You suddenly feel the urge to delete one row. Somewhat distracted by the drone in the next cubicle mumbling about a lost stapler, you type

```
Delete From Opps;
```

You look on your screen, and you see this:

```
perkins=# Delete From Opps;
DELETE 8
```

Delete 8! Oops! Without a WHERE clause, DELETE FROM deletes all the rows in the table. No warning, no recovery—unless you used the COMMIT statement covered in Chapter 4, "Interactive PostgreSQL Using psql." This is an important thing to remember about DELETE FROM.

> Standard SQL does not include a COMMIT statement. PostgreSQL extends SQL with the BEGIN, COMMIT, ROLLBACK, and END statements. See the `psql /h` command, covered in Chapter 4, for further information on these extensions.

DELETE FROM can also be used for good stuff. Using the WHERE clause, type

```
perkins=# DELETE FROM customers00 WHERE Age = -999;
DELETE 2
```

Now check your work.

```
perkins=# SELECT * FROM customers00;
 firstname | lastname | age
-----------+----------+----
 Alton     | Perkins  | 21
 Leslie    | Perkins  | 26
 Laura     | Perkins  | 21
 Kelly     | Perkins  | 18
 Jeff      | Perkins  | 45
 Ruth      | Perkins  | 16
(6 rows)
```

Remember, always use a WHERE with a DELETE FROM, unless you intend to remove every row in the table.

Altering Database Objects

For those rare occasions when you have to make a change to a table after its creation, you use the statement ALTER TABLE. Here is the syntax:

```
ALTER TABLE table [ * ]
    ADD [ COLUMN ] column type
ALTER TABLE table [ * ]
    ALTER [ COLUMN ] column { SET DEFAULT value | DROP DEFAULT }
ALTER TABLE table [ * ]
    RENAME [ COLUMN ] column TO newcolumn
ALTER TABLE table
    RENAME TO newtable
ALTER TABLE table
    ADD table constraint definition
```

If you need to change the name of Customers00 to Family, you type

```
perkins=# ALTER TABLE Customers00 RENAME TO Family;
```

Use the \dt command to see whether this worked.

```
perkins=# \dt
          List of relations
        Name        | Type  |  Owner
--------------------+-------+---------
 address            | table | perkins
 customerscheck     | table | perkins
 customersdrone     | table | perkins
 customersmultikey  | table | perkins
 customersnotnull   | table | perkins
 customersprimarykey| table | perkins
 customersunique    | table | perkins
 family             | table | perkins
 opps               | table | perkins
(9 rows)
```

The other common use of ALTER TABLE is to add a column. To add a column named MiddleInitial use this:

```
perkins=# ALTER TABLE FAMILY ADD COLUMN MiddleInitial varchar(3);
ALTER
perkins=# SELECT * FROM Family;
 firstname | lastname | age | middleinitial
-----------+----------+-----+--------------
 Alton     | Perkins  |  21 |
 Leslie    | Perkins  |  26 |
 Laura     | Perkins  |  21 |
 Kelly     | Perkins  |  18 |
 Jeff      | Perkins  |  45 |
 Ruth      | Perkins  |  16 |
(6 rows)
```

ALTER TABLE doesn't facilitate deleting a column. Deleting a column would leave the database confused about what to do with the data. If you want to delete a column, use the SELECT INTO TABLE method to copy data to a temporary table. Then use the SELECT INTO TABLE method again to copy all the fields but the deleted one back to the table name after the original TABLE has been dropped. Confused? See the example in the next section.

Deleting Tables

To delete a table, use the DROP TABLE statement with this syntax:

```
DROP TABLE name [, ...]
```

To continue with the example from the preceding section, copy the Family table to FAMILYTMP.

```
perkins=# SELECT * INTO TABLE FAMILYTMP FROM Family;
SELECT
```

Now, DROP the Family table.

```
perkins=# DROP TABLE FAMILY;
DROP
```

Now select all the fields back into a new Family table.

```
perkins=# SELECT FirstName, LastName, Age INTO TABLE FAMILY FROM FAMILYTMP;
SELECT
```

Check your work.

```
perkins=# Select * FROM FAMILY;
 firstname | lastname | age
-----------+----------+----
 Alton     | Perkins  |  21
 Leslie    | Perkins  |  26
 Laura     | Perkins  |  21
 Kelly     | Perkins  |  18
 Jeff      | Perkins  |  45
 Ruth      | Perkins  |  16
(6 rows)
```

Finally, clean up the FAMILYTMP.

```
perkins=# DROP TABLE FAMILYTMP;
DROP
```

You can avoid the last step, dropping the Familytmp table, by using the clause TEMP in the SELECT INTO statement. Remember, TEMP tables are automatically dropped at the end of a session—one more thing to cover.

Updating Data

The ability to update data rounds out your newly acquired SQL knowledge to create and manipulate data in your PostgreSQL database. UPDATE uses this syntax:

```
UPDATE table SET col = expression [, ...]
    [ FROM fromlist ]
    [ WHERE condition ]
```

Suppose that a year has passed, so now the ages in the table are a year behind. You change them by typing

```
perkins=# UPDATE FAMILY SET Age = Age + 1;
UPDATE 6
```

See whether it worked.

```
perkins=# Select * from FAMILY;
 firstname | lastname | age
-----------+----------+----
 Alton     | Perkins  |  22
 Leslie    | Perkins  |  27
 Laura     | Perkins  |  22
 Kelly     | Perkins  |  19
 Jeff      | Perkins  |  46
 Ruth      | Perkins  |  17
(6 rows)
```

Now everybody is a year older. If you want to make only me a year older, use this:

```
perkins=# UPDATE FAMILY Set Age = Age + 1
perkins-# WHERE FirstName = 'Jeff';
UPDATE 1
```

which is verified by this:

```
perkins=# select * from family;
 firstname | lastname | age
-----------+----------+----
 Alton     | Perkins  |  22
 Leslie    | Perkins  |  27
 Laura     | Perkins  |  22
 Kelly     | Perkins  |  19
 Ruth      | Perkins  |  17
```

```
Jeff      | Perkins  | 47
(6 rows)
```

which is about how fast the years seem to go by.

Summary

You have covered much ground and worked many examples. If you are new to SQL and PostgreSQL, these will be the foundation for your database manipulation skills. If you have worked with SQL but are new to PostgreSQL, you have verified that the basic SQL statements work. In any case, you are ready to move on to Chapter 9, where you will learn the basic data types that make up PostgreSQL. The next chapter also describes how SQL is used as a programming language inside PostgreSQL.

Chapter 9: Basic PostgreSQL Data Types and SQL Functions

T he normal procedure here would be to cover the data types by themselves and then move on to creating functions with SQL. However, the data types are inherently dry, a little boring, and hard to illustrate. This chapter is not boring—it teaches you how to write functions using SQL and then shows you the PostgreSQL data types, illustrated with SQL. This chapter covers the basic data types: numbers, characters, and boolean. Other PostgreSQL data types are covered in Chapter 17, "Advanced Data Types."

Writing SQL Functions in PostgreSQL

An *SQL function* in PostgreSQL is a collection of SQL statements that can be written and stored to a database and called from within an SQL statement (such as those covered in Chapter 8, "Basic SQL") or called from within another function. PostgreSQL can use functions written in several languages, PL/PGSQL (a structured way of using SQL, covered in Chapter 10, "Programming with PL/PGSQL"), PL/Tcl (using the TCL programming language, covered in Chapter 11, "Programming with PL/Tcl and Tcl), and PL/Perl (using the Perl programming language, covered in Chapter 15, "Programming with Perl"). In addition to these built-in languages, you can use the C languages to add functions. Adding functions in the C languages is covered in Chapter 12, "Programming with C" SQL functions are the simplest to implement and don't require any previous programming experience, just what you learned in Chapter 8. Therefore, let's start with SQL functions.

There are two ways to write SQL functions in PostgreSQL: the easy way and the hard way. I'll show you the hard way first.

Using the CREATE FUNCTION SQL Statement

The hard way to create SQL is to use the CREATE FUNCTION SQL statement. Log into psql, and type /h CREATE FUNCTION. Your session will look something like this:

```
perkins=# \h CREATE FUNCTION
Command:     CREATE FUNCTION
Description: Defines a new function
Syntax:
CREATE FUNCTION name ( [ ftype [, ...] ] )
    RETURNS rtype
    AS definition
    LANGUAGE 'langname'
    [ WITH ( attribute [, ...] ) ]
```

```
CREATE FUNCTION name ( [ ftype [, ...] ] )
    RETURNS rtype
    AS obj_file , link_symbol
    LANGUAGE 'C'
    [ WITH ( attribute [, ...] ) ]
```

Ignore the second definition for now; it is covered in Chapter 12. Use the first definition to create your first function. Type the following:

```
perkins=# CREATE FUNCTION myfirstfunction()
perkins-# RETURNS unknown
perkins-# AS 'SELECT ''Hello World'' '
perkins-# LANGUAGE 'sql'
perkins-# WITH (iscachable);
```

which returns

```
CREATE
```

Before examining the details, look at what the function does.

```
perkins=# select myfirstfunction();
```

This returns

```
myfirstfunction
----------------
 Hello World
(1 row)
```

How did this work? The first line, CREATE FUNCTION myfirstfunction(), tells PostgreSQL that you want to create a function named *myfirstfunction* that has no parameters. You will look at functions with parameters in the next section.

The second line, RETURNS unknown, tells PostgreSQL which data type this function returns. Because you haven't discussed any data types, unknown is appropriate here. You will see many examples returning various data types in the following sections.

The third line, AS 'SELECT ''Hello World'' ', is the function definition. The tricky bit here is the use of the character '. The function definition begins and ends with the character '. If the character ' is used inside the definition, then, it has to be either doubled up, as shown here at either end of Hello World, or escaped. *Escaped* means that it is written as \' instead of ' '.

The fourth line, LANGUAGE 'sql', specifies the language used in the function. The SQL language is built in to PostgreSQL. Other languages are available and are covered in the following chapters.

The last line, WITH (iscachable), passes special attributes to PostgreSQL. Currently, only one attribute is available, iscachable. The iscachable attribute tells PostgreSQL that this function will return the same value for any given inputs. In the case of myfirstfunction, which doesn't have any inputs and always returns Hello World, iscachable lets PostgreSQL know that it is okay to optimize this function to improve performance.

Why is this the hard way to create a function? If you make a typing error in psql, you pretty much have to start over from the top. When you create more complex functions this can become frustrating, unless you are a perfect typist. You can use an external text editor to write your functions and then paste them into psql, but that is not the easy way. The easy way is to use pgaccess.

Using the pgaccess Program

To use the pgaccess program to view or create functions, log in to your database and select the Functions tab. You should see an entry for myfirstfunction(). Double-click on it. You will see something like that in Figure 9.1.

The pgaccess program simplifies function entry, letting you concentrate on the programming details instead of the CREATE FUNCTION syntax. Notice the normal use of the ' character. pgaccess adds any additional 's that are needed. The only thing you don't get with pgaccess is the WITH clause, where currently you can set the iscachable attribute. There is a way to set this attribute, though. Let's create another function and see how to do it.

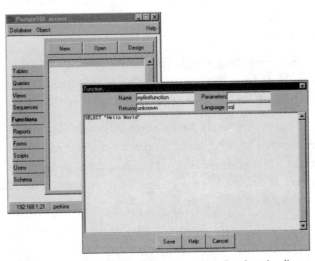

Figure 9.1   *The PostgreSQL Access view of myfirstfunction()*

Before starting the next example, choose SQL Window from the Database menu in pgaccess. A window like that in Figure 9.2 will appear.

Recall from Chapter 5, the pgaccess chapter, that the SQL window shows the transactions between pgaccess and PostgreSQL. Watch this window as you build the next function.

Click the New button on the PostgreSQL Access Functions tab. Build a function named mypi, returning a float8 (I will get to the specifics of all the numeric data types in the next section), using the SQL language. Make the description of the function read SELECT 22.0/7.0. (I vaguely remember from some long-ago math course that this is an approximation of pi.) Now click the Save button. You will get a Function Saved message, and the Function dialog box will disappear. The SQL window will contain messages that look like this:

```
create function MyPI () returns float8 as 'SELECT 22.0/7.0
' language 'sql'
...select * from pg_proc where proname='mypi'
...
```

There are a couple of very useful features here. The first line is your function expressed in the CREATE FUNCTION format. This is convenient if you need to create this function in a script (or to paste it into a book you are writing about PostgreSQL).

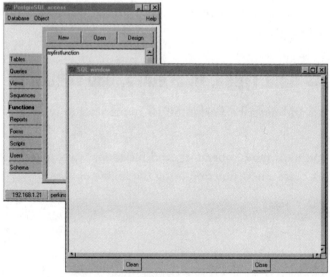

Figure 9.2   *The pgaccess SQL window*

The line `select * from pg_proc where proname='mypi'` points you to the pg_proc table. This is where information about each function is stored. Open psql and type

```
perkins=# select proiscachable from pg_proc where proname='mypi';
```

which will return

```
proiscachable
--------------
 f
(1 row)
```

Change the `iscachable` attribute to true, using the following UPDATE statement:

```
perkins=# update pg_proc set proiscachable='t' where proname='mypi';'
UPDATE 1
```

Now check your work:

```
select proiscachable from pg_proc where proname='mypi';
 proiscachable
--------------
 t
(1 row)
```

As you see, you don't have to use pgaccess to write functions in PostgreSQL, but it can simplify your coding. For the remainder of the book, when you create functions I will give you the CREATE FUNCTION syntax, because the screen shots of pgaccess are hard to read and because doing so will reinforce what you have learned about the syntax. I will begin by explaining in detail the data types available in PostgreSQL, beginning with numeric data types.

PostgreSQL Numeric Data Types, Operators, and Functions

Tables 9.1 through 9.3 list and describe PostgreSQL's numeric data types and their operators.

Let's see how the most common types, operators, and functions work together, starting with the integers. Create a new function using the following:

```
create function add2int (int2 , int2)
returns int2 as 'select $1 + $2
' language 'sql'
```

Table 9.1   PostgreSQL Numerical Data Types

Type	Description
int2	An integer from -32,768 to 32,767
int4	An integer from -2,147,483,648 to 2,147,483,647
int8	An integer from -9,223,372,036,854,775,808 to 9,223,372,036,854,775,807 (roughly the same as my daughter's college costs)
float4	A floating-point number with five significant digits after the decimal
float8	A floating-point number with 14 significant digits after the decimal
decimal	A user-defined decimal with a limit of about 8,000 digits
numeric	A user-defined number
serial	A special type used to create sequences

Table 9.2   Numerical Data Type Operators

Operator	Description
+ - * /	The usual plus, minus, multiply, and divide operators
! !!	Factorials
%	Modular division
^	Exponential
@	Absolute value
|/	Square root
||/	Cube root

Table 9.3   Numerical Data Type Functions

Function	Description
abs(n)	Returns the absolute value of n
degrees(n)	Returns n expressed in degrees
exp(n)	Raises the mathematical constant e to the n power
ln(n)	Returns the natural logarithm of n
log(n)	Returns the base 10 logarithm of n
pi()	Returns a rather long version of the mathematical constant pi
pow(x, y)	Raises x to the y power
radians(n)	Converts n from degrees to radians
round(n)	Returns n rounded to the nearest integer
sqrt(n)	Returns the square root of n
cbrt(n)	Returns the cube root of n
truc(n)	Returns the integer value of n
acos(n)	Returns the arccosine of n
asin(n)	Returns the arcsine of n
atan(n)	Returns the arctangent of n
cos(n)	Returns the cosine of n
cot(n)	Returns the cotangent of n
sin(n)	Returns the sine of n
tan(n)	Returns the tangent of n

Arguments passed into a function are referenced using $1, $2, and so on. This is okay for shorter functions but can cause readability and debugging problems in more complex functions. In the following chapters, you will see that more complex programming languages, such as PL/pgsql, PL/Perl, and PL/Tcl, have a more sophisticated way of handling variables.

Then type

```
perkins=# select add2int(5, 99);
```

which will return

```
add2int
--------
    104
(1 row)
```

which is what you would expect. For something you might not expect, try this:

```
perkins=# select add2int(1, 32767);
```

which you might expect to result in 32768, but instead you get this:

```
add2int
--------
  -32768
(1 row)
```

How did this happen? Remember, `int2` only goes up to 32767. Rather than throw an error, this addition rolls over to -32678. If you ever have a problem with the numbers looking wrong, but no error is thrown, check for this kind of rollover.

It can also happen with big numbers. Consider this function:

```
create function mult2int (int4, int4) returns int4 as 'select $1 * $2
' language 'sql'
```

Now plug in the numbers 2 and 1,073,741,824. If you have ever worked in the Department of Defense, or for any of the larger state governments, you know that that second number is not ridiculously big. Leave out the commas. If you don't, PostgreSQL will think that you are entering extra arguments and won't be able to find a `mult2int` that takes five `int4`'s.

```
perkins=# select mult2int(2, 1073741824);
  mult2int
------------
 -2147483648
(1 row)
```

An `int2` is probably okay for tracking the dollars in your high school band fund but bad for tracking federal grant money.

Remember that when you divide integers, you get some rounding, as illustrated by the following:

```
create function div2int (int4, int4) returns int4 as 'select $1 / $2
' language 'sql'
```

> White space in the definition is important here. If you write `select $1/$2`, PostgreSQL will see the `/` as an escape character instead of a divide by. Make sure that you use `select $1 / $2`.

Now use the numbers 4 and 3, like this:

```
perkins=# select div2int(4, 3);
 div2int
--------
       1
(1 row)
```

Reverse them now to get this:

```
perkins=# select div2int(3, 4);
 div2int
--------
       0
(1 row)
```

If you want numbers after the decimal point, use floats:

```
create function div2floats (float4, float4) returns float4 as 'select $1 / $2
' language 'sql'
```

Using 4 and 3 again, you get this:

```
perkins=# select div2floats(4, 3);
 div2floats
-----------
    1.33333
(1 row)
```

For more decimal points, use a float8—for instance:

```
create function div2floats (float8, float8) returns float8 as 'select $1 / $2
' language 'sql'
```

Again, using 4 and 3:

```
perkins=# select div2floats(4, 3);
    div2floats
-----------------
 1.33333333333333
(1 row)
```

Note that PostgreSQL doesn't balk at having two functions with the same name. PostgreSQL allows you to use the same function names, as long as the argument list is different. It does not allow the same function name if only the return values are different. To illustrate this, create a table:

```
create table "tableoffloats" ("float4val1" float4,"float4val2" float4,
"float8val1" float8,"float8val2" float8)
insert into "tableoffloats" ("float4val1","float4val2","float8val1","float8val2")
values ('4','3','4','3')
```

Don't forget that you can use pgaccess to do this. Now try the two float4 columns:

```
perkins=# select div2floats(float4val1, float4val2) from tableoffloats;
 div2floats
------------
    1.33333
(1 row)
```

Notice that the five decimals, showing that `div2floats` returned a float4, indicate that the first `div2floats` function was used. Now try the float8's:

```
perkins=# select div2floats(float8val1, float8val2) from tableoffloats;
    div2floats
------------------
  1.33333333333333
(1 row)
```

Those of you who delight in finding ways to break things might try mixing a float4 and a float8:

```
perkins=# select div2floats(float8val1, float4val2) from tableoffloats;
    div2floats
------------------
  1.33333333333333
(1 crow)
```

In this case, PostgreSQL has promoted the float4 to a float8. When working with data in which every decimal counts, watch out for these kinds of automatic promotions!

The decimal and numeric data types allow you to roll your own numbers. The SQL92 standard (I found this copy at http://www.informatik.uni-essen.de/Lehre/Material/GdI3/sql92.html) defines numeric and decimal as follows:

```
NUMERIC [ <left paren> <precision> [ <comma> <scale> ] <right paren> ]
DECIMAL [ <left paren> <precision> [ <comma> <scale> ] <right paren> ]
```

This means that a value defined as `numeric(3,2)` or `decimal(3,2)` will have three total digits (the decimal is not considered a digit), with two of the digits after the decimal.

There are a couple of quirks. Consider the following:

```
create function div2decimals (numeric,numeric)
```

returns numeric as `'select($1 / $2)::decimal(3,2)`

Again with the 4 and the 3:

```
perkins=# select div2decimals(4, 3);
 div2decimals
--------------
         1.33
(1 row)
```

If you try to make the return value `numeric(3,2)`, PostgreSQL will accept your function but change the return value to numeric. Therefore, if you want to have just two decimal points in your return value, you have to cast the return value using the syntax `::decimal(3,2)`, as shown in the CREATE FUNCTION used to make `div2decimals`. For those of you familiar with C, C++, or Java, casting is a familiar concept. If you're not familiar with casting, you need to make sure that you are not adding or taking away digits you need in your answer.

If you need to use the geometric functions (sin, cos, and so on), remember that their arguments are in radians, as shown by the following:

```
perkins=# select sin(pi()/4);
        sin
-------------------
 0.707106781186547
(1 row)


perkins=# select sin(45);
        sin
-------------------
 0.850903524534118
(1 row)


perkins=# select sin(radians(45));
        sin
-------------------
```

```
0.707106781186547
(1 row)
```

Two of the only things I remember from geometry class is that the sine of 45 degrees is .707 and that pi/4 is the radian equivalent of 45 degrees.

PostgreSQL Character Data Types, Operators, and Functions

Tables 9.4 through 9.6 list and describe PostgreSQL character data types, operators, and functions.

Table 9.4   PostgreSQL Character Data Types

Data Type	Description
char	A single character
char(n)	A string with the width specified by n, padded with blanks
text	An unbound number of characters. Don't think of text as unlimited unless your database storage space is unlimited.
varchar(n)	A string with a width up to n, not padded by blanks

Table 9.5   Character Data Type Operators

Operator	Description
||	Concatenates two strings
~~	Returns true if both character types match—the same as LIKE in SQL
!~~	Returns true if the character types do not match
~	Returns true if the left character type matches the regular expression
~*	Returns true if the left character type matches the regular expression, disregards case

Table 9.6   Character Data Type Functions

Function	Description
`char_length(s)`	Returns the length of character type s
`lower(s)`	Returns a string just like s except that all uppercase characters are changed to lowercase
`octet_length(s)`	Returns the amount of storage needed for character type s
`position(x in y)`	Returns the position of string x in string y
`substring(s from x to y)`	Returns a string from position x to y of string s
`trim(p s from bigs)`	Returns a string from which character x is trimmed from character type bigs according to p, which can be leading, trailing, or both
`upper(s)`	Returns a string where all characters in s have been changed to uppercase

Knowing what things *are* doesn't show you how they *work*. I will clarify some of these character-related objects with a few examples. Create this table containing all the char types:

```
create table "chartypes" ("charval" char,"charval2" char(6), "varcharval"
varchar(6),"textval" text)
```

Now, populate the table:

```
insert into "chartypes" ("charval","charval2","varcharval","textval") values
('abcd','abcd','abcd','abcd')
```

After the insert, if you look at the charval field (use `select charval from chartypes`), a single-character data type, you will see that the requested `'abcd'` was truncated to `'a'` without a warning. This is a common cause of errors in database applications, in which the database designer allows x characters for a column and the user tries to stuff in x * 100 and then wonders where the data went.

Write a new function, also named `chartypes`, as follows:

```
create function chartypes (bpchar,bpchar,varchar,text)
returns text as 'Select ''char lengths = '' || char_length($1) || '','' ||
char_length($2) || '','' || char_length($3)||'','''||char_length($4)
```

Notice the use of the || to link the strings together and the use of the `char_length()` function. Let's see how the data in the chartypes table looks:

```
perkins=# select chartypes(charval, charval2, varcharval, textval) from chartype
s;
      chartypes
-----------------------
 char lengths = 1,6,4,4
(1 row)
```

The column `charval`, of type char, is what one would expect—one character long. The column `charval2`, type `char(6)`, is six characters wide, even though you put in only four characters. Both `varcharval` and `textval`, `varchar(6)` and text, respectively, are four characters long.

Now see which side `charval2` has the padding. Using both the trim and `char_length` functions, type

```
perkins=# select char_length(trim(leading ' ' from charval2)) from chartypes;
 char_length
-------------
           6
(1 row)


perkins=# select char_length(trim(trailing ' ' from charval2)) from chartypes;
 char_length
-------------
           4
(1 row)
```

This padding can cause some problems. For example, if you used `char(6)` to store a value and then made a comparison, you could get some unexpected results. Consider this:

```
perkins=# select 'abcd'~~charval2 from chartypes;
 ?column?
----------
 f
(1 row)


perkins=# select 'abcd  '~~charval2 from chartypes;
 ?column?
----------
```

```
 t
(1 row)
```

Here the ~~ (same as LIKE) operator shows that the string `'abcd'` will not match the value put into charval2 because the two blanks from the padding are considered part of charvar2. Be careful in your use of char. Give strong consideration to using varchar or text for character columns.

Choosing between varchar and text depends on your degree of optimism. I tend toward the pessimistic side when it comes to database design. For example, if you use a text data type, your user can stuff in some really big file that overflows your storage space. A varchar allows you to limit per-item storage. (Of course, varchar doesn't guard against a user's depositing a large number of varchars that overflow your system memory—will this horror never end?)

The PostgreSQL Boolean Data Type

The PostgreSQL boolean data type is very straightforward: if the value of the type is `true`, it returns a y. If the value is `false`, it returns an n. True values can be entered in as `TRUE`, `t`, `true`, `y`, `yes`, or `1`. False values can be entered as `FALSE`, `f`, `false`, `n`, `no`, or `0`.

Summary

Well, at least it wasn't boring. As you begin to use PostgreSQL, you will use numerical, character, and boolean data types in every table and function you create. You will write SQL functions to maintain control of the data flow in and out of your database. When you need a more advanced environment, you will use one of the higher-level languages covered in the following chapters.

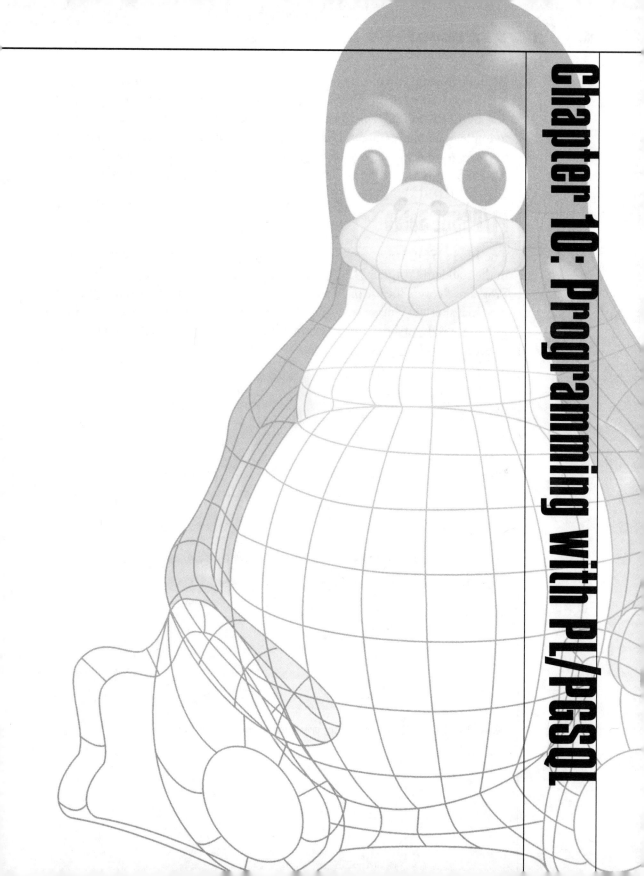

Chapter 10: Programming with PL/PgSQL

sing the SQL language to create functions, as you did in Chapter 9, is okay for simple tasks, but PL/PGSQL is a more structured approach to working with SQL. PL/PGSQL provides more functionality, making complex tasks easier to implement and maintain. PL/PGSQL has a low learning curve, enabling you to leverage your knowledge of SQL and SQL functions into the ability to use PL/PGSQL. This chapter is an overview of the PL/PGSQL language.

PL/PGSQL Setup

The PL/PGSQL language is one of the two external language modules included in the standard PostgreSQL installation. Chapter 2, "PostgreSQL Administrative Programs," covers the use of createlang and droplang, the administrative programs used to install and remove languages in PostgreSQL. Before installing PL/PGSQL in PostgreSQL, first determine whether it is already installed. Type `createlang -1` to list the installed languages.

```
[perkins@laura perkins]$ createlang -l perkins
    Procedural languages
 Name | Trusted? | Compiler
------+----------+----------
(0 rows)
```

If the language is not installed, type

```
createlang -L /usr/pgsql/lib plpgsql perkins
```

as in the following:

```
[perkins@laura pgsql]$ createlang -L /usr/lib/pgsql plpgsql perkins
```

Now check your work. List the installed languages.

```
[perkins@laura pgsql]$ createlang -l perkins
      Procedural languages
  Name   | Trusted? | Compiler
--------+----------+----------
 plpgsql | t        | PL/pgSQL
(1 row)
```

Now that PL/PGSQL is set up, you can see how it works.

General Syntax

Use the CREATE FUNCTION syntax to create PL/PGSQL functions. Here is the general syntax:

```
CREATE FUNCTION myfunction (var, var, ...)
RETURNS var AS '
DECLARE
   var;
   var;
BEGIN
 statement;
 RETURN var;
END;'
LANGUAGE 'plpgsql';
```

Notice that PL/PGSQL adds a few features not present in SQL functions. First, the body of a PG/PLSQL function is contained in a block, defined by BEGIN and END tags:

```
create function myfirstplpgsqlfunction (int4,int4) returns int4 as 'DECLARE
   FirstVal ALIAS FOR $1;
   SecondVal ALIAS FOR $2;
   Sumofvals int4;
BEGIN
   Sumofvals := FirstVal + SecondVal;
   RETURN SumofVals;
END;
```

Check your work using psql with the query:

```
perkins=# select myfirstplpgsqlfunction(2,2);
 myfirstplpgsqlfunction
------------------------
                      4
(1 row)
```

> Remember, you don't have to build the CREATE FUCTION statements by hand. You can use pgaccess to build your functions, as described in Chapter 9. pgaccess takes care of all the required syntax, including quotation marks.

NOTE

PL/PGSQL adds a section that starts with the word DEFINE and ends with the BEGIN tag. In this section, all the variables used in the function, except those from the function's argument list, are defined. The section "Variables" covers this in detail.

Note that lines are terminated with a semicolon (;), except for the DECLARE and BEGIN statements. This enables those of you who revel in confusion and chaos to put more than one statement on a line.

```
create function myfirstplpgsqlfunction (int4,int4) returns int4 as 'DECLARE
  FirstVal ALIAS FOR $1;
  SecondVal ALIAS FOR $2;
  Sumofvals int4;
BEGIN
  Sumofvals := FirstVal + SecondVal;RETURN SumofVals;
END;
```

You could even write

```
create function myfirstplpgsqlfunction (int4,int4)
returns int4 as 'DECLARE   FirstVal ALIAS FOR $1; SecondVal ALIAS FOR $2; Sumofvals
int4;
BEGIN   Sumofvals := FirstVal + SecondVal;RETURN SumofVals; END;
```

With the only loss being readability, I strongly suggest one statement to a line. The function doesn't run any faster if you crowd it all into one line. I also suggest using comments.

PostgreSQL Commenting

Comments come in two forms in PL/PGSQL. The first form is a double dash (--):

```
--This is my first plpgsql funtions
--Here are some comments so that I don''t forget
```

This form of comment makes everything from the -- to the end of the line a comment. You can also put a comment with this format at the end of a statement:

```
RETURN SumofVals; --Glad this is done
```

The other type of comment starts with a /* and ends with a */. This type of comment is familiar to those of you programming in C. For those of you who don't spend 60 percent of your programming time hunting down memory leaks, these symbols are used to make one or more lines of text into comments. Consider the following:

```
/*This is my first plpgsql function
Here are some comments so that I don''t forget */
```

> Remember that any quotation marks used in a function have to be doubled, such as don''t in the preceding comment. If not doubled, the compiler will think that it has found the quotation mark that ends the function definition.

There is a common "gotcha" with this kind of comment. If you forget the closing */, your entire program becomes a comment, which is a good way to stop those pesky compiler warnings but doesn't contribute to the original goal of your code.

Also, be careful not to embed and end comments (*/) inside a comment block:

```
/*This is my first plpgsql function
Here are some comments opps (*/) so that I don''t forget */
```

This results in your program thinking that the bit after the inadvertent end comment is code instead of remarks.

PL/PGSQL is not case sensitive. Look at the lines from the function you wrote:

```
Sumofvals := FirstVal + SecondVal;
   RETURN SumofVals;
```

Notice that Sumofvals and SumofVals do not have the same capitalization, but the function still returns the expected value.

The callme() Function

You can call other functions within the body of a PL/PGSQL function. Here is a new function named callme() that does just that:

```
create function callme () returns int4 as 'DECLARE
 retval int4;
BEGIN
 retval := myfirstplpgsqlfunction(2,2);
 retval := retval * 3;
 RETURN retval;
END;
```

Now call it in psql to see whether it returns the number 12.

```
perkins=# select callme();
 callme
--------
     12
(1 row)
```

The functions called aren't limited to other PL/PGSQL functions. Look at this new version of `callme`:

```
create function callme () returns int4 as 'DECLARE
 retval int4;
BEGIN
 retval := mult2int(2,2);
 retval := retval * 3;
 RETURN retval;
END;
```

This version of `callme` calls the function `mult2int`, which is an SQL function you made in Chapter 9. This is important because it means that you can use different languages to solve your programming problems.

Variables

Any variable used within the body of a PL/PGSQL function is required to be declared in the DECLARE section. The variables passed in to the function are automatically named $1, $2, and so on, just as they are in SQL functions. In PL/PGSQL, though, you can rename them in the DECLARE section. Consider the DECLARE section from the `myfirstplpgsqlfunction()`:

```
DECLARE
    FirstVal ALIAS FOR $1;
    SecondVal ALIAS FOR $2;
    Sumofvals int4;
```

In the first line of the DECLARE section the first variable passed into the function, automatically named $1, is renamed to `FirstVal`. This is done using the term ALIAS FOR. The same thing is done in the next line, assigning variable $2 to the name `SecondVal`. The third variable, `Sumofvals`, is declared as an int4.

Most of the variable types used in PL/PGSQL are the PostgreSQL data types detailed in Chapter 9. Recall that the PostgreSQL data types include various sizes of integers and floats, as well as types for character and text. PL/PGSQL also includes the ROWTYPE and RECORD data types. The ROWTYPE is for handling rows from specific tables in the database. The RECORD type is for general row handling. Don't worry about these two right now; both ROWTYPE and RECORD data types are covered in the following sections.

You can also declare a variable to have a type assigned from a column of an existing table. Look at the chartypes table created in Chapter 9.

```
perkins=# \d chartypes
         Table "chartypes"
 Attribute  |    Type    | Modifier
------------+------------+----------
 charval    | char(1)    |
 charval2   | char(6)    |
 varcharval | varchar(6) |
 textval    | text       |
```

Write a function that assigns text to a variable based on charval2.

```
create function testchar (text) returns text as 'DECLARE
  textin ALIAS FOR $1;
  retval chartypes.charval2%TYPE;
BEGIN
  retval := textin;
  RETURN retval;
END;
```

Now test it:

```
perkins=# select testchar('Here is some long text');
 testchar
----------
 Here i
(1 row)
```

Notice how the input text is truncated to six characters, the length of charval2. Now, alter the table, making the length of charval2 10:

```
perkins=# CREATE TABLE temp AS Select charval, varcharval, textval from chartype
s;
SELECT
perkins=# DROP TABLE chartypes;
DROP
perkins=# CREATE TABLE chartypes AS Select * from temp;
SELECT
perkins=# ALTER TABLE chartypes ADD charval2 char(10);
ALTER
```

```
perkins=# \d chartypes
        Table "chartypes"
 Attribute  |    Type    | Modifier
------------+------------+----------
 charval    | char(1)    |
 varcharval | varchar(6) |
 textval    | text       |
 charval2   | char(10)   |
```

This looks like the long way around, but there is no ALTER statement that allows you to change the type of a column. Now drop out of psql, then get back into psql, and run the testchar() function.

```
perkins=# select testchar('Here is some long text');
  testchar
------------
 Here is so
(1 row)
```

Note that you now have 10 characters without having to rewrite the function. You did have to recycle your connection to PostgreSQL because the function had been run, and the value of retval set, before the table was changed. When the connection was reset and the function called again, the type of retval was set to char(10). Use this kind of variable declaration whenever your function is tied closely to a specific table. That way, when the table is changed, the function is also updated.

All programming languages deal with the issue of variable scope. The scope of a variable covers the places where the variable is visible. In PL/PGSQL, all the variables in the DECLARE statement are local. *Local* variables are visible only in their own functions. For example, if function foo has a variable foovar and function footoo also has a variable foovar, the two variables do not interfere with each other, even if the functions interact. Study the following:

```
create function foo () returns int2 as 'DECLARE
  foovar int2;
BEGIN
  foovar := 20;
  RETURN foovar;
END;
create function footoo () returns int2 as 'DECLARE
DECLARE
  foovar int2;
```

```
BEGIN

  foovar := 10;

  RETURN foovar;

END;
```

The value returned, 30, shows that the variable `foovar` in function `foo` is not affected by its namesake in function `footoo`.

PL/PGSLQ declares the variables passed in with the argument list as CONSTANT. A constant variable cannot change its assigned value within the body of a function. Observe these rewrites of `foo` and `footoo`:

```
create function foo () returns int2 as 'DECLARE

  foovar int2;

BEGIN

  foovar := 10;

  PERFORM footoo(foovar);

  RETURN foovar;

END;
create function footoo (int2) returns int2 as 'DECLARE

  foovar ALIAS FOR $1;

BEGIN

  --foovar := 20 * $1;

  foovar := foovar * 2;

  RETURN $1;

END;
```

Before running this from psql, look at the code and see what you expect it to do. From the look of things, the variable `foovar` in `foo` will be changed when it is passed into the `footoo` function.

Note the use of the PERFORM command. PERFORM executes the function `footoo` and disregards the result. PL/PGSQL requires every function to return a value and doesn't allow you to call a function without assigning its return value to some variable, unless you use PERFORM.

```
perkins=# select foo();

NOTICE:  plpgsql: ERROR during compile of footoo near line 3

ERROR:  $1 is declared CONSTANT
```

The expected reassignment doesn't happen because PL/PGSLQ makes `foovar` CONSTANT when it is passed into `footoo`, and then refuses to change it.

PL/PGSQL also has a few dozen special variables and one type, OPAQUE, that come into play when the function is used as a database trigger. These variables and this type are covered later in the chapter in the section "Dealing with Data: Database Triggers."

Control Structures

The PG/PLSQL language has three types of control structures: IF, LOOP, and FOR.

Give Me an IF!

The IF statement has two possible syntaxes:

```
IF expression THEN
   Statement...
   Statement...
END IF;
OR
IF expression THEN
   Statement...
   Statement...
ELSE
   Statement...
END IF;
```

IF logic is straightforward. If the expression evaluates to true (see Chapter 9 for a rundown on possible boolean values), the statements between the IF and the ELSE (if there is an ELSE) are executed. If there is no ELSE, the statements between the IF and the END IF are executed. If the expression evaluates to false, and there is an ELSE, the statements between the ELSE and the END IF are executed. In the absence of an else clause, all the statements are skipped, and execution is passed to the statement after the END IF. Here is a simple example:

```
create function testpos (int2) returns bool as 'DECLARE
   retval boolean;
   target ALIAS FOR $1;
BEGIN
   IF target > 0 THEN
     retval := true;
   ELSE
     retval := false;
```

```
    END IF;
    RETURN retval;
END;
```

Give the function a 5, and see what happens:

```
perkins=# select testpos(5);
 testpos
--------
 t
(1 row)
```

Now try a negative number or zero:

```
perkins=# select testpos(-10);
 testpos
--------
 f
(1 row)
```

This function can be written without the return values, like this:

```
IF target > 0 THEN
    RETURN true;
  ELSE
    RETURN false;
  END IF;
```

This returns the same value and eliminates the retval variable, but the function has multiple exit points. Multiple exit points can add time to debugging long, complicated functions and, as a general rule, should be avoided.

Another way to write this function is

```
create function testpos (int2) returns bool as 'DECLARE
  target ALIAS FOR $1;
BEGIN
  RETURN target > 0;
END;
```

However, that doesn't illustrate using the IF statement.

The FOUND Variable

PL/PGSQL has a built-in boolean variable named FOUND. FOUND and IF work together like this:

```
create function checkfor (text) returns boolean as 'DECLARE
  targetrecord RECORD;
  targetperson ALIAS FOR $1;
  retval       boolean;
BEGIN
  SELECT * into targetrecord FROM address where nickname = targetperson;
  IF FOUND THEN
    retval = true;
  ELSE
    retval = false;
  END IF;
  RETURN retval;
END;
```

where the table address is defined as follows:

```
perkins=# \d address
          Table "address"
 Attribute |    Type     | Modifier
-----------+-------------+----------
 nickname  | varchar(10) |
 street    | varchar(15) |
 state     | varchar(2)  |
 zipcode   | varchar(10) |
 city      | varchar(25) |
Index: address_zipcode
```

I can find my Dad, but there is no *Dodah* here:

```
perkins=# select checkfor('Alton');
 checkfor
----------
 t
(1 row)
' language 'plpgsql'
perkins=# select checkfor('Dodah');
 checkfor
----------
```

```
       f
(1 row)
```

Note the use of the RECORD variable type. The result of the select statement is se-lected into the targetrecord variable. The targetrecord variable is defined as a RECORD type. Look at the following:

```
create function getzip (text) returns text as 'DECLARE
  targetname ALIAS FOR $1;
  targetrecord RECORD;
  retval text;
BEGIN
  SELECT * into targetrecord FROM address where nickname = targetname;
  IF FOUND THEN
    retval = targetrecord.zipcode;
  ELSE
    retval = ''?????'';
  END IF;
  RETURN retval;
END;
' language 'plpgsql'
```

Find my Dad's zip code:

```
perkins=# select getzip('Alton');
 getzip
--------
 45454
(1 row)
```

where the name *Dodah* returns this:

```
perkins=# select getzip('Dodah');
 getzip
--------
 ?????
(1 row)
```

RAISE Statements

Say that you wanted to do more than return ????? when an address is not found. In that case, you would use a RAISE statement. Here is a rewritten getzip:

```
create function getzip (text) returns text as 'DECLARE
  targetname ALIAS FOR $1;
```

```
    targetrecord RECORD;
    retval text;
BEGIN
    SELECT * into targetrecord FROM address where nickname = targetname;
    IF FOUND THEN
       retval = targetrecord.zipcode;
    ELSE
       RAISE EXCEPTION ''No address for %'', targetname;
    END IF;
    RETURN retval;
END;
' language 'plpgsql'
```

Now try `'Dodah'`:

```
perkins=# select getzip('Dodah');
ERROR:  No address for Dodah
```

The EXCEPTION keyword, used after the RAISE, causes the system to write an error to a log and abort the transaction. Look at the log:

```
010306.00:15:44.132    [333] ProcessQuery
010306.00:15:44.147    [333] query: SELECT  * FROM address where nickname =  $1
010306.00:15:44.188    [333] query: SELECT   $1
010306.00:15:44.190    [333] ERROR:  No address for Dodah
010306.00:15:44.191    [333] AbortCurrentTransaction
```

To make the database write to a log file, change the line in /etc/rc.d/init.d/ postgresql from this:

```
su -l postgres -c "/usr/bin/pg_ctl  -D $PGDATA -p /usr/bin/postmaster start >/
dev/null 2>&1" < /dev/null
```

to this:

```
su -l postgres -c "/usr/bin/pg_ctl  -D $PGDATA -p /usr/bin/postmaster start >/
var/log/postgresql 2>&1" < /dev/null
```

This causes the postmaster to send messages to the file /var/log/postgresql. Because this file can get big fast, you might want to have two scripts that launch PostgreSQL: one script that writes to the debug file and another that doesn't. Also, note that this modification causes a new file to be written every time PostgreSQL is started, which would overwrite your preceding log. If you need to save the preceding log, consider adding a line in the shutdown part of the script that runs the logrotate command.

The other two keywords you can use in front of RAISE are DEBUG and NOTICE. They also cause lines to be written to the log, but they do not stop the transaction. Here is the function rewritten with DEBUG:

```
create function getzip (text) returns text as 'DECLARE
  targetname ALIAS FOR $1;
  targetrecord RECORD;
  retval text;
BEGIN
  SELECT * into targetrecord FROM address where nickname = targetname;
  IF FOUND THEN
    retval = targetrecord.zipcode;
  ELSE
    RAISE DEBUG ''No address for %'', targetname;
  END IF;
  RETURN retval;
END;
' language 'plpgsql'
```

When this function is run, a value is never set for retval, so you get this:

```
perkins=# select getzip('Dodah');
 getzip
--------


(1 row)
```

and you get this in the error log:

```
010306.00:19:46.422   [333] query: SELECT  * FROM address where nickname =  $1
010306.00:19:46.442   [333] query: SELECT   $1
010306.00:19:46.444   [333] DEBUG:  No address for Dodah
010306.00:19:46.444   [333] query: SELECT   $1
010306.00:19:46.444   [333] CommitTransactionCommand
```

What this means is that DEBUG and NOTICE are more suitable for recording the value of variables or the progress through a function.

You might be wondering what happens to the value of targetrecord if more than one row of data is found: Only the first row is kept in the RECORD variable. To work with multiple rows from a database, use the FOR statement.

The For . . . In Statement

To work with multiple rows of data, use the FOR...IN statement. The first syntax for the FOR...IN statement is

```
[Label]
FOR name IN [REVERSE] expression .. expression LOOP
   Statement...
   Statement...
END LOOP;
```

The Label field and the REVERSE tags are optional. The Label field is part of the EXIT statement (you will learn about it in a moment). The REVERSE tag causes the rows to be accessed in reverse order. The name tag is a counter, bounded by the two expressions. Here is an example:

```
create function forexample () returns int2 as 'DECLARE
   retval int2;
BEGIN
   FOR count IN 10 .. 15  LOOP
     retval := count;
     RAISE DEBUG ''count is %'', count;
   END LOOP;
   RETURN retval;
END;


' language 'plpgsql'
```

which runs like this:

```
perkins=# select forexample();
 forexample
------------
         15
(1 row)
```

Here are the DEBUG lines from the log:

```
010306.01:01:15.154    [333] DEBUG:  count is 10
010306.01:01:15.154    [333] DEBUG:  count is 11
010306.01:01:15.154    [333] DEBUG:  count is 12
010306.01:01:15.154    [333] DEBUG:  count is 13
010306.01:01:15.154    [333] DEBUG:  count is 14
010306.01:01:15.155    [333] DEBUG:  count is 15
```

Now try REVERSE:

```
create function forexample () returns int2 as 'DECLARE
  retval        int2;
  targetrecord RECORD;
BEGIN
  FOR count IN REVERSE 15 .. 10 LOOP
    retval := count;
    RAISE DEBUG ''count is %'', count;
  END LOOP;
  RETURN retval;
END;
' language 'plpgsql'
```

Notice how the limits are also reversed. Running this function returns 10.

```
perkins=# select forexample();
 forexample
------------
         10
(1 row)
```

The log shows how you got from 15 to 10.

```
010306.01:07:40.188   [333] DEBUG:  count is 15
010306.01:07:40.188   [333] DEBUG:  count is 14
010306.01:07:40.188   [333] DEBUG:  count is 13
010306.01:07:40.188   [333] DEBUG:  count is 12
010306.01:07:40.188   [333] DEBUG:  count is 11
010306.01:07:40.188   [333] DEBUG:  count is 10
```

This form of FOR...IN is useful if you want to do some processing over a range of values, and it's often used to populate table data for testing. The other form of FOR...IN is

```
[Label]
FOR RECORD||ROW in Select statement LOOP
  Statements...
END LOOP;
```

The Label is the same as the other FOR...IN syntax (EXIT is covered in the next section). The variable after the FOR can be either a RECORD or ROW type. The select statement is any SQL select clause. If you want to examine a bunch of rows, you can write

```
create function instate (text) returns int2 as 'DECLARE
  targetstate ALIAS FOR $1;
```

```
   retval int2 := 0;
   targetrecord RECORD;
BEGIN
   FOR targetrecord IN SELECT * FROM address LOOP
     IF targetrecord.state = targetstate THEN
       retval := retval + 1;
     END IF;
   END LOOP;
   RETURN retval;
END;
' language 'plpgsql'
```

Then, if you look for addresses in Florida, you get this:

```
perkins=# select instate('FL');
 instate
--------
       3
(1 row)
```

Notice that retval is initialized to 0. This is so that the statement retval := retval + 1; doesn't have to deal with a null value (all uninitialized variables are set to NULL). More often than not, when you are dealing with data, you will use this structure.

LOOP forever

There are two kinds of loops: the LOOP forever and the WHILE LOOP. The LOOP forever has this syntax:

```
[Label]
LOOP
  Statements...
END LOOP;
```

This is a dangerous statement to use because it allows a LOOP to be started without an exit condition. In other programming languages, these kinds of loops are used to monitor computer ports or check on the health of a running program. PL/PGSQL doesn't have any features that allow real-time process or port monitoring, so I suggest that you don't use this function. If you do find a use for it, though, you will also need to know how to use the EXIT statement.

The Exit Statement

The EXIT statement syntax looks like this:

```
EXIT [Label] [WHEN expression];
```

Without the optional bits, Label and WHEN, EXIT causes the program to break out of the current LOOP, IF, or FOR control structure and pass program execution to the next statement after the control structure. If the Label bit is used, control is passed to the structure bearing the given label. If the WHEN clause is used, the EXIT occurs only if the expression evaluates to true. Consider the following:

```
create function loops (int2) returns int2 as 'DECLARE
  maxcount ALIAS FOR $1;
BEGIN
  LOOP
    EXIT WHEN maxcount = 0;
    --Make sure we tend toward zero
    IF maxcount > 0 THEN
      maxcount := maxcount - 1;
    ELSE
      maxcount := maxcount + 1;
    END IF;
  END LOOP;
  RETURN maxcount;
END;
' language 'plpgsql'
```

which, when given a value, looks like this:

```
perkins=# select loops(5);
 loops
------
     0
(1 row)
```

Pretty routine. If you have ever used a do...until loop in another language, this is similar. The danger here is that the exit condition will never be reached. For example—and don't ask how I know this—if the exit condition is changed to maxcount < 0, a condition that is never reached, your process will run (and tie up your server) until you recycle PostgreSQL.

A couple other programming notes: The value passed in is set to maxvalue in the first line after the BEGIN. There are two reasons for this. First, remember that all variables passed in are declared constant, so you can't use varin directly because it can't be changed. Second, varin cannot be assigned to maxval in the DECLARE block because it is undefined until after that block.

The WHILE LOOP

The last control structure in PL/PGSQL is the WHILE LOOP. It looks like this:

```
[Label]
WHILE expression LOOP
  Statements...
END LOOP;
```

This means that this structure will enter the loop only if the expression is true and exit the loop only when the expression is false. Here is a rewritten loops function:

```
create function loops (int2) returns int2 as 'DECLARE
  varin ALIAS FOR $1;
  maxcount int2 ;
BEGIN
  maxcount := varin;
  WHILE maxcount != 0 LOOP
    --Make sure we tend toward zero
    IF maxcount > 0 THEN
      maxcount := maxcount - 1;
    ELSE
      maxcount := maxcount + 1;
    END IF;
  END LOOP;
  RETURN maxcount;
END;
```

This looks the same in psql as the preceding version.

Be careful when using the loops function. You don't want your production database stopping because you don't reach your exit case.

Dealing with Data: Database Triggers

You already saw, in the FOR...LOOP section, how to manipulate data using PL/PGSQL. Unlike the rest of the languages covered in the programming section, PL/PGSQL does not have a life outside PostgreSQL. Now you move on to using PL/PGSQL as a database trigger.

A *database trigger* is a special database function that is linked to a table and called whenever there is an UPDATE, INSERT, or DELETE on the table. Triggers are traditionally used to check the values of incoming data to make sure that things such as negative salaries or two-digit years don't get into a database. Triggers can also be used to write information about transactions to the log or to call other functions in PostgreSQL.

Following are the commonly used variables available to a function called as a trigger:

- **NEW.** A RECORD type referenced to the new row in the database, used when the TG_OP is UPDATE or DELETE
- **OLD.** A RECORD type referenced to the old row in the database, used when the TG_OP is UPDATE or DELETE
- **TG_WHEN.** A text type of BEFORE or AFTER, indicating when the trigger is called
- **TG_OP.** A text type of INSERT, UPDATE, or DELETE, indicating the type of database operation that fired the trigger

To create a trigger, make a function with no arguments and a return type of OPAQUE. Look at the following:

```
create function triggerme () returns unknown as 'DECLARE
  testme RECORD;
BEGIN
  --If called before an operation, then
  --Return either NULL or a RECORD with the value to INSERT or UPDATE
  IF TG_WHEN = ''BEFORE'' THEN
    --check for valid state
    Select * into testme from validstates WHERE NEW.state = validstate;
    IF FOUND THEN
      return NEW;
    ELSE
      RAISE EXCEPTION ''State % not in validstates table'', NEW.state;
    END IF;
  ELSE --We are called after the opp
    RAISE DEBUG ''Database Name %'', TG_NAME;
    RAISE DEBUG ''Operation is %'', TG_OP;
    RETURN NULL;
  END IF;
END;
' language 'plpgsql'
```

Here, the value of the new state is checked against a table of valid states. The validstates table looks like this:

```
create table "validstates" ("validstate" varchar(2),"fullname" text)
```

Now, tie the trigger to a table. Notice how a third name is used so that if you have to drop the trigger, you don't have to drop the function.

```
perkins=# CREATE TRIGGER check_state BEFORE INSERT or UPDATE on address
perkins-# FOR EACH ROW EXECUTE PROCEDURE triggerme();
CREATE
```

Now, insert data with a valid state.

```
perkins=# insert into "address" ("nickname","street","state","zipcode","city")
values ('Jeff','1600 Penn','FL','55599','Niceville');
INSERT 413249 1
```

That worked. Now try a brand XX state.

```
perkins=# insert into "address" ("nickname","street","state","zipcode","city")
values ('Biff','1600 Penn','XX','88888','Arlington');
ERROR:  State XX not in validstates table
```

If you make changes to your trigger function, drop the relationship, using this:

```
perkins=# DROP TRIGGER check_state on address;
```

Then reattach the trigger as before. If you don't do this, PostgreSQL will use a cached copy of your function. It's very frustrating to make changes to a function and not see them take effect.

Summary

PL/PGSQL is a good, straightforward language, extending naturally out of SQL. It uses the same data types as PostgreSQL and is especially suited to data manipulation, especially triggers. Make PL/PGSQL the next step after you become familiar with SQL. PL/PGSQL handles most of what you need to do with a database. When the program problems you must solve become more complex, move to PL/Tcl.

Chapter 11: Programming with PL/Tcl and Tcl

he next evolution in this language drill is Tcl. *Tcl* stands for *Tool Command Language*. It is a popular language for writing scripts, especially scripts that manipulate text data. PL/Tcl is an implementation of the Tcl language, like SQL and PL/PGSQL, used to write PostgreSQL functions. This chapter covers the basics of the Tcl language, enough to get a newbie started. Then, for both the newbies and those already familiar with Tcl, this chapter demonstrates PostgreSQL's PL/Tcl implementation of Tcl and how to manipulate PostgreSQL data from Tcl scripts. There's something for everyone.

PL/Tcl Setup

The PL/Tcl language is one of the two external language modules included in the standard PostgreSQL installation. Chapter 2 covered the use of createlang and droplang, the administrative programs used to install and remove languages in PostgreSQL. Before installing PL/Tcl in PostgreSQL, first check to determine whether it is already installed. Type `createlang -1` to list the installed languages.

```
[perkins@laura perkins]$ createlang -l perkins
    Procedural languages
  Name  | Trusted? | Compiler
--------+----------+----------
 plpgsql | t        | PL/pgSQL
(1 row)
```

If the language is not installed, type `createlang -L /usr/pgsql/lib plpgsql perkins`.

```
[perkins@laura pgsql]$ createlang -L /usr/lib/pgsql pltcl perkins
```

Now check your work. List the installed languages.

```
[[perkins@laura pgsql]$ createlang -l perkins
    Procedural languages
  Name  | Trusted? | Compiler
--------+----------+----------
 plpgsql | t        | PL/pgSQL
 pltcl   | t        | PL/Tcl
(2 rows)
```

That sets up PL/Tcl inside PostgreSQL. If you are interested in using Tcl as a stand-alone language, check out the Scriptics Web site, at http://www.scriptics.com. At the site, you can download the most recent versions of the Tcl language for a variety of software platforms. If you are using Linux, Tcl is probably already installed. To check for Tcl on a Linux machine, type

```
[perkins@laura lib]$ which tclsh
/usr/bin/tclsh
```

This shows that you have the Tcl shell program (tclsh). If you intend to use Tcl as a scripting language, you need this program. If you don't have Tcl, get it from the Scriptics Site.

Data-aware Tcl comes from the postgresql-tcl packages, available in various formats at postgresql.readysetnet.com/sites.html. This package installs an enhanced Tcl interpreter, pgtclsh. To see whether this is already installed, type

```
[perkins@laura lib]$ which pgtclsh
/usr/bin/pgtclsh
```

If you need to use Tcl scripts that access your PostgreSQL database, you will need pgtclsh.

> When I installed the Red Hat Package Manager (RPM) version of postgresql-tcl on my Red Hat 7.0 installation, I had to create a new link, libtcl8.0.so, to the shared library libtcl8.3.so.

PL/Tcl General Syntax

The CREATE FUNCTION syntax is used to create PL/Tcl functions. Here is the general syntax:

```
CREATE FUNCTION myfunction (var, var, ...)
RETURNS va
r AS '
  Statement...
  Statement...
'
LANGUAGE 'plpgsql';
```

PL/Tcl functions don't have a rigid format. Consider the following:

```
create function basicpltclfunction (int4,int4) returns int4 as '
  expr $1 + $2
' language 'pltcl'
```

Check your work, using psql with this query:

```
perkins=# select basicpltclfunction(42, 2);
 basicpltclfunction
--------------------
                 44
(1 row)
```

> Remember, you don't have to build the CREATE FUCTION statements by hand. You can use pgaccess to build your functions, as described in Chapter 9, "Basic PostgreSQL Data Types and SQL Functions." pgaccess takes care of all the required syntax, including quotation marks.

Notice the lack of a return statement. In PL/Tcl and Tcl, a function without a return statement returns the result of the last statement. Here is the statement rewritten with a return:

```
create function basicpltclfunction (int4,int4) returns int4 as '
  set retval [expr $1 + $2]
  return $retval
' language 'pltcl'
```

which gives the same result:

```
perkins=# select basicpltclfunction(42, 2);
 basicpltclfunction
--------------------
                 44
(1 row)
```

Statements in PL/Tcl and Tcl are terminated by a newline. You cannot stack multiple statements on a single line. One statement per line is generally a good thing. The use of comments is even better.

PL/Tcl and Tcl Commenting

Comments in PL/Tcl and Tcl are denoted by a pound sign (#):

```
#This is my first pltcl function
```

The # must be the first character, other than a blank, on a line. Otherwise, the # is treated like any other symbol. You cannot write something like this:

```
return $retval #Glad this is done
```

If you tried it, you would get this:

```
perkins=# select basicpltclfunction(42, 2);
ERROR:  pltcl: bad option "44": must be -code, -errorcode, or -errorinfo
```

PL/Tcl is case sensitive; the keyword *return* cannot be typed as *Return*:

```
create function basicpltclfunction (int4,int4) returns int4 as '
  set retval [expr $1 + $2]
  Return $retval
' language 'pltcl'
```

PostgreSQL will not recognize Return as a command and will throw an error:

```
perkins=# select basicpltclfunction(42, 2);
ERROR: pltcl: invalid command name "Return"
```

PL/Tcl Functions

You can call other functions within the body of a PL/Tcl function—you can even call a function written in a different language.

```
create function tclcallme () returns int4 as '
  spi_exec " select add2int(2,2) as retval"
  return $retval
' language 'pltcl'
```

You can't call the function directly; you need to use the SQL syntax, as you do when calling a function from psql. See the section "Dealing with Data: PL/Tcl vs. Tcl" for more details on the spi_exec function.

Working with Tcl from the command line starts with the tclsh command shell.

```
[perkins@laura lib]$ tclsh
% set x 3
3
% set y 4
4
% expr $x + $y
7
%
```

When you invoke the tclsh shell, you get a new command-line prompt, the ampersand (%). As demonstrated, the tclsh shell is interactive. As you type in commands, you get results. This is a very good way to learn the basics of Tcl. The "Tcl Variable Types," uses the tclsh shell to demonstrate the various types of variables. If you want to write and execute programs in Tcl, you need to use a script.

Tcl Scripts

Start a Tcl script with the line `#!/usr/bin/tclsh`. On a Linux system, this causes your script to be called by the tclsh shell. When your script is called, the following four variables are created and passed in:

- **argv.** The list of arguments passed to the function.
- **argc.** The number of arguments passed to the function.
- **argv0.** The name of the file that called tclsh.
- **tcl_interactive.** Returns 1 if tclsh is running in the interactive mode and returns 0 otherwise.

Here is a simple script example:

```
[root@laura /tmp]# cat tcltestscript.tcl
#!/usr/bin/tclsh
 #Do some math
  set x 1
  set y 2
  puts "$x + $y =  [expr $x + $y]"
 #See what was passed to us
  puts "argv = $argv"
  puts "argc = $argc"
  puts "argv0 =  $argv0"
  puts "tcl_interactive = $tcl_interactive"
```

Running this script with some random arguments results in the following:

```
[root@laura /tmp]# ./tcltestscript.tcl 3 5 7
1 + 2 =  3
argv = 3 5 7
argc = 3
argv0 =  ./tcltestscript.tcl
tcl_interactive = 0
```

Don't worry about the syntax; it will all be covered as the chapter progresses.

Tcl Variable Types

The variable types used inside a PL/Tcl function are the same, straightforward variable types use in Tcl. There are only three types of variables to learn: Elements, Lists, and Arrays.

Tcl Elements

Each element starts out life as a string and must have its value assigned using a set statement. Element variables can be set anywhere in a script or function. To set the variable x to the value `Hello World`, you use

```
% set x "Hello World"
Hello World
```

> The set command might look unsophisticated to those of you with lots of pro-
> gramming experience, but it saves Tcl from having to deal Fortran-like
> variable-naming mistakes. Fortran creates variables on-the-fly, so if you have a
> variable named `foo` with a value of 5 and later in your program you misspell *foo*
> as *fooo*, a new variable `fooo` will be created with a default value. This can't hap-
> pen in Tcl because of the set function. If you set `foo` to 5 and later try to use `fooo`,
> the parser will point out that you are using an uninitialized variable.

NOTE

The puts command prints a variable to the standard output, but you have to be careful how the variable is referenced. The following command doesn't print out the expected "Hello World":

```
% puts x
x
```

If you want to print out the value of an element variable, preface it with a dollar sign ($). This syntax should be familiar to those of you who have done batch file programming in Linux or DOS. To print out the value of x, use

```
% puts $x
Hello World
```

Tcl has several useful commands for manipulating strings. Each command starts with the word *string*, as in this function, which finds the length of a string:

```
% string length $x
11
```

The most commonly used string functions are `bytelength`, `compare`, `equal`, `first`, `index`, `is`, `last`, `length`, `map`, `match`, `range`, `repeat`, `replace`, `tolower`, `toupper`, `totitle`, `trim`, `trimleft`, `trimright`, `wordend`, and `wordstart`. See the Tcl appendix for a complete reference.

Here is a sampling of string functions:

```
% set y "Hello World"
Hello World
% set z "Bye"
Bye
% string compare $x $y
0
% string compare $x $z
1
% string toupper $x
HELLO WORLD
```

Not everything in life and programming is a string. In Tcl, to evaluate an expression as a number, you use the *expr* keyword—for example:

```
% set x 3
3
% set y 4
6
% puts "$x + $y"
3 + 4
```

If you want the sum of the two numbers, you type

```
% puts [expr $x + $y]
7
```

The brackets ([ ]) cause the contained expression to be evaluated. If you want to output the value of the variables, use double quotes (" "):

```
% puts "$x + $y"
3 + 4
```

To treat the expression as a string without substituting the values of the variables, use braces, { }:

```
% puts {$x + $y}
$x + $y
```

For manipulating numbers, Tcl contains an assortment of math functions. For a detailed listing, see the Tcl appendix. To get a general feel for what is available, study the following examples:

```
% set pi 3.1415
3.1415
```

This sets up an approximate value for pi. You need this because the geometric functions deal in radians. For those of you who haven't had to deal with radians, 360 degrees is equal to 2pi radians (about 6.283). To get the cosine of 45 degrees, you use

```
% expr sin($pi/4)
0.707090402001
```

or to get the cosine of 60 degrees, you use

```
% expr cos($pi/3)
0.500026746549
```

Random numbers come two ways:

```
% expr rand()
0.610539645707
% expr srand(1)
7.82636925943e-06
% expr rand()
0.131537788143
% expr srand(1)
7.82636925943e-06
```

Notice that the srand function returns the same value when given the same seed, whereas the rand function returns a different value every time it is called.

Tcl Lists

In Tcl, a *list* is a collection of values. Take the days of the week:

```
% set weekdays {Monday Tuesday Wednesday Thursday Friday}
Monday Tuesday Wednesday Thursday Friday
% puts $weekdays
Monday Tuesday Wednesday Thursday Friday
```

When you have a list, you can manipulate it with one of the Tcl list functions. (A complete list of Tcl list functions can be found in the Appendix C.) For example, get a list of all the Tcl commands using the Tcl's info function:

```
% set commands [info commands]
tell socket subst open eof pwd glob list exec pid auto_load_index time unknown e
val lrange fblocked lsearch auto_import gets case lappend proc break variable ll
ength auto_execok return linsert error catch clock info split array if fconfigur
e concat join lreplace source fcopy global switch auto_qualify update close cd f
or auto_load file append format read package set binary namespace scan trace see
```

```
k while flush after vwait uplevel continue foreach rename fileevent regexp upvar
 unset encoding expr load regsub history interp exit puts incr lindex lsort tclL
og string
```

For some reason, these aren't in alphabetical order. You can fix that.

```
% lsort $commands
after append array auto_execok auto_import auto_load auto_load_index auto_qualif
y binary break case catch cd clock close concat continue encoding eof error eval
 exec exit expr fblocked fconfigure fcopy file fileevent flush for foreach forma
t gets glob global history if incr info interp join lappend lindex linsert list
llength load lrange lreplace lsearch lsort namespace open package pid proc puts
pwd read regexp regsub rename return scan seek set socket source split string su
bst switch tclLog tell time trace unknown unset update uplevel upvar variable vw
ait while
```

To find the info command in this list, use

```
% lsearch $commands info
31
```

To do a reverse find, using the index:

```
% lindex $commands 31
info
```

or all on one line:

```
% lindex $commands [lsearch $commands info]
info
```

Creating a list out of a string is the job of the `split` command. Consider this:

```
% set filename [split "myfile.txt" .]
myfile txt
```

`split` takes the given phrase and divides it, using a supplied character, in this case, a period. To split this phrase by the character *t*, you use

```
% set filename [split "myfile.txt" t]
myfile. x {}
```

The {} at the end denotes the space occupied by the last *t*.

Tcl Arrays

An *array* is a list with an index. Make the weekday list into a weekday array:

```
% set weekday(1) Monday
Monday
% set weekday(2) Tuesday
Tuesday
% set weekday(3) Wednesday
Wednesday
% set weekday(4) Thursday
Thursday
% set weekday(5) Friday
Friday
% puts $weekday
can't read "weekday": variable is array
```

Notice that puts can't be used to show the members of an array. To see the values, use

```
% puts $weekday(1)
Monday
% puts $weekday(2)
Tuesday
```

One of the really useful things about Tcl arrays is that you don't have to use a number as an index. Try this:

```
% set weekday(Mon) Monday
Monday
% set weekday(Tue) Tuesday
Tuesday
% puts $weekday(Mon)
Monday
```

Here, the abbreviations for each day are used as an index. This is called an *associative array*.

Array functions are always prefaced by the word *array*. For example:

```
#!/usr/bin/tclsh
#array test

set week(1) Monday
```

```
set week(2)  Tuesday
set week(3)  Wednesday
set week(4)  Thursday
set week(5)  Friday
set week(6)  Saturday
set week(7)  Sunday


puts [array get week]


set result [array get week {[1-3]}]


puts $result


puts [array size week]
```

This script returns

```
4 Thursday 5 Friday 1 Monday 6 Saturday 2 Tuesday 7 Sunday 3 Wednesday
1 Monday 2 Tuesday 3 Wednesday
7
```

Notice how the search, `array get week{[1-3]}`, operates on the index, 1-7, and not the value. The statement, `array get week {[S]*}`, won't return all the days starting with *S* because days are the values in this array. All the array functions are listed in Appendix C.

Procedures and Variable Scope

Writing a procedure in PL/Tcl is slightly different from writing a procedure in Tcl, but variable scope is the same in both. First, look at procedures and variable scope in Tcl. From the tclsh, a procedure looks like this:

```
% proc addtwoints {x y} { return [expr $x + $y]}
% addtwoints 3 4
7
```

Tcl uses a `source` statement to import procedures. Here is a file, addone.tcl, built with a text editor:

```
# This procedure adds one to x


proc addone x {
```

```
    return [incr x]
}
```

Using the `source` statement to import the function into the tclsh session and then calling addone looks like this:

```
% source addone.tcl
% addone 4
5
```

If a variable x is declared and passed into addone, will addone change its value? Let's see:

```
% set x 5
5
% addone $x
6
% set x
5
```

The procedure addone doesn't change the value of the variable x. Addone acts on a copy of the variable. What if a function needs to change the value of the variable on the argument list? Tcl has the command `upvar` for just this occasion. Look at a modified version of addone:

```
# This procedure adds one to x
proc addone x {
  upvar $x a
  return [incr a]
}
```

Set a variable y, and see whether it is changed:

```
% set y 5
5
% addone y
6
% set y
6
```

When a variable is part of an argument for a procedure, as in `incr x` or `addone y`, it does not use the `$` prefix.

NOTE

Any variable declared outside a procedure is *global*. A procedure can reference a global variable by using upvar:

```
# Returns a global variable
proc getglobal { } {
  upvar #0 my_global a
  return $a
}
```

Load the program, declare the my_global, and then run getglobal:

```
% source getglobal.tcl
% set my_global 76
76
% getglobal
76
```

You can declare global variables from inside a procedure using the *global* keyword. For example, an initialization script looks like this:

```
#Sets up Global variables for some program
proc setglobals { } {
    global my_global1
    global my_global2
    global my_global3
    set my_global1 15
    set my_global2 5
    set my_global3 55
}
```

Check your work using

```
% source setglobals.tcl
% setglobals
55
% set my_global1
15
% set my_global2
5
% set my_global3
55
```

PL/Tcl Procedures

The general syntax and a few examples of PL/Tcl procedures are given at the beginning of the chapter. Now try a slightly more complex example. First, make a procedure that initializes some global variables.

```
create function initglobals () returns int2 as '  global my_global1
  global my_global2
  global my_global3
  set my_global1 15
  set my_global2 5
  set my_global3 55
' language 'pltcl'
```

Read those variables from a different procedure:

```
create function useglobals () returns text as 'upvar #0 my_global1 a
upvar #0 my_global2 b
upvar #0 my_global3 c
lappend mylist "$a $b $c"
return $mylist
' language 'pltcl'
```

Initialize the global variables, and then call them.

```
perkins=# select initglobals();
 initglobals
------------
         55
(1 row)
perkins=# select useglobals();
 useglobals
------------
 {15 5 55}
(1 row)
```

> In PL/Tcl, all the procedures share a common Tcl interpreter.

PL/Tcl also has a couple dozen special variables and one type, OPAQUE, that come into play when the function is used as a database trigger. These are covered later in the chapter.

Control Structures

The PL/PGSQL language has four types of control structures: if, for, foreach, switch, and while.

The if Statement

The if statement has three possible syntaxes:

```
if expression then {
   Statement...
   Statement...
}
```

or

```
if expression then {
   Statement...
   Statement...
}else{
   Statement...
}
```

or

```
if expression then {
   Statement...
}elseif expression {
   Statement...
}elseif expression {
   Statement...
} else {
   Statement...
   Statement...
}
```

The if statement is straightforward. An if statement must have an expression to evaluate and statements to execute if the expression is true. An if statement can contain an unlimited number of ifelse clauses. An if statement can also contain one else clause. If the expression evaluates to true, the statements contained in the braces after the keyword then are executed. If the expression evaluates to false and there is an elseif statement, the expression of the elseif is evaluated. If there is an else clause and all the other expressions have evaluated to false, the statements between the braces after the else are executed. Here is a simple example:

```
proc testif x {
  set retval "none"
  if {$x > 0} {
    set retval "Positive"
  } elseif {$x == 0} {
    set retval "Zero"
  } else {
    set retval "Negative"
  }
  return "The value $x is $retval"
}
```

Now load the procedure and try some values:

```
% source testif.tcl
% testif 4
The value 4 is Positive
% testif 0
The value 0 is Zero
% testif -10
The value -10 is Negative
```

The for Statement

The syntax of the for will be familiar to those who have programmed in C.

```
for {start} {test} {increment} {
  statement...
  statement...
}
```

The following example shows how this works:

```
proc testfor x {
  for {set i 0} {$i <= $x} {incr i} {
    puts "The variable i is $i"
  }
}
```

which runs like this:

```
% source testfor.tcl
% testfor 5
The variable i is 0
The variable i is 1
The variable i is 2
The variable i is 3
The variable i is 4
The variable i is 5
```

The foreach Statement

The Tcl `foreach` statement works with lists. There are two forms of syntax. The first is

```
foreach var list {
   statement...
   statement...
}
```

This form of the `foreach` statement iterates through each of the items in the list. The value of the list item is assigned to the variable and the statements inside the braces are executed. Then the value of the next item in the list is assigned to the variable, and so on. Here is an example:

```
proc testforeach inList {
   upvar $inList aList
   foreach x $aList {
      puts $x
   }
}
```

Make a list and run this procedure:

```
% set mylist {one two three four}
% source testforeach.tcl
% testforeach mylist
one
two
three
four
```

> The `upvar` statement has to be used when a list or an array is an argument for a procedure.

The single variable and list are a specialized form of the general foreach syntax:

```
foreach variablelist list variablelist list...{
  Statement...
  Statement...
}
```

This form of `foreach` runs all the values in the list into the variables in the variable list. Here is a modified version of the `testforeach` procedure:

```
proc testforeach inList {
  upvar $inList aList
  foreach {x y} $aList {
    puts "x = $x, y = $y"
  }
}
```

Running this with the same list used in the first `foreach` example yields

```
% testforeach mylist
x = one, y = two
x = three, y = four
```

If there aren't enough list values to go around, the variable is assigned an empty value. An empty value is the same as using a `set x {}`.

If you want to run the entire list through each variable, try this:

```
proc testforeach inList {
  upvar $inList aList
  foreach {x} $aList {y} $aList {
    puts "x = $x, y = $y"
  }
}
```

which results in this:

```
% source testforeach.tcl
% testforeach mylist
x = one, y = one
x = two, y = two
```

```
x = three, y = three
x = four, y = four
```

The switch Statement

Tcl contains a very useful switch control structure. The Tcl switch control structure allows you to take actions based on either exact or partial matches. The syntax is

```
switch -option string {
  pattern {
    statement...
  }
  pattern {
    statement...
  }
  default {
    statement...
  }
}
```

The key to the `switch` statement is in the `-option` clause. There are three options: `exact`, `regexp`, and `glob`. The first option, `exact`, requires an exact match to trigger one of the pattern clauses. The `exact` clause is the default option. Here is an example:

```
proc testswitch x {
  #The -exact option is the default
  switch $x {
    Monday { puts "English and History" }
    Friday { puts "Tennis and Golf"}
    default { puts "nothing scheduled"}
  }
}
```

Load `testswitch` and run some days through it.

```
% source testswitch.tcl
% testswitch Tuesday
nothing scheduled
% testswitch Monday
English and History
```

If you want to run the statements in the pattern clause, based on a partial match, use either the `glob` or `regexp` option. These options differ only in the syntax used to determine a match. (See the Appendix C for details.) Here is an example that gives a little more latitude on entering the date:

```
proc testswitch x {
  #The -exact option is the default
  switch -regexp $x {
    Mon* { puts "English and History" }
    Fri* { puts "Tennis and Golf"}
    default { puts "nothing scheduled"}
  }
}


% source testswitch.tcl
% testswitch Monday
English and History
% testswitch Mon
English and History
% testswitch Thursday
nothing scheduled
```

The while Statement

The `while` statement in Tcl is a loop, entered if a condition is true (see the section earlier on the for statement for values that evaluate to true) and executed until the condition becomes false. The syntax is

```
while {expression} {
  Statement...
  Statement...
}
```

Here is an example of using `while` to search the contents of an array:

```
proc testwhile {inArray target} {
  #Remember to use upvar for lists or arrays
  upvar $inArray theArray
  set retval "false"
  set srch [array startsearch theArray]
  while {[array anymore theArray $srch]} {
    set arrayVal [array nextelement theArray $srch]
```

```
    #watch our work
    if {$arrayVal == $target} {
      set retval "true"
      #clean up the search variables
      array donesearch theArray $srch
    }
    # If we are done, break out of the loop
    if {$retval} break
  }
  return $retval
}
```

Now load it and test it.

```
% source testwhile.tcl
% array set myarray {Monday Mon Tuesday Tue Wednesday Wed}
% source testwhile.tcl
% testwhile myarray Monday
true
% testwhile myarray Friday
false
```

Notice how the break command is used to end the loop when a match is found. Be careful using while statements. If the test condition is never met, your statement will loop forever!

Dealing with Data: PL/Tcl vs. Tcl

PL/Tcl and Tcl have slightly different ways of manipulating PostgreSQL data. In the next sections you will first learn how PL/Tcl procedures access PostgreSQL data, then examine how database triggers are built using PL/Tcl. Finally, you will see what the pgtclsh shell adds to your data manipulation toolkit.

Data Access from a PL/Tcl Function

To access data from within a PL/Tcl function, use the spi_exec procedure. The syntax is

```
spi_exec {-count n} {-array name} query {
  Statement...
}
```

The optional -count argument tells PostgreSQL the maximum number of rows to return. The optional -array argument is used with an SQL select statement. It creates an associative array with the given name and drops in the first row of data. The query statement contains an SQL statement. If there are any statements between the braces after the query, they are executed in the same manner as a foreach statement, with each new row of data placed in the named array. Here is an example:

```
create function getrow () returns text as '
  spi_exec -array firstrow "select * from address"
  return [array get firstrow]
' language 'pltcl'
```

This gets the first row of the table and dumps it and the column names out.

```
perkins=# select getrow();
                                 getrow


-------------------------------------------------------------------------------
----------
 .tupno 0 city {Fair Oaks} state CA zipcode 95555 nickname Leslie street {1313 M
Bird Lane}
(1 row)
```

Notice the .tupno column. This is an internal PostgreSQL column that is not normally available and represents the row number.

Now do something with multiple rows:

```
create function getrows () returns text as '#make an empty list
list retval {}
spi_exec -array firstrow "select * from address" {
  lappend retval $firstrow(zipcode)
}
return $retval
' language 'pltcl'
```

This function throws out a space-delimited list of the zip codes in the table:

```
perkins=# select getrows();
                     getrows
-------------------------------------------------
 95555 55555 77555 88888 45454 99955 99955 55599
(1 row)
```

A Tcl Example

To make queries more specific, say, to get a row with a particular name, use the `spi_prepare` statement. The `prepare` statement syntax is

```
spi_prepare query vartypes
```

The query is a normal SQL query, with the variables embedded using the syntax `\$1`, `\$2`, and so on. If there are embedded variables, their PostgreSQL types are given. For example, to prepare a query to search for names, you would use a statement such as the following:

```
set plan [spi_prepare "select * from address where nickname = ''$1''" text]
```

The plan could then be executed in a statement using the `spi_execp` function. The `spi_execp` function has this syntax:

```
spi_execp -count n -array arrayname -null nullvars query varlist {
Statement...
Statement...
}
```

The optional `-count`, `-array`, and statements contained in braces work the same as `spi_exec`. The optional `-null` field contains a variable made of spaces and *n*'s. This variable must be exactly as long as the number of columns returned and contain an *n* where the column is null. The query is the variable created with `spi_prepare`. If `spi_prepare` uses the variable, the varlist is a list of the variables to insert. Here is an example:

```
create function getname (text) returns text as '
set plan [spi_prepare "select * from address where nickname = ''$1''"  text]
spi_execp -array firstrow $plan [list $1]
return [array get firstrow]
' language 'pltcl'
```

This function runs like this:

```
perkins=# select getname('Jeff'::text);
                                  getname
----------------------------------------------------------------------------
.tupno 0 city Orlando state FL zipcode 99955 nickname Jeff street {555 Dodah Dr}
(1 row)
```

Notice that the value passed to `getname` is cast as text. This cast wouldn't have to be done if the variable came from another function with a return value of text or if the value was the result of a select statement.

PL/Tcl even offers a convenient global array, called *GD*. GD is a convenient place to put things such as plans, so you don't have to create them again and again. Look at the modified `getname`:

```
create function getname (text) returns text as 'if {![ info exists GD(plan9) ]} {
   # Plan9 is not saved, so we need to build it
      set GD(plan9) [spi_prepare "select * from address where nickname = ''$1''"
text]
}
spi_execp -array firstrow $GD(plan9) [list $1]
return [array get firstrow]
' language 'pltcl'
```

Now, `plan9` is created only once but can be executed from a PL/Tcl function. Using the `spi_prepare` method for repeated queries means faster overall execution of the queries because PostgreSQL doesn't have to waste CPU cycles setting up a repeated query. PostgreSQL can focus on getting the data rather than make a map to the data.

Database Triggers

A database *trigger* is a special database function that is linked to a table and called whenever there is an UPDATE, an INSERT, or a DELETE on the table. Triggers are traditionally used to check the values of incoming data to make sure that things such as negative salaries or two-digit years don't get into a database. Triggers can also be used to write information about transactions to the log or to call other functions in PostgreSQL.

Following are the commonly used variables available to a PL/Tcl function called as a trigger:

- **$NEW.** A RECORD type referenced to the new row in the database, used when the TG_op is UPDATE or DELETE.
- **$OLD.** A RECORD type referenced to the old row in the database, used when the TG_op is UPDATE or DELETE.
- **$TG_when.** A text type of BEFORE or AFTER, indicating when the trigger is called.
- **$TG_op.** A text type of INSERT, UPDATE, or DELETE, indicating the type of database operation that fired the trigger.
- **$GD.** A global status array.

A trigger can have one of the following three return values:

- **OK.** Completed the operation on the NEW record.
- **SKIP.** Does not complete the operation on the NEW record.
- A list of Record values, commonly generated using the array `get NEW`.

To create a trigger, make a function with no arguments and a return type of OPAQUE. Look at the following:

```
create function tcltriggerme () returns OPAQUE as '#If called before an operation
then
#Return either NULL or a RECORD with the value to INSERT or UPDATE
  if {$TG_when == "BEFORE"} then {
    #check for valid state, short list - save trees
    list validstates {AL CA TX FL}
    set result [lsearch -exact validstates $NEW(state)]
    if {$result} {
      return [array get NEW]
    } else {
      return {}
    }
  } else {
    elog DEBUG "Database Name $TG_name";
    elog DEBUG "Operation is TG_op";
    return{};
  }
' language 'pltcl'
```

Here, the value of the new state is checked against a list of valid states. This list of states can also be imported from a select statement on a table of state abbreviations.

Now tie the trigger to a table. Notice how a third name is used so that if you have to drop the trigger, you don't have to drop the function.

```
perkins=# CREATE TRIGGER check_state before insert or update on address
perkins-# for each row execute procedure tcltriggerme();
CREATE
```

Now insert data with a valid state.

```
perkins=# insert into "address" ("nickname","street","state","zipcode","city") v
alues ('Puder','1456 Old Rd','FL','8990','St Augustine');
INSERT 413730 1
```

That works. Now try a brand XX state.

```
perkins=# insert into "address" ("nickname","street","state","zipcode","city") v
alues ('Biff','1600 Penn','XX','88888','Arlington');
INSERT 0 0
```

Notice that PL/Tcl doesn't have the capability to raise an error. It will not save the record, but it won't stop the program.

If you make changes to your trigger function, drop the relationship, using this:

```
perkins=# DROP TRIGGER check_state on address;
```

Then reattach the trigger as before. If you don't do this, PostgreSQL will use a cached copy of your function. It's very frustrating to make changes to a function and not see them take effect.

Data Access from Tcl

When PL/Tcl is installed, a PostgreSQL-enabled command shell pgtclsh is also installed. This shell works just like `tclsh`, except that it has built-in procedures for accessing PostgreSQL. A complete list of the PostgreSQL functions in pgtclsh is available in Appendix C. Here, you will focus on the basics.

- Opening a connection to a database
- Executing a SQL query
- Manipulating data
- Closing a database connection

The first step is to type **pgtclsh** from the command line to start the shell. After the shell is started, the `pg_conndefaults` command can be used to see how your shell is configured:

```
% set connlist [pg_conndefaults]
{authtype Database-Authtype D 20 {}} {user Database-User {} 20 perkins} {passwor
d Database-Password * 20 {}} {dbname Database-Name {} 20 perkins} {host Database
-Host {} 40 {}} {hostaddr Database-Host-IPv4-Address {} 15 {}} {port Database-Po
rt {} 6 5432} {tty Backend-Debug-TTY D 40 {}} {options Backend-Debug-Options D 4
0 {}}
```

Here, you see that my user name and the database name are already set to what I want. Now, make a connection using `pg_connect`. If you did not set up your user to need a password (see Chapter 3, "PostgreSQL Basic Security"), you won't need an entry on the `conninfo` string.

```
% set conn [pg_connect -conninfo "host=localhost password=yourpasswordhere"]
pgsql3
```

Executing a query is done with the `pg_exec` function:

```
% set result [pg_exec $conn "Select * from address"]
pgsql4.0
```

If you executed a `select` statement, you can get the column names using the `pg_result` procedure and the `-attributes` flag:

```
% set resultslist [pg_result $result -attributes]
nickname street state zipcode city
```

When you have a result set in hand, you can assign it to an array for manipulation using the `pg_result` command and the `-assign` switch:

```
% pg_result $result -assign resultarray
resultarray
```

Here is a dump of the array:

```
% array get resultarray
6,zipcode 99955 5,street {555 Dodah Dr} 3,state CA 7,zipcode 55599 7,nickname Je
ff 4,city Waco 4,state TX 8,zipcode 8990 7,street {1600 Penn} 5,state FL 0,nickn
ame Leslie 6,city Orlando 6,state FL 0,street {1313 MBird Lane} 7,state FL 2,nic
kname Kelly 8,city {St Augustine} 8,state FL 2,street {1010 Pudder Ln} 4,nicknam
e Alton 1,city {Big Pine} 4,street {1872 Waco} 6,nickname Jeff 3,city {Fair Oaks
...
```

Row number and column name are used to access the result array values:

```
% set resultarray(0,nickname)
Leslie
```

> There can be no spaces between the indices of the array. If you use the command `set resultarray(0, nickname)`, you will not get `Leslie`. You will get `nickname)`. Tcl doesn't support true multidimensional arrays. To simulate a multidimensional array, Tcl uses associative arrays. In this case, the value `0,nickname` is the true index. It just looks like a multidimensional array.

When you are done with a result set and database, use `pg_result` with the `-clear` option (`pg_result $results -clear`) and `pg_disconnect` (`pg_disconnect $conn`) to release the database resources. If you don't release resources after you use them, you will eventually lose the ability to connect to the database because of lack of database connection and result resources.

Summary

Tcl is a widely used scripting and programming language. The pgaccess program in Chapter 5 is written in Tcl, using a graphics library called *Tk*. In this chapter, you have learned the basics of the Tcl language, how to write a PL/Tcl procedure, the methods used to bring PostgreSQL data into a PL/Tcl procedure, the mechanics of building database triggers in PL/Tcl, and how to use pgtclsh to write data-enabled Tcl programs—a good start. You should now know enough about Tcl and PL/Tcl to write basic programs and database functions.

PostgreSQL's PL/Tcl and the pgtclsh shell provide a workbench, stocked with powerful string manipulation and relational database tools, from which you can craft efficient solutions to your database programming problems.

If you want to learn more about Tcl, I suggest that you download TclPro from sourceforge.net/projects/tclpro/. This no-cost tool includes a debugger and extensive Tcl help files. Also, the site at http://dev.scriptics.com/ is a good starting point for all things Tcl.

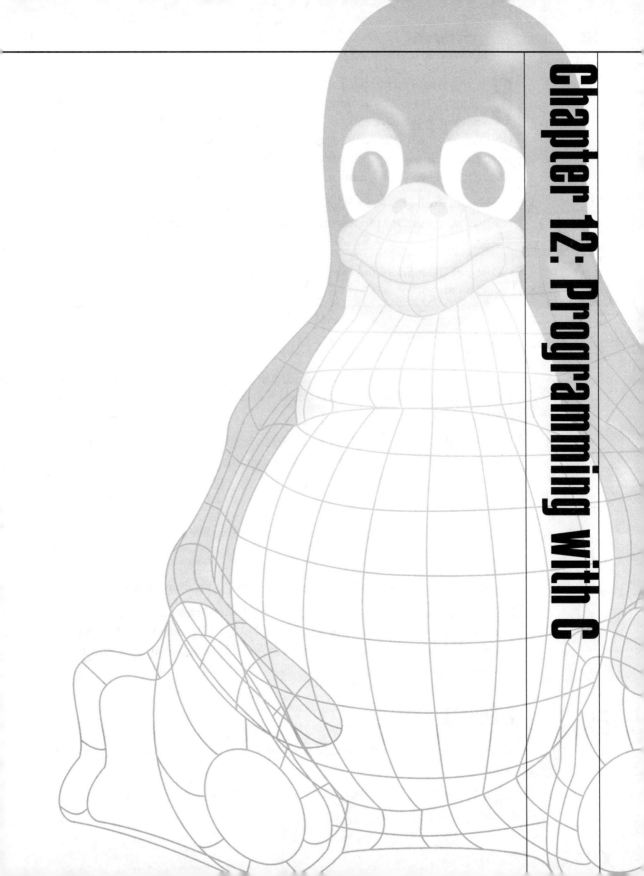

Chapter 12: Programming with C

C is the language of speed. If you need a program that rotates graphics or manipulates a mathematical matrix, you should consider creating your solution in the C language. C is the stuff that PostgreSQL—and most other UNIX, Linux, and Windows programs—are made of. PostgreSQL allows for the construction of stored procedures in C. The PostgreSQL system also includes a library that allows C programs to do business with a PostgreSQL database.

This chapter will give you a brief overview of the C language, then will teach you how to construct stored procedures in C and access a PostgreSQL database using it.

> PostgreSQL support for the C++ language is covered in the PostgreSQL documentation.

C Setup

The C language is automatically included as a stored procedure language in your PostgreSQL installation—you don't need to use the createlang and droplang programs covered in Chapter 2.

Most installations of UNIX and Linux include a C compiler. This C compiler is typically the GNU C compiler (http://gcc.gnu.org/). To test for a GNU C compiler on your Linux system, type

```
[root@laura pgsql]# which gcc
```

If you have a GNU C compiler, you'll get something like this:

```
/usr/bin/gcc
```

If you don't have a compiler and you want to use C, get it from http://gcc.gnu.org/.

The libpq library is included in your PostgreSQL installation. It contains the functions required to connect a C program to a PostgreSQL database. On a Redhat installation, the libpq library is located in /usr/lib/libpq.so (shared object) and /usr/lib/libpq.a (static library).

C General Syntax

The CREATE FUNCTION syntax is used to create C functions. Following is the general syntax:

```
CREATE FUNCTION myfunction (var, var, ...)
RETURNS var AS
```

```
' /dir/dir/lib.so
LANGUAGE 'c';
```

The item contained inside the single quotes, /dir/dir/lib.so, is the path to and name of a shared object (more about how to create a shared object a little later). The shared object contains the C function named in the first line of the CREATE FUNCTION statement. Most of the prebuilt functions included in PostgreSQL are C shared objects. Type:

```
perkins=# \df
```

```
                           List of functions
   Result   |         Function         |              Arguments
------------+--------------------------+-------------------------------------
 _bpchar    | _bpchar                  | _bpchar int4
 _varchar   | _varchar                 | _varchar int4
 float4     | abs                      | float4
 float8     | abs                      | float8
 int2       | abs                      | int2
 int4       | abs                      | int4
 int8       | abs                      | int8
 numeric    | abs                      | numeric
```

Now, use the abs function:

```
perkins=# select abs(5.6);
 abs
----
 5.6
(1 row)
```

You can see that you have already used several C-based stored procedures. Below is a quick example. Don't worry about the syntax—I will cover that shortly.

```
[perkins@laura examples]$ cat functs.c
#include <string.h>
#include "postgres.h"

/* Globals */
int MAXLEN = 20;

/*prototypes*/
int4 x_squared(int4);
```

```
text * hello_world(void);

/* Simple Math*/

int4 x_squared(int4 x)
{
    return(x * x);
}

/* Every C tutorial must have a Hello World */
text * hello_world()
{
  char * hellostring = "Hello World";
  text * retval = (text *) palloc(MAXLEN);
  memset((void *) retval, 0, MAXLEN);
  VARSIZE(retval) = MAXLEN;
  strncpy(VARDATA(retval), hellostring, MAXLEN);
  return retval;
}


[perkins@laura examples]$ gcc -I/usr/include/pgsql -O2 -Wall -Wmissing-prototype
s -Wmissing-declarations -c -o functs.o functs.c
[perkins@laura examples]$ gcc -shared -o functs.so functs.o
perkins=# CREATE FUNCTION hello_world() RETURNS text AS '/tmp/examples/functs.so'
LANGUAGE 'c';
CREATE
perkins=# select hello_world();
 hello_world
------------
 Hello World
(1 row)
perkins=# CREATE FUNCTION x_squared(int4) returns int4 as '/tmp/examples/functs.
so' language 'C';
CREATE
perkins=# select x_squared(16);
 x_squared
----------
       256
(1 row)
```

Remember, you don't have to build the CREATE FUCTION statements by hand. You can use pgaccess to build your functions, as described in Chapter 5, "Getting Graphical with PostreSQL." pgaccess takes care of all the required syntax, including quotes.

Notice the `return` statement in the C function. Return statements are mandatory in a PostgreSQL stored procedure written in the C language.

Statements in C are terminated by a semicolon (`;`). You can stack multiple statements on a single line, like this:

```
char * hellostring = "Hello World"; text * retval = (text *) palloc(MAXLEN);
memset((void *) retval, 0, MAXLEN); VARSIZE(retval) = MAXLEN;
strncpy(VARDATA(retval), hellostring, MAXLEN); return retval;
```

I recommend one statement per line because it makes your code more readable. When you use comments, your code becomes even more readable.

Comments in C start with a `/*` and end with a `*/`, as in

```
/*This is my first c function*/
```

Comments can come after a semicolon. You can write something like this:

```
return retval; /*Glad this is done*/
```

C is case-sensitive; the keyword *return* cannot be typed as *Return*. Changing the `x_squared` function,

```
/* Simple Math*/

int4 x_squared(int4 x)
{
    Return(x * x);
}
```

and then compiling it results in this:

```
[perkins@laura examples]$ gcc -I/usr/include/pgsql -O2 -Wall -Wmissing-prototype
s -Wmissing-declarations -c -o functs.o functs.c
functs.c: In function 'x_squared':
functs.c:15: warning: implicit declaration of function 'Return'
```

Notice that the error is caught in the C compiler. The C program must compile correctly, or the shared object will not be produced. If the shared objects are not produced, the CREATE FUNCTION statement cannot create a new function. This is different from PL/PGSQL and TCL, in which syntax errors aren't found until you try to run the stored procedure.

If *compiler* and *shared object* are new terms for you, you should spend a couple minutes looking at how to use the C compiler to produce a shared object.

The general syntax for compiling a C program from the command line is

```
[root@laura pgsql]# gcc --help
Usage: gcc [options] file...
Options:
  -pass-exit-codes          Exit with highest error code from a phase
  --help                    Display this information
  (Use '-v --help' to display command line options of sub-processes)
  -dumpspecs                Display all of the built-in spec strings
  -dumpversion              Display the version of the compiler
  -dumpmachine              Display the compiler's target processor
  -print-search-dirs        Display the directories in the compiler's search path
  -print-libgcc-file-name   Display the name of the compiler's companion library
  -print-file-name=<lib>    Display the full path to library <lib>
  -print-prog-name=<prog>   Display the full path to compiler component <prog>
  -print-multi-directory    Display the root directory for versions of libgcc
  -print-multi-lib          Display the mapping between command-line options and
                            multiple library search directories
  -Wa,<options>             Pass comma-separated <options> on to the assembler
  -Wp,<options>             Pass comma-separated <options> on to the preprocessor
  -Wl,<options>             Pass comma-separated <options> on to the linker
  -Xlinker <arg>            Pass <arg> on to the linker
  -save-temps               Do not delete intermediate files
  -pipe                     Use pipes rather than intermediate files
  -time                     Time the execution of each subprocess
  -specs=<file>             Override built-in specs with the contents of <file>
  -std=<standard>           Assume that the input sources are for <standard>
  -B <directory>            Add <directory> to the compiler's search paths
  -b <machine>              Run gcc for target <machine>, if installed
  -V <version>              Run gcc version number <version>, if installed
  -v                        Display the programs invoked by the compiler
  -E                        Preprocess only; do not compile, assemble, or link
  -S                        Compile only; do not assemble or link
  -c                        Compile and assemble, but do not link
```

```
-o <file>                Place the output into <file>
-x <language>            Specify the language of the following input files
                         Permissible languages include: c c++ assembler none
                         'none' means revert to the default behavior of
                         guessing the language based on the file's extension
```

```
Options starting with -g, -f, -m, -O, or -W are automatically passed on to
the various sub-processes invoked by gcc.  In order to pass other options
on to these processes, the -W<letter> options must be used.
For bug reporting instructions, please see:
<URL:http://bugzilla.redhat.com/bugzilla/>.
```

The lines used to produce the shared object in the examples are

```
gcc -I/usr/include/pgsql -O2 -Wall -Wmissing-prototypes -Wmissing-declarations -c -
o functs.o functs.c
```

and

```
gcc -shared -o functs.so functs.o
```

The first line creates an object file from the source file, functs.c. The `-I/usr...` flag tells the compiler where to find the C language include files necessary to compile a PostgreSQL C stored procedure. A header file in C normally contains type definitions. The `-o` and `-W` switches pass lower level information to the compiler. The `-c` switch tells the compiler not to link in other libraries. The `-o` switch tells the compiler to create a file named *functs.o* out of functs.c.

The second time `gcc` is called, the `-shared` directive is used to create a shared object, functs.so, out of the functs.o file.

As a programmer, you must perform three tasks to compile a shared object for use as a PostgreSQL stored procedure:

- Include postgres.h in your C program.
- Use the two compile statements just covered to create the shared object.
- Use the CREATE FUNCTION syntax to incorporate your function into PostgreSQL.

Notice that all three of these are done in the simple example. The C program includes the line `#include postgres.h`, the compile line creates a shared object, and the CREATE FUNCTION adds the new functions to PostgreSQL as stored procedures. Notice that one shared object can contain many functions and that CREATE FUNCTION can reference the same shared object for each stored procedure.

The required include files and libraries for accessing PostgreSQL from inside a C program are covered in the section "Dealing with Data" later in this chapter.

C Variables

The C language supports all the basic data types:

- **int.** An integer (precision varies by platform).
- **long.** A long integer (precision varies by platform).
- **float.** A floating-point number (precision varies by platform).
- **double.** A decimal number, normally twice the precision of a floating point.
- **char.** A character.
- **Boolean.** True or false. Zero (0) evaluates to false. All other numbers evaluate to true.

> One drawback to using the C language is the difference in numerical representation and precision from platform to platform. See your platform notes for specifics on your platform. In general, you will be okay if you stay under 32K for integers. You can also use longs instead of integers and use doubles instead of floating points. This gives you the maximum precision on any particular platform but uses up twice as much memory for variable storage.

The PostgreSQL data types supported by C are listed in the /usr/include/pgsql/postgres.h file. Here is a partial listing from that file:

```
typedef int16 int2;
typedef int32 int4;
typedef float float4;
typedef double float8;
```

In general, the postgres.h file uses the C typedef statement to redefine PostgreSQL data types to C data types. Some of the data types are defined as pointers.

Pointers and Passing Variables by Reference or Value

Remember the C code for your simple function. There was a * behind the return value. In the C language, the * symbol represents a pointer. A *pointer* in C is a reference to a memory location. Pointers allow variables to be passed by reference instead of value. For example, if a function is passed a variable, `int y`, it is getting a copy of the variable. The function can then change this variable without changing the original value of y. If a function is passed `int * y`, which translates as an integer pointer to y, the function has a direct connection to the original variable.

If you are new to C and want to do commercial-grade programming in it, either take a course or read one of the many available texts on the C language. C is not like any of the scripting languages you have learned in this book. It is like a very large power tool with no safety guard. Used properly, it can do a lot of work in a very short time, but a wrong move can cost you dearly. The dark side of C's capability to manipulate bits and bytes is that C has little internal protection against inadvertently corrupting your system's memory. Misusing a pointer or even stuffing 11 things into a 10-thing array can cause your system to lose memory and resources (C's infamous memory leaks) and your machine to crash. Entire industries thrive on C's capability to leak memory.

NOTE

C Arrays

C arrays are an N-dimensional collection of variables. An array is declared like this:

```
int myarray[10];
```

The elements of an array are accessed using brackets (`[ ]`):

```
myarray[1] = 1;
```

Multidimensional arrays are allowed:

```
int myarray[5][5][5]
myarray[1][1][1] = 3;
```

Arrays in C are *zero-based*. This means that if you declare an integer array with a size of 10, the first value is accessed using

```
myarray[0]
```

and the last element is accessed with

```
myarray[9]
```

A common error in C is to declare an array, forget that it is zero-based, and put something into what you think is the last position. If, in the preceding array, you did something like this:

```
myarray[10] = 4;
```

the compiler wouldn't complain, and the program would compile and quite possibly run. When the program started running, you would be playing Russian Roulette with your system because every time this line is run, a value is placed into memory next to the memory allotted for the array. Sometimes this memory location is benign, sometimes it contains other variables, and sometimes it contains important program or system information. Be careful when you declare and use arrays.

Structures

The C language structure is a collection of variable types grouped under one name.

```
struct genericstrucname {
  vartype var, var;
  vartype var;
} stucture name;
```

Structures are very useful for representing row data from a database table. See the section "Dealing with Data: C Stored Procedures and Programs" for an example of using a structure to contain the results of a query.

Procedures and Variable Scope

Writing a procedure in C is straightforward. The general syntax is as follows:

```
Returnvalue procedurename(variabletype variable name, variabletype
variablename...){ Statement;
Statement;
}
```

Note that the closing brace (}) doesn't use a semicolon as a terminator. Here is an example:

```
/* This procedure adds one to x */


int addone(int x)
{
  return int + 1;
}
```

C has a special function named *main* used to create stand-alone programs. So far, you have looked at functions contained in a shared library. If you use C to create a stand-alone program, you need a `main` function. Here is an example:

```
/*stdio.h is the Header file where the function printf is defined*/
#include <stdio.h>
/* Example of a program with a main */
```

```
main()
{
  printf("Hello World\n");
}
```

Now compile and run mainexample:

```
[perkins@laura examples]$ gcc -o mainexample mainexample.c
[perkins@laura examples]$ ./mainexample
Hello World
```

Only three special variables, `argv`, `argc`, and `env`, are used in the `main` declaration. These are the only three variables allowed as arguments to a main function. The `argc` contains the number of arguments on the command line, plus one. The character array, `argv`, contains the name of the program in its zero value (`argv[0]`) and the text of any command-line variables in the following values. The character array `env` contains the system's environmental variables. Together, these three variables are used to pass data into the `main` function. For example, the file argtest.c,

```
#include <stdio.h>

int main(int argc, char *argv[], char *env[])
{
  int i;
  printf("According to argc, %d arguments were passed in\n",argc);
  for(i = 0;i < argc; i++)
  {
    printf("arg %d is %s\n", i, argv[i]);
  }

/*reset i so that we can reuse it*/
  i = 0;
  while(env[i] != NULL)
  {
    printf("env %d is %s\n", i, env[i]);
    /*increment i*/
    i++;
  }
}
```

compiles and runs like this:

```
[perkins@laura examples]$ gcc -o argtest argtest.c
[perkins@laura examples]$ ./argtest one two three
```

```
According to argc, 4 arguments were passed in
arg 0 is ./argtest
arg 1 is one
arg 2 is two
arg 3 is three
env 0 is PWD=/tmp/examples
env 1 is REMOTEHOST=aries.1.168.192.in-addr.arpa
env 2 is HOSTNAME=laura.perkinsfamily
env 3 is PVM_RSH=/usr/bin/rsh
env 4 is QTDIR=/usr/lib/qt-2.2.0
env 5 is LESSOPEN=|/usr/bin/lesspipe.sh %s
env 6 is XPVM_ROOT=/usr/share/pvm3/xpvm
...
```

I will return to stand-alone programs in the section "Dealing with Data: C Stored Procedures and Programs" later in the chapter.

The C language mandates that all variables be declared. You cannot get past the compile stage without declaring all the variables used in your program or function. Variables declared inside a function are visible only inside that function unless they are exported using a pointer. Here is a rewritten argtest.c, using two functions with their own version of i to print out the argv and env arrays:

```c
#include <stdio.h>
/*prototypes*/
void printargs(int, char *[]);
void printenv(char *[]);

int main(int argc, char *argv[], char *env[])
{
  int i = 9;
  printf("According to argc, %d argument(s) were passed in\n",argc);
  printargs(argc, argv);
  printenv(env);
  printf("Check i is still %d\n", i);


}


void printargs(int numargs, char *myargs[])
{
  int i;
```

```
  for(i = 0;i < numargs; i++)
  {
    printf("arg %d is %s\n", i, myargs[i]);
  }
}


void printenv(char *myenv[])
{
  int i = 0;
  while(myenv[i] != NULL)
  {
    printf("env %d is %s\n",i , myenv[i]);
    /*increment i*/
    i++;
  }


}
[perkins@laura examples]$ ./argtest
According to argc, 1 argument(s) were passed in
arg 0 is ./argtest
env 0 is PWD=/tmp/examples
env 1 is REMOTEHOST=aries.1.168.192.in-addr.arpa
env 2 is HOSTNAME=laura.perkinsfamily
env 3 is PVM_RSH=/usr/bin/rsh
env 4 is QTDIR=/usr/lib/qt-2.2.0
env 5 is LESSOPEN=|/usr/bin/lesspipe.sh %s
env 6 is XPVM_ROOT=/usr/share/pvm3/xpvm
env 7 is KDEDIR=/usr
env 8 is USER=perkins
...
env 25 is HOME=/home/perkins
env 26 is PATH=/usr/local/bin:/bin:/usr/bin:/usr/X11R6/bin:/usr/local/java/bin:/
home/perkins/bin
env 27 is _=./argtest
Check i is still 9
```

If a variable is declared outside the main function or any other function, it is handled as a global variable, as shown in the following example:

```
#include <stdio.h>
/*prototypes*/
```

```
void showme();

char *GLOBALTEXT = "This is some Global Text";

int main(int argc, char *argv[], char *env[])
{
  printf("From in main GLOBALTEXT is %s\n", GLOBALTEXT);
  showme();
}
void showme()
{
    printf("From in showme GLOBALTEXT is %s\n", GLOBALTEXT);
}
```

The preceding code, compiled and run, looks like this:

```
[perkins@laura examples]$ gcc -o vistest vistest.c
[perkins@laura examples]$ ./vistest
From in main GLOBALTEXT is This is some Global Text
From in showme GLOBALTEXT is This is some Global Text
```

C Control Structures

The C language has five types of control structures: if, for, do, while, and switch.

The if Statement

The if statement has two forms:

```
if ( <condition> )
{
  <statement1>;
}
```

OR

```
if ( <condition> )
{
  <statement1>;
}
else
{
```

```
<statement2>;

}
```

The `if` statement is straightforward. It must have an expression to evaluate and statements to execute if the expression is true. An `if` statement can also contain an `else` clause. If the expression evaluates to true, the statements contained in the braces after the `then` are executed. If there are no braces, only the next statement is executed.

> Forgetting to use the braces to enclose all the statements you want to run if the condition is true is a common cause of logic errors in C. I recommend using braces to enclose every `if` and `else` clause. Your code becomes more readable, and you avoid this class of logic errors.

If the expression evaluates to false, and there is an `else` clause, the statements between the braces after the `else` are executed. Here is a simple example:

```
boolean testif (int x
{
  boolean retval;
  if (x > 0)
  {
    retval = true;
  }
  else
  {
    retval = false;
  }
  return retval;
}
```

This function returns `true` if the given number is greater than zero; otherwise, it returns `false`.

The for Statement

The syntax of the `for` statement in the C language is

```
for ( [<initialization>] ; [<condition>] ; [<increment>] )
{
  <statement>
}
```

The following example shows how this works:

```
void testfor(int x)
{
  int i;
  for (i=0;i <= x; i=i+1)
{

    printf( "The variable i is %d", i);

}
}
```

When this function is called, it prints out the value of i as it moves from 0 to the value of x. If x is negative, nothing is printed.

The do and while Statements

The keywords *do* and *while* can be combined in two ways. The first is

```
Do
{
 statement
}while ( condition );
```

This results in a loop that will be executed at least once and until the condition is true. The second form results in a loop that cannot be executed if the expression is false upon the first evaluation.

```
While( expression) do
{
 statement;
}
```

If the expression is true upon its first evaluation, this second form will execute until the statement becomes false. The break statement can be used to exit either form. However, it is not good programming practice to have multiple exits from a function or stucture. Use break only if you cannot find any other way out of your control structure.

The switch Statement

The C language contains a very straightforward switch control structure. The Tcl switch control structure allows you to take actions based on exact character matches. The syntax is

```
switch (variable ){
  case varvalue :
```

```
    statement;
  break;
  case varvalue :
    statement;
  break;
  default:
    statement;
}
```

This `switch` statement is not as flexible as the Tcl switch. Remember, the Tcl switch statement can use strings and pieces of strings to route execution to a particular case (review Chapter 11, "Programming with PL/Tcl and Tcl" for details). The C `switch` statement routes execution based on the value of a single character. If no cases match, execution is routed to the optional default statement. Here is an example:

```
void testswitch(char x)
{
  switch x
{
    case 'M':
    case 'W':
    case 'F':
      printf("English and History" );
      break;
    case 'T':
      printf("Tennis and Golf");
    break;
    default :
     printf("nothing scheduled");
  }/* end switch x */
}
```

This function prints *English and History* if passed the characters M, W, or F. Notice how the `break` statement is absent from the M and W cases. A case that matches the switch without a break executes its own statement and every subsequent statement until a break, the default case, or the end of the switch statement is encountered.

C Stored Procedures as Database Triggers

A database *trigger* is a special database function that is linked to a table and called whenever there is an UPDATE, INSERT, or DELETE on the table. Triggers are traditionally used to check the values of incoming data to make sure that things like negative salaries or two-digit years don't get into a database. Triggers can also be used to write information about transactions to the log or to call other functions in PostgreSQL.

Trigger data is passed to a C stored procedure in the form of a structure.

```
typedef struct TriggerData
{
    TriggerEvent  tg_event;
    Relation      tg_relation;
    HeapTuple     tg_trigtuple;
    HeapTuple     tg_newtuple;
    Trigger       *tg_trigger;
} TriggerData;
```

A trigger can have one of two return values:

- **A pointer to a new row.** Completes the operation on the NEW record
- **NULL.** Doesn't complete the operation on the NEW record

To create a trigger, make a function with no arguments and a return type of OPAQUE. Look at the following C code:

```
#include "executor/spi.h"
#include "commands/trigger.h"
#include <string.h>


bool isvalidstate(HeapTuple, TupleDesc);
HeapTuple   ctriggerme(void);


HeapTuple ctriggerme(void)
{
  HeapTuple  retval = NULL;
  /*See if there is any reason to go on*/
  if(!CurrentTriggerData)
  {
    elog(ERROR, "In ctriggerme, CurrentTriggerData not initialized");
  }
  /*Only need to check if the user is adding or updating a record*/
  if(TRIGGER_FIRED_BY_UPDATE(CurrentTriggerData->tg_event) )
  {
    if(isvalidstate(CurrentTriggerData->tg_newtuple,
                CurrentTriggerData->tg_relation->rd_att))
```

```
    {
      retval = CurrentTriggerData->tg_newtuple;
    }
  }
  if(TRIGGER_FIRED_BY_INSERT(CurrentTriggerData->tg_event))
  {
    if(isvalidstate(CurrentTriggerData->tg_trigtuple,
                  CurrentTriggerData->tg_relation->rd_att))
    {
      retval = CurrentTriggerData->tg_trigtuple;
    }
  }
  /* return the proper value*/
  return retval;
}
/*check to see if state is valid*/
bool isvalidstate(HeapTuple tgtRecord, TupleDesc recordDesc)
{
  bool retval = false;
  bool connected = false;
  int ret;
  char query[80];
  char tgtstate[3];
  ret = SPI_connect();/* Step 1 - Connect to the database */
  if(ret < 0)/* we have a problem; log and return a zero */
  {
    elog(ERROR, "In ctriggerme/isvalidstate - cant connect to database");
    return false;
  }
  else /* we have a good connection; check for the state */
  {
    connected = true;
    strcpy(tgtstate, SPI_getvalue(tgtRecord, recordDesc, 3));
    sprintf(query, "select * from validstates where validstate ='%s'",tgtstate);
    ret = SPI_exec(query, 0);
    if(SPI_processed > 0)/*We have a match*/
    {
      retval = true;
    }
    else
```

```
    {
      retval = false;
    }
  }
  if(connected)
  {
    SPI_finish();/* Close our connection */
  }
  return retval;
}
```

Here, if the user is doing an UPDATE or INSERT, the value of the new state is checked against a table of valid states abbreviations. If the value of the new state is in the validstates table, the new record is added. If not, the function returns a NULL, and the action is skipped. The validstates table looks like this:

```
perkins=# \d validstates
        Table "validstates"
 Attribute  |    Type    | Modifier
------------+------------+----------
 validstate | varchar(2) |
 fullname   | text       |
```

and contains the following values:

```
perkins=# select * from validstates;
 validstate |  fullname
------------+------------
 FL         | Florida
 CA         | California
(2 rows)
```

These are all the states my tiny mind can remember, but you might want more. Now compile the shared object:

```
[perkins@laura examples]$ gcc -I/usr/include/pgsql -O2 -Wall -Wmissing-prototype
s -Wmissing-declarations -c -o ctriggerme.o ctriggerme.c
[perkins@laura examples]$ gcc -shared -o ctriggerme.so ctriggerme.o
```

Then log in to psql and create the stored procedure:

```
perkins=# CREATE FUNCTION ctriggerme() RETURNS opaque AS '/tmp/examples/
ctriggerme.so' LANGUAGE 'c';
CREATE
```

Now tie the trigger to a table. Notice how a third name is used so that if you have to drop the trigger, you don't have to drop the function. If you ran the trigger examples in the previous chapters, you will need run the statement DROP TRIGGER check_state on address before creating the new C trigger:

```
perkins=# CREATE TRIGGER check_state before insert or update on address
perkins-# for each row execute procedure ctriggerme();
CREATE
```

Now you insert data with a valid state:

```
perkins=# insert into "address"
("nickname","street","state","zipcode", "city")
values('Tyler', '567 Doggy Heaven', 'FL', '34444','Niceville');
INSERT 414370 1
```

That worked. Now try a brand XX state:

```
perkins=# insert into "address" ("nickname","street","state","zipcode","city")
values ('Biff','1600 Penn','XX','88888','Arlington');
INSERT 0 0
```

Notice that C doesn't have the capability to raise an error. It does not save the record, but it won't stop the program.

If you make changes to your trigger function, drop the relationship, using this:

```
perkins=# DROP TRIGGER check_state on address;
```

Then reattach the trigger as before. If you don't do this, PostgreSQL will use a cached copy of your function. It's frustrating to make changes to a function and not see them take effect.

You will deal with all the SPI functions in the isvalidstate function in the next section. The other items in the trigger structure are covered in detail in both the PostgreSQL documentation (Chapter 47).

Dealing with Data: C Stored Procedures and Programs

There are three issues to cover in this section:

- How to deal with a row of data from an SQL query that is passed into a C stored procedure
- How to access the database from a C stored procedure
- How to access the database from a C program

SQL Data Passed to a C Stored Procedure

Data is passed into a C stored procedure using a structure named *TupleTableSlot*. The definition of this structure is located in the /usr/include/pgsql/executor/ tuptable.h file and looks like this:

```
typedef struct TupleTableSlot
{
        NodeTag         type;
        HeapTuple       val;
        bool            ttc_shouldFree;
        bool            ttc_descIsNew;
        TupleDesc       ttc_tupleDescriptor;
        Buffer          ttc_buffer;
        int                     ttc_whichplan;
} TupleTableSlot;
```

Two functions provide a way to contain the data contained in each data row. Here are their rototypes:

```
char *GetAttributeByNum(TupleTableSlot *slot, AttrNumber attrno,
                                bool *isNull);
char *GetAttributeByName(TupleTableSlot *slot, char *attname, bool *isNul
l);
```

Here is the source code for the C program:

```
#include "postgres.h"
#include "executor/executor.h" /* for the getAttributeByName() */
#include <string.h>

/*Prototypes*/
bool isflorida(TupleTableSlot *);

bool isflorida(TupleTableSlot * targetRecord)
{
  bool retval = false;
  bool isnull = false;
  int ret = 0;
  text *tgtstate = (text *)palloc(3);
  char *mystate = "FL";

  tgtstate = (text *) GetAttributeByName(targetRecord, "state", &isnull);
```

```
if(!isnull)/*target column is not null, so let's check for a match*/
{
  /*elog(ERROR, "The tgtstate is about %s long", VARDATA(tgtstate))*/;
  ret = strncmp(mystate, VARDATA(tgtstate), 2);
  if(ret == 0)/* we have a match*/
  {
    retval = true;
  }
}
return retval;
}
```

> In a C stored procedure, use the text type for importing data via the
> `GetAttributeByName()` **function for table columns with type varchar.**

Now compile to a shared object:

```
[perkins@laura examples]$ gcc -I/usr/include/pgsql -O2 -Wall -Wmissing-prototype
s -Wmissing-declarations -c -o isflorida.o isflorida.c
[perkins@laura examples]$ gcc -shared -o isflorida.so isflorida.o
```

Log in to psql and create the new stored procedure:

```
perkins=# CREATE FUNCTION isflorida(ADDRESS) RETURNS bool AS '/tmp/examples/isfl
orida.so' LANGUAGE 'c';
CREATE
```

Finally, use the `isflorida` function:

```
perkins=# select nickname, isflorida(ADDRESS) from ADDRESS;
 nickname | isflorida
----------+----------
 Tyler    | t
 Leslie   | f
 Laura    | f
 Kelly    | t
 Ruth     | f
 Alton    | f
 Valerie  | t
 Jeff     | t
 Jeff     | t
```

```
 Puder    | t
(10 rows)
perkins=# select nickname, state from address where isflorida(ADDRESS);
 nickname | state
----------+------
 Tyler    | FL
 Kelly    | FL
 Valerie  | FL
 Jeff     | FL
 Jeff     | FL
 Puder    | FL
(6 rows)
```

> To make the database write to a log file, change the line in /etc/rc.d/init.d/
> postgresql from
>
> ```
> su -l postgres -c "/usr/bin/pg_ctl  -D $PGDATA -p /usr/bin/postmaster start >/
> dev/null 2>&1" < /dev/null
> ```
>
> **to**
>
> ```
> su -l postgres -c "/usr/bin/pg_ctl  -D $PGDATA -p /usr/bin/postmaster start >/
> var/log/postgresql 2>&1" < /dev/null
> ```
>
> This causes the postmaster to send messages to the file /var/log/postgresql.
> Because this file can get big fast, you might want to have two scripts that launch
> PostgreSQL: one script that writes to the debug file and another that doesn't.
> Also, note that this modification causes a new file to be written every time
> PostgreSQL is started, which would overwrite your preceding log. If you need to
> save the preceding log, consider adding a line in the shutdown part of the script
> that runs the logrotate command.

A useful item to note is that when the calling query returns more than one row of
data, your function is called for each row! This is like the `foreach` statement in Tcl
(refer to Chapter 11).

Data Access from inside a C Stored Procedure

PostgreSQL has a *Server Programming Interface* (SPI) that allows C stored procedures to access PostgreSQL. SPI basics include

- Opening the SPI connection
- Executing a query

- Manipulating data
- Closing the SPI connection

The isvalidstate function from the trigger example earlier in the chapter illustrates all four items. Here is the code:

```
/*check to see if state is valid*/
bool isvalidstate(HeapTuple tgtRecord, TupleDesc recordDesc)
{
  bool retval = false;
  bool connected = false;
  int ret;
  char query[80];
  char tgtstate[3];
  ret = SPI_connect();/* Step 1 - Connect to the database */
  if(ret < 0)/* we have a problem; log and return a zero */
  {
    elog(ERROR, "In ctriggerme/isvalidstate - cant connect to database");
    return false;
  }
  else /* we have a good connection; check for the state */
    connected = true;
    strcpy(tgtstate, SPI_getvalue(tgtRecord, recordDesc, 3));
    sprintf(query, "select * from validstates where validstate ='%s'",tgtstate);
    ret = SPI_exec(query, 0);
    if(SPI_processed > 0)/*We have a match*/
    {
      retval = true;
    }
    else
    {
      retval = false;
    }
  }
  if(connected)
  {
    SPI_finish();/* Close our connection */
  }
  return retval;
}
```

First, the `SPI_connect()` function is called, and its return value is checked to make sure that there is a valid connection. Then the state value is extracted from the target record, using the `SPI_value()` function. The `SPI_value()` function takes the record, record description, and an integer representing the number (starting from 1) of the column of data. `SPI_value()` returns a pointer to an array of characters. Numeric value is returned as an array of characters. Then the query is formed and executed using the `SPI_exec()` function. `SPI_exec()` takes an array of characters containing the query and a number of rows on which to act if the query is a delete, insert, or update or to return if the query is a select.

In a stored procedure, the record data and its description are stored in the global structure, CurrentTriggerData (see the trigger example for details). If you wanted to select a column from the results of the query in isvalidstate, or any other SELECT query, you would first see whether `SPI_processed` is greater than 0. A positive `SPI_processed` value indicates a successful query that returned the number of rows of data contained in `SPI_processed`. Then you would use the `SPI_tuptable->tupdesc` to get the record description and `SPI_tuptable->vals[index]` to access a zero-based array of the records returned. You could then use the `SPI_valuefunction`—and the other SPI functions described in the C/C++ appendix—to manipulate the data.

If the query is not a SELECT, SPI_processed contains the number of records DELETEd, UPDATEd, or INSERTed.

> In database speak, a *tuple* is a row of data from a query. *Tuple* and *record* refer to the same thing, a row of data.

Data Access from inside a C Program

PostgreSQL provides several functions for database access from inside a standalone C program. These functions are contained in the library libpq, which comes with the standard PostgreSQL installation. The functions are covered in detail in the PostgreSQL documentation, Chapter 53. To get started, you need to know how to do the following things:

- Connect to the database
- Execute a query
- Manipulate data
- Close the database
- Compile using libpq

Here is a program that demonstrates the basics:

```c
#include <stdio.h>
#include "libpq-fe.h" /*types and prototypes for libpq*/

/*Prototypes*/
void shutdown(PGconn *conn);

int main(int argc, char *argv[], char *env[])
{
  PGconn    *conn; /*Connection to the Database*/
  PGresult *result;/*Result set*/
  int numfields, i, j;

  /*See if there are enough arguments*/
  if(argc != 6)
  {
    printf("Usage:  cdatamain host  dbname usrname password query\n");
    exit(1);
  }
  conn = PQsetdbLogin(argv[1], "5432", NULL, NULL, argv[2], argv[3], argv[4]);
  /*See if we connected*/
  if(PQstatus(conn) == CONNECTION_BAD)
  {
    printf("Connection to database '%s' failed \n", argv[2]);
    printf("Error was:  %s", PQerrorMessage(conn));
    shutdown(conn);
  }
  /*Try a query*/
  result = PQexec(conn, argv[5]);
  if(!result)/*query didn't work*/
  {
    printf("Query Problems\n");
    printf("Error was: %s", PQerrorMessage(conn));
    shutdown(conn);
  }
  /* get some descriptive data */
  numfields = PQnfields(result);
  for(i = 0; i < numfields; i++)
  {
    printf("|%-10s|", PQfname(result, i));
```

```
    }
    printf("\n");/*Line Feed*/
    for(i = 0;i < PQntuples(result);i++)
    {
       for(j = 0;j < numfields;j++)
       {
          printf("|%-10s|", PQgetvalue(result, i, j));
       }
          printf("\n");/*Line Feed*/
    }
       /*Clear out Result set
    PQclear(result);
    PQfinish(conn);
    exit(0);/*Normal Exit*/
}


    /*Close connection and indicate an abnormal exit*/
void shutdown(PGconn *conn)
{
    PQfinish(conn);
    exit(1);
}
```

Now compile it. Notice the use of `-lpq` to use the libpq library:

```
[perkins@laura examples]$ gcc -I/usr/include/pgsql -lpq -o cdatamain cdatamain.c
```

Now run it:

```
[perkins@laura examples]$ ./cdatamain 192.168.1.21 perkins perkins 17jeff25 "SEL
ECT * FROM ADDRESS"
```

nickname	street	state	zipcode	city
Tyler	567 Doggy Heave	FL	34444	Niceville
Leslie	1313 MBird Lane	CA	95555	Fair Oaks
Laura	Rt 66	AZ	55555	Big Pine
Kelly	1010 Pudder Ln	FL	77555	Really NiceVille
Ruth	4624 Minn	CA	88888	Fair Oaks
Alton	1872 Waco	TX	45454	Waco
Valerie	555 Dodah Dr	FL	99955	Orlando
Jeff	555 Dodah Dr	FL	99955	Orlando
Jeff	1600 Penn	FL	55599	Niceville
Puder	1456 Old Rd	FL	8990	St Augustine

Opening the database is accomplished with the `PQsetdbLogin()` function. If you don't need a user name and password, you can use the `Pqsetdb()` function. After checking whether the connection was successful (`PQStatus(conn) == CONNECTION_BAD`), the query is executed using `PQexec`. If there are results, they are manipulated using the `PQnfields`, `PQntuples`, and the `PQgetvalue` functions, as shown.

Finally, the result set , `Pqclear(result)`, is released, and the connection, `Pqfinish()`, is ended.

This example covers about 90 percent of the stand-alone C programs PostgreSQL data requires.

Summary

The C language is simple and complex at the same time. Do not consider this chapter a comprehensive C tutorial. It is intended as an introduction to C in the PostgreSQL environment. This chapter provides a starting point for experienced C programmers and enough information for those of you new to the C language to understand its basic structure and strengths.

Besides the basics of C, this chapter showed by example how to create stored procedures from C and to connect to the database from inside a stored procedure and from a stand-alone C program. It's a lot to absorb, but if you focus on the basics covered here, you'll be on your way.

Chapter 13: Programming with Python

U sing the SQL language to create functions, as you did in Chapter 9, "Basic PostgreSQL Data Types and SQL Functions," is okay for simple tasks but can make more complex tasks harder than they have to be. Python is another interpreted scripting language, like Perl. It was developed by Guido van Rossum with the intention of creating a generalized language that is system-aware and object-oriented. Contrary to the commonly accepted belief that Python was named for the snake, it was named for the comedic group of six actors who performed the comedy show "Monty Python's Flying Circus," which aired on BBC from 1969 to 1974. With that trivia out of the way, let's look at the characteristics of the Python scripting language and how you can use it to give you more functionality with your PostgreSQL applications.

The incorporation of Python into the picture gives you the options of processing data with PL/PGSQL trigger functions or externally using Python code after the data is retrieved. Depending on the specific goal, one option can achieve better performance or be significantly easier to implement than the other. Python has a very low learning curve, largely because of its inherent simplicity, yet it is an extremely powerful tool. This chapter is an overview of the Python language in general and how the PyGreSQL module incorporates this powerful language into the PostgreSQL picture. By the end of the chapter, you will be able to write functions to interface with your PostgreSQL database, using the PyGreSQL module.

Python Setup

The Python language is external to the standard PostgreSQL installation. Determine whether Python is installed on your system by executing the following command:

```
which python
```

If the system responds with the path to the Python binary, you're almost there. Otherwise, you must download the Python package from http://www.python.org or a mirror site. The latest version, 2.1, is available as a compressed tar archive, requiring that you run `tar` to decompress it and then run `configure` and `make` to generate the necessary binaries. You must have the header files and development libraries for both PostgreSQL and Python; they are necessary for the next step. If you use a system with a package manager, such as the Red Hat Package Manager, the Python headers and libraries might be contained in a separate Python-devel file.

To use Python to interface with your PostgreSQL database, you must download a package named *PyGreSQL*. PyGreSQL is a version of the PostgreSQL query library, written to be called from a Python script. You can download PyGreSQL 2.1, the current version, from ftp://ftp.druid.net/pub/distrib/PyGreSQL.tgz. Installation requires that you use the `tar` command to decompress the file, change to the directory created for the decompressed files, and perform the following steps:

1. Change to the newly created PyGreSQL directory (/usr/local/packages/ PyGreSQL-3.1, in my case).

2. Compile using this command, replacing the /usr/local/packages/python1.5 with the appropriate path to your Python source:

   ```
   cc -fpic -shared -o _pg.so -I/usr/include/packages/python1.5 -lpq pgmodule.c
   ```

3. Test the build by starting the interpreter in the PyGreSQL directory where you just built the PyGreSQL module. I am assuming that your PostgreSQL database is named *test* and that you are logged in as a valid user.

```
[prompt] python
Python 1.5.2 (#2, Jun 11 2001, 09:17:54) [GCC 2.96 20000731 (Red Hat Linux 7.0)] on
linux2
Copyright 1991-1995 Stichting Mathematisch Centrum, Amsterdam
>>>import _pg
>>>db = _pg.connect('dbname','localhost')
```

Now that PyGreSQL is set up, you can see how it works.

Python General Syntax

Python is a very readable language. Those who have not yet learned to program in Python can often read and follow Python code. The key to well-written Python code is simplicity. Code blocks are indicated by indentation, rather than awkward characters like braces. The absence of these characters greatly enhances Python's readability and even provides a minor performance increase because the braces don't have to be loaded at execution time (every byte counts).

Python code begins with no indentation at the highest level of code. After that, each increase in indentation indicates the beginning of a new code block. The end of a block is indicated by the backing out of the indentation to the preceding level. No longer do you have to worry about setting an indentation policy, except for perhaps deciding whether to use tabs or spaces and how many at each indentation. Although those who have worked in more syntactically demanding languages might be put off at first by Python's simplicity, in time you will find yourself pleased by the readability of your Python programs.

Line Termination

Statements in Python are terminated with a newline in most cases. There is no need to put a semicolon at the end of each line, as in C or C++, although doing so generally does not generate an error message. Python interprets the following two statements identically:

```
print 'Hello World.'
print 'Hello World.';
```

Semicolons can be used to join two statements on the same line, so the second line simply parses an empty statement. This consumes resources unnecessarily but does not generate an error. Care should be taken that the joining does not make the program more difficult to read.

Case Sensitivity

Python is a case-sensitive language. `MyVaRiAbLe` is not the same as `myvariable` or `MYVARIABLE`; each is a unique variable because of case. This gives you the flexibility to create rules that make your code even easier to read. For instance, a class can begin with a capital letter, and its members be lowercase, enabling you to distinguish the two immediately.

Python Commenting

In Python, comments are identified by a preceding pound or hash symbol (#) and can begin anywhere on a line. Any characters between the hash symbol and the end of the line are ignored by the interpreter. Even though Python is very readable, the use of comments must be sufficient to ensure that those who need to understand the code, whether for maintenance or enhancement, can follow it with ease.

Object-Orientation

Python was designed to be *object-oriented*. This means that you can design code to take advantage of multiple inheritance, polymorphism, and operator overloading, which is not possible with many scripting languages. If you are just learning about object-oriented programming, it might be easier within the uncomplicated Python framework.

User-Defined Functions

Whereas Python's built-in functions are compiled into the interpreter and loaded as part of the built-in namespace, user-defined functions are either defined at the top-level part of a module, and therefore loaded into the global namespace, or defined within another function, and therefore loaded into the function's local scope. User-defined functions have five standard attributes. Table 13.1 shows these attributes for the function `foo`.

Table 13.1   Python's User-Defined Functions

Attribute	Description
foo._doc_	Documentation string
foo._name_	Function name in string form
foo.func_code	Byte-compiled code object
foo.func_defaults	Default argument tuple
foo.func_globals	Global namespace definitions

> An interpreted language is slower than a compiled language at runtime because execution requires an additional step to get to the system's native binary language. Python, like Java, is *byte-compiled*, meaning that it is stored in a form that is closer to machine language than if it were not byte-compiled. This speeds up the process without losing the advantages offered by an interpreted language.

User-defined functions are defined with the *def* keyword, as shown here:

```
def is_prime():
    count = num / 2
    while count > 1:
        if num % count == 0: return 0
        count = count -1
    return -1
```

You can execute other Python scripts within the body of a Python function using either the `import` command or `execfile` command. The `import` command version looks like this:

```
#My Python script
import otherscript
```

Importing a module the first time causes the module's top-level code to be executed. If the `import` statement is run again, its code is not executed. Sometimes this is the desired effect. Often it is achieved by checking the name of the script to determine when it is called by the main script, as shown here:

```
#My Python script
import otherscript
if _name_ == "_main_":
    perform the rest of the script
```

If you want to execute that code again within the current script, you use the reload command, like this:

```
#My Python script
reload(otherscript)
```

An alternative to the import command is the `execfile()` command, which has the following syntax:

```
#My new Python script
execfile("/path/to/otherscript.py")
```

Now, every time this script is called, the otherscript.py file is executed as well, regardless of how many times it's been called before.

Python Variables

The Python scripting language uses *dynamically typed* variables, meaning that the variables do not have to be predefined. When the variable is assigned a value, it is automatically defined and initialized. The variable types supported by Python are numbers, strings, lists, tuples, and dictionaries. The examples in this section use the Python interpreter because that is the easiest way to illustrate the function of the variable types. The Python interpreter prompt (>>>) precedes anything that is to be typed in as user input. Lines in the example that are not preceded by the interpreter prompt are the output returned by the interpreter.

Numbers

In Python, there are four numerical types: int, float, long, and complex. The *int* type represents signed integers, such as -231 or 0×80, just as in other languages; likewise, the float type represents floating-point real numbers, such as 3.14159 or -1.609E-19. Where Python is different is with the long and complex types. Python longs, unlike C longs, which are typically 32 bit, are limited only by the amount of virtual memory your system contains. Python also allows the programmer to cope with *imaginary* numbers (numbers involving the square root of -1), the *complex* number type in Python offers greater flexibility.

Strings

A Python *string* is any series of characters in between either single or double quotation marks. You can specify any subset of the string, using the slice operators (`[ ]` and `[:]`), with indexes from 0 (the beginning of the string) to -1 (the end of the string). The first character of the string would be `string[0]`, and the last would be `string[-1]`. If the string were set equal to the word *Python*, `string[1:4]` would represent the subset *yth*. Remember that the first character of the string is numbered 0, so counting past 1 starts the subset at the *y* up to, but not including, the character with index 4. Leaving a blank after the colon means to begin at the character whose number precedes the colon and to include the rest of the string, as demonstrated by `string[2:]`, which equals *thon* in the example. If the blank is before the colon and a number follows, simply start at the first character and include each character up to, but not including, that represented by the number that follows the colon, as in `string[:2]`, which in the example equals the string `'Py'`.

There is no char type in Python. Instead, Python uses a string of one character.

Python allows for the use of the + operator to concatenate strings and the * operator to repeat strings, as in: `'Pyt' + 'hon' = 'Python'` and `'My' * 2 = 'MyMy'`. A string can also be formatted using string formatting codes like those used with printf in the C language. The most common codes are `%s`, `%d`, `%i`, `%u`, and `%x`, which are used for string, decimal, integer, unsigned integer, and hexadecimal integer, respectively. Here is an example:

```
>>>number = 4
>>>"I have %d brothers and sisters." % number
'I have 4 brothers and sisters.'
```

Lists and Tuples

Both lists and tuples in Python are ordered collections of any object type to include other lists. They are extremely flexible and are accessed by offset. A Python list is enclosed in brackets, and its elements and size are variable and changeable.

The indexing is identical to what you saw with strings in the preceding section. The following are some examples:

```
>>>List = [0,1,2,3,'dog']
>>>List[0]
0
>>>List[3:]
[3,'dog'] (element three through the end)
>>>List[:3]
[0,1,2] (up to but not including element three)
>>>List[2]=99 (set second element equal to 99)
>>>List (show the list)
[0,1,99,3,'dog']
```

Tuples, on the other hand, are enclosed in parentheses and have values that cannot be changed. See the following examples:

```
>>>Tuple = ('blue', 3, 'sky', 44)
>>>Tuple[0]
'blue'
>>>Tuple[2:]
('sky,44)
>>>Tuple[:2]
('blue',3)
```

If you try to reset the value of a tuple element, you get an error:

```
>>>Tuple = (1,2,3,4,5,6)
>>>Tuple[3] = 14
Traceback (innermost last):
  File "<stdin>", line 1, in ?
TypeError: object doesn't support item assignment
```

Dictionaries

Python uses dictionary structures to hold unordered variable-length key-value pairs of data, separated by commas and enclosed in braces. Dictionaries are comparable to associative arrays or hashes and are stored as hash tables. Because the dictionary entries are not sequenced, operations such as concatenation and slicing do not work on dictionaries. The values do not have to be ordered because the search for a value is key-based; find the key and take the associated value. For instance, the key can be the name of an item in inventory, and the value its price in cents:

```
>>>inventory = {'socks': 150, 'shoes': 2500, 'comb': 35}
```

For a more complicated inventory, dictionaries can be nested as follows:

```
>>>inventory = {'socks': {'blue':150,'red':100},'shoes': 2500, 'comb': 35}
```

To return the value for shoes, type the dictionary name, followed by the key value in brackets:

```
>>>inventory['comb']
35
```

Several built-in functions work on dictionaries. To test whether a certain key is contained within a dictionary, use the has_key function, which returns a value of 1 if the key exists and 0 if it doesn't:

```
>>>inventory.has_key('comb')
1
```

To list the keys from the dictionary, use the keys function:

```
>>>inventory.keys()
['combs','socks','shoes']
```

To find the number of items in the dictionary, use the len function:

```
>>>len(inventory)
3
```

To add an item to an existing dictionary, simply set the key equal to the value, like this:

```
>>>inventory['hat']=1200
>>>inventory.keys()
['socks','shoes','hat','comb']
```

Attempting to add an item to a nonexistent dictionary results in an error:

```
>>>new['item']=200
Traceback (innermost last):
  File "<stdin>", line 1, in ?
NameError: new
```

To delete an entry, use the del function:

```
>>>del inventory['comb']
```

To change an entry, simply set the key to a new value:

```
>>>inventory['hat']=400
```

Control Structures

Python has three types of control structures: IF, WHILE, and FOR.

Give Me an If!

The if statement in Python is similar to if statements in other languages. Indentation is used to tell Python which statements go with which clause. Here is an example:

```
x = 3
if x < 0:
    print 'Your number is negative'
elif x == 0:
    print 'Your number is zero'
elif x > 1:
    print 'Your Number is positive'
else:
    print 'Propbably not a number'
```

Which Produces:

```
Your Number is positive
```

The if statement has two clauses after the if. The elif clause is a combination of the else and if statement. If none of the clauses above an elif have been executed then the statement after the elif is evaluated. If the statement is true then the lines after the elif are executed. The else clause is executed if the original if and any optional elif clauses evaluate to false.

The Two Loops

There are two kinds of loops in Python: the for loop and the while loop. The for loop has this syntax:

```
for [object] in [object_list]:
    Python Block
else:
    Other Python Block
```

The for loop allows you to compare a target object against a list of objects and run the subsequent block of code only if your object is contained in the list of objects. The for loop works with strings, lists, tuples, and new objects that you create with classes.

If the specified target object is not found, the `else` loop (if one exists) is executed.

The `while` loop continues to execute the included code block until a condition is no longer true. At this point, it executes the code block included in the `else` statement (if one exists) or simply continues the code that follows. The while loop has this syntax:

```
while expression:
    Python Block...
else:
    alternate Python Block
```

Sometimes during a `while` loop you might want to test for a given condition and not execute the remaining statements. To facilitate this, the `continue` statement can be used. The `continue` statement causes the execution of the loop to go back to the `while`. If the condition for the `continue` (usually an if statement) is not met, execution progresses past it to the next statement. In the next example, the `while` loop is executed five times, printing the even numbers between 0 and 5:

```
count = 0
while  count < 5:
    count = count + 1
    if count % 2 == 0: continue # print if even
    print count
```

In other cases, you might want to leave the loop if a certain condition is met, rather than take the time to finish the rest of the loop and go back to the while at the top. To do this, you use the `break` command, which skips the remainder of the `while` loop and executes the code that immediately follows the end of the loop. In the preceding example, if you wanted to find only one prime number, you could do this:

```
count = num / 2
while count > 1:
    if count % num == 0: #there is a remainder
        break #no need to continue
    count = count + 1
else:
    print count
```

[*******]

Dealing with Data Using Python

For the sake of the next few examples, I'm going to assume that you have an existing PostgreSQL database named *dbname* and that you are on the hosting system. The following examples will not work if you are not logged in as a valid user who has been given access to the database dbname. To add a user to dbname, simply log in as the Postgres user who is running the postmaster, and use the createuser command as follows:

```
bash-2.04$ createuser vicki
```

There are a couple of configuration questions to answer before the user is created. Database and user creation are covered in Chapter 2, "PostgreSQL Administrative Programs." Here is a short sample program to get the ball rolling:

```
#! /usr/bin/python
import _pg
db = _pg.connect(dbname='perkins',host='localhost',user='perkins')
print db.query('select * from county')
db.close()
```

Running this example on a table containing the county data for the state of Florida results in

```
[perkins@lilsony perkins]$ ./ch13basic.py
id|name
--+-------------------------------------------------
 1|Alachua
 2|Baker
 3|Bay
 4|Bradford
 5|Brevard
 6|Broward
 7|Calhoun
 8|Charlotte
 9|Citrus
10|Clay
...
64|Volusia
65|Wakulla
66|Walton
```

```
67|Washington
(67 rows)
```

This simple example illustrates some very important points. The first is how to get a database connection.

Getting a Database Connection

To connect to the database, you must import the _pg module already installed by your PostgreSQL installation. Then execute the connection command as follows:

```
import _pg
db = _pg.connect(dbname='perkins',host='localhost',user='perkins')
```

The basic example is run as a script, but you can use the same commands from the Python command line. The syntax for the connect statement is

```
connect([dbname], [host], [port], [opt], [tty], [user], [passwd])
```

You don't have to use all the arguments. You can use the syntax shown in the basic example to pick the arguments you need.

```
db = _pg.connect(dbname='perkins',host='localhost',user='perkins')
```

Executing a Query

After you have a connection, you can use it to execute any standard Postgres query by enclosing the command in a dquery statement.

In the basic example, you used

```
db.query('select * from county')
```

but you could just as easily used the query statement to accomplish the following:

- Insert values into a table:

  ```
  db.query("INSERT INTO simple VALUES ('MeMyself&I',12,'Stillme')")
  ```

- Select values from a table:

  ```
  db.query("SELECT * FROM simple")
  ```

- Create a table:

  ```
  db.query("""CREATE TABLE simple (name varchar(80), age int, ID varchar(8)""")
  ```

Manipulating Data

As far as manipulating data goes, all the sample program does is use the Python print statement to take advantage of the query statement's capability to stream out the query results. If you need finer control of the data, the _pg library has a pgqueryobject. The basic example, rewritten to include the pgqueryobject, looks like this:

```
#! /usr/bin/python
import _pg
db = _pg.connect(dbname='perkins',host='localhost',user='perkins')
result = db.query('select * from county')
print result.listfields()
print result.fieldname(0)
print result.fieldname(1)
print result.fieldnum('ID')
print result.ntuples()
db.close()
```

The pgquerobject is created in this line:

```
result = db.query('select * from county')
```

Then its functions—listfields, fieldname, fieldnum, and numtuples—are exercised:

```
[perkins@lilsony perkins]$ ./ch13intermediate.py
('id', 'name')
id
name
0
67
```

Listfields does what its name implies. The fieldname function trades an integer value, starting at 0, for the field name as a string. The fieldnum does just the opposite, trading a string for the field name. The numtuples (remember, *tuples* is another word for a database row) returns the number of rows of data.

The pgqueryobject contains two more functions. The first is getresult. The getresult function returns a listing of the data. The last pgqueryobject function is the dictresult, which returns the data as a Python list of dictionaries.

Closing a Database Connection

It is always a good idea to clean up after yourself. If you leave too many database connections open, you degrade PostgreSQL performance and, eventually, run out of database connections. To prevent this, use

```
db.close()
```

Summary

Python is a popular and powerful language. This chapter introduced you to the basics of both Python and the PostgreSQL library for Python. The scope of Python's capabilities far exceeds what this chapter describes. With what you just learned, though, you can perform PostgreSQL queries from within the Python environment. You can make simple Python scripts for a Web site, and you have a hand on a very long lever called *Python* that can be used to move your programming world.

Chapter 14: Programming with PHP

by Julie Meloni

PHP is a very popular and easy-to-learn server-side scripting language. By making use of a parsing engine in conjunction with a Web server, raw PHP scripts are run through the parsing engine when a URL is requested. The resulting output is sent by the Web server to the Web browser, where you see it in all its glory.

Inside these PHP scripts, you can do many wonderful things, including accessing a PostgreSQL database to perform queries, retrieve and display data, and generally make your Web site dynamic. This chapter gives you a brief overview of installing and configuring PHP with a Web server and PostgreSQL and then delves a little into the PHP language and how to write simple scripts. Ultimately, you will learn how to access a PostgreSQL database using the numerous functions built in to PHP.

Installation of PHP and a Web Server

If you are hosting your Web site with an Internet service provider that already has a working version of PHP, a Web server, and PostgreSQL, you can skip this section. If you are using PHP and PostgreSQL on a development machine in-house or at a colocation facility, or you have some other arrangement that allows you to manage your own development environment, this section gives you an overview of how to get these pieces working together.

The most common implementation of PHP and a Web server is to run PHP as a Dynamic Shared Object (DSO) module as part of an Apache Web Server 1.3.x release. You can also configure PHP as a static module for Apache or for the AOLServer or Roxen Web servers. You can also install an ISAPI module version of PHP for Zeus, an NSAPI module for the Netscape Enterprise Server, or a CGI binary that will enable PHP in any of these Web servers.

> If you want to configure PHP as anything other than a DSO for Apache, read the installation instructions in the PHP Manual at http://www.php.net/manual/.

You most often find PHP used on a non-Windows OS, running as a module of the Apache Web server. This means that when you compile PHP from the source, using either the-with-apache or-with-apxs configuration options, you're creating a separate file that goes in the Apache modules directory. You then need to recompile Apache, activating your PHP module in the process. When you recompile Apache, the PHP parsing engine becomes part of the Web server, making request processing quicker and more streamlined.

Preparing for Installation

To install PHP and Apache, you have to go grab a few files first. To get PHP, go to the PHP Web site at http://www.php.net/, and head to the Downloads section. Grab the latest release of the source code. As of this writing, the latest release is 4.0.5. Download the source code to somewhere on your hard drive, such as /usr/local/.

To get the source code for Apache, visit the Apache Web site at http://httpd.apache.org/dist/httpd/ and the source code for version 1.3.x. As of this writing, the latest release is 1.3.19. You will see something named *Apache 2.0*, but do not download it yet because it's currently a beta version and not ready for prime time. Put the source code somewhere on your hard drive, such as /usr/local/, and remember that this is where you put it.

Finally, ensure that PostgreSQL is installed and you know the path to the installation directory. These instructions assume that everything is located under /usr/local/, but if you have your files in other places, you will have to substitute those directories where applicable in the instructions.

Installing Apache

Installing the dynamic version of PHP will save you time and headaches later in life, for if you decide to recompile a PHP DSO to add or delete functionality, you won't have to recompile Apache when you re-create the DSO. For example, suppose that you build a simple version of PHP with just database support. A few days later, you decide that you want to install encryption support. All you have to do is type `make clean` (to get rid of previous configuration settings and makefiles), add the new configuration option to your configuration command, and then type `make` and `make install` to build a new module. This new PHP module is dumped in the proper location for Apache. For the proper module to be loaded, all you have to do is restart Apache, rather than fully recompile the server software.

If you already have a version of Apache installed, check whether you have mod_so. If you do, you can skip through this section. To check for mod_so, do the following:

1. cd to the Apache bin directory (/usr/local/apache_[version]/bin/ or wherever you installed Apache originally).

2. Type `./httpd -1`. You should see a list of enabled modules, and if mod_so.c shows up in that list, you can skip ahead to the PHP installation section. If mod_so.c doesn't show up in your list, you can skip ahead to step 6 in the second list after this to enable mod_so in Apache.

NOTE

Time to extract the source code and build a Web server! Just follow these simple steps.

1. gunzip or uncompress the file so that you're left with the *.tar file.
2. Type the following to un-tar the file into a directory named *apache_[version]*:

   ```
   tar -xvf apache_[version].tar
   ```

3. cd into /usr/local/apache_[version] (or wherever you un-tar'd it).
4. Type the following to prepare for building, replacing [path] with your own path, such as /usr/local/apache[version]—no trailing slash:

   ```
   ./configure --prefix=[path] --enable-module=so
   ```

The configuration script checks for requirements and then builds the makefiles. When the configuration process is complete, your shell prompt returns. If you have any warnings or errors, try to decipher the problem from the messages that appear, and attempt the configuration again.

If you make it through compilation without errors, continue the build process by typing **make** at the prompt. The makefiles will run and compile Apache. The goal is to get through this step without warnings and fatal errors. When you're back at the prompt, type **make install** to create the final set of directories and files and to return a message from the Apache Group, thanking you for installing Apache on your system.

Alternatively, you will see errors and warnings in the installation, which, if you can't decipher them, should be the big red flag prompting you to visit http://www.apache.org/ and read through the FAQs and documentation.

Assume that Apache built itself properly. During the installation process, a default set of configuration files was placed in the conf directory, under the installation directory. If you make a few minor changes to the httpd.conf file (the master Apache configuration file), you can start Apache and prove that it's working properly:

1. In your text editor of choice, open httpd.conf and find a line starting with ServerAdmin.
2. Change the default entry to real values, such as

   ```
   ServerAdmin joe@schmo.com
   ```

3. Find a line starting with ServerName.
4. Change the default entry to real values, such as

   ```
   ServerName localhost
   ```

> If you have a real machine name, such as `mybox.yourdomain.com`, go ahead and
> use it instead of `localhost`:
>
> `ServerName mybox.yourdomain.com`

5. Save the file.

6. cd up a directory (type `cd ..`).

7. Start Apache using the following command:

    `./bin/apachectl start`

This command starts Apache. You should see a message like *httpd started*. Follow
that up by opening your Web browser and typing http://localhost/ in the location
bar. If you used a `ServerName` other than `localhost`, type that in the location bar
instead. You should see the default Welcome! page for the Apache installation.

I can't stress enough that if your installation fails at any point, you should visit the
Apache Web site at http://www.apache.org/ and read the FAQs and documentation in an attempt to pinpoint your problem. If everything looks, walks, and smells
like a working Web server, move on to the next section to compile PHP.

Installing PHP

You should already have the source code for PHP sitting on your hard drive somewhere. All you have to do is unpack it and create the Apache module. The build
process creates this module and puts it where it needs to go inside the Apache
installation directories. You restart your Web server after the module has been
added, but you will cross that bridge when you get there.

Go to the directory in which you placed the PHP source code, and follow these
steps to install this bad boy:

1. gunzip or uncompress the file so that you're left with the *.tar file.

2. Type the following to un-tar the file into a directory named `php-[version]`:

    `tar -xvf php-[version]`

3. cd into /usr/local/php-[version].

The build process for PHP follows the same sequence as the build process for
Apache: configure, make, and make install.

Let's stop here for a moment. If you are using a PostgreSQL release greater than 7.1,
you must do a tweaky little thing for compilation to be successful. This might be fixed

in later versions of PHP; if you have any doubts, always check the Bug Fixes section of the PostgreSQL documentation, at http://techdocs.postgresql.org/bugsfixes.php.

This change is to a line in the PHP 4 source code. You will be changing the line where it refers to <postgres.h>, to be <postgres_fe.h>, using these steps:

1. Change directories to /usr/local/php-[version]/ext/pgsql/.

2. Type the following to make the change and create a backup file:

   ```
   sed "s/postgres.h/postgres_fe.h/" php_pgsql.h > php_pgsql.h.tmp
   ```

3. Type the following to copy the backup file to the active file:

   ```
   mv php_pgsql.h.tmp php_pgsql.h
   ```

Now you're ready to configure PHP. For your own edification, this next step shows you the numerous configuration options you have when building PHP. Change directories back to the top level of the installation directory (/usr/local/php-[version]) and type `./configure --help` to see a list of the 150 or so configuration options for PHP. It makes for interesting reading, but you will use only a few of them to create the DSO version of PHP with PostgreSQL support.

Type the following configuration line, replacing `[/path/to/postgresql]` with your own path (such as `/usr/local/postgresql`) and changing `[/path/to/apxs]` to be the actual path to your apxs file (look in the Apache installation bin directory):

```
./configure --with-pgsql=/[/path/to/postgresql] --with-apxs=/[path/to/apxs]
```

Now, watch the configuration file do its thing and then create a set of makefiles before you get back to prompt. If you have warnings or errors, try to decipher the problem from the messages that appear, and attempt the configuration again. You can also check the PHP FAQs at http://www.php.net/FAQ.php.

If you have made it to this point without fatal errors or other bad warnings, type **make** to run the makefiles created in the configuration step, and begin to build PHP. When you're back at the prompt, type **make install**. This final step in the compilation sequence compilation creates the DSO, plops it in the Apache modules directory, modifies some parts of the Apache httpd.conf file for you, and returns you to the prompt.

When you're back at the prompt, you must go back to the Apache httpd.conf and make one more modification—tell Apache what to do with *.php or *.phtml files.

With httpd.conf open in your text editor, find a section that looks like the following:

```
# And for PHP 4.x, use:

#
```

```
#AddType application/x-httpd-php .php
#AddType application/x-httpd-php-source .phps
```

Just take away the # before the two `AddType` lines, and add `.phtml` on the line with `.php`. The section should now look something like this:

```
# And for PHP 4.x, use:
#
AddType application/x-httpd-php .php .phtml
AddType application/x-httpd-php-source .phps
```

> If you want to parse *.html files as PHP, just add the file extension to the list in your `AddType` line so that it ends up looking like this:
>
> ```
> AddType application/x-httpd-php .php .phtml .html
> ```

Save this file, navigate to the Apache installation directory, and restart the server by typing `./bin/apachectl restart`.

Provided that there are no issues on startup, you can learn how to test your installation in the next section. However, if you get an error at startup about Apache not being able to load the PHP module because it can't find a corresponding named library (such as libpq.so), here's what you do:

1. Use find to locate the file that it says it can't find.
2. Using a text editor, open /etc/ld.so.conf.
3. Add the directory in which the problematic file exists.
4. Save the file.
5. Type `ldconfig`.
6. Return to the PHP directory, and type `make clean`.
7. Issue the configuration command, followed by the make and make install steps.

After telling your system where the libraries are, the build sequence should be successful, or at least closer to finishing. If your build does not complete without failing, you can search the php-install mailing list archives at http://marc.theaimsgroup.com/?l=php-install for a similar problem and possible solution. Of course, if the installation looks successful, you should test it.

Testing Your Installation

After you get through the build process, there's one good way to test your install, besides creating a "Hello World" script—use the `phpinfo()` function to display system information. Open a text editor, and type the following:

```
<? phpinfo() ?>
```

Save this file as phpinfo.php, and put it in Apache's document root (htdocs). Then fire up your Web browser, and go to http://localhost/phpinfo.php, where you should see a long page of variables and their values. The `phpinfo()` function automatically produces this page, which shows you what sorts of things are installed, your environment, your settings, and so on.

If you now have a working installation of PHP and Apache, with PostgreSQL support built in to PHP, take a moment to learn the basic structure and syntax of the language. Then, you will be creating dynamic Web sites with PHP and PostgreSQL in no time flat.

General PHP Syntax

PHP happily cohabitates with HTML in simple text files that sit on your Web server, waiting to be parsed. The sequence goes something like the following, assuming that you're working with files with the extension.php:

1. The Web browser requests a document with a .php extension.
2. The Web server realizes that it's a PHP file, based on the extension (and because you assigned that extension to a type in the Apache configuration file), and sends the request on to the PHP parser.
3. The PHP parser finds the requested file and scans it for PHP code.
4. When the PHP parser finds PHP code, it executes that code and places the resulting output (if any) into the place in the file formerly occupied by the code.
5. This new output file is sent back to the Web server.
6. The Web server sends it along to the Web browser.
7. The Web browser displays the output.

To combine PHP code with HTML, the PHP code must be set apart from the HTML. This is done using PHP start and end tags. The PHP parser will attempt to execute anything between these tags, which usually look like this: `<?php` and `?>` or `<?`   and `?>`.

Now you will try the basic "Hello World" script, which is primarily HTML, with a section of PHP thrown in for good measure. Type the following in your text editor:

```
<HTML>
<HEAD>
<TITLE>"Hello World" Script</TITLE>
</HEAD>
<BODY>
<? echo "<P><em>Hello World!</em></P>"; ?>
</BODY>
</HTML>
```

Save the file with the name *helloworld.php*, and place it in the document root of your Web server. Next, open your Web browser, and type **http://localhost/ helloworld.php** to see whether it executes properly. If it does, you should see the following in italicized text:

Hello world!

If you view the HTML source in your Web browser, you will see that it contains only HTML code. This block of PHP was executed:

```
<? echo "<P><em>Hello World!</em></P>"; ?>
```

The `echo` function is used to output information, in this case, to print the HTML output:

```
<P><em>Hello World! I'm using PHP!</em></P>
```

As with most programming languages, the instruction terminator (the semicolon) is necessary to tell the parsing engine that the instruction is over and to move on to the next one. One of the most common errors in PHP programming is simply to forget to use the instruction terminator.

In the next section, I'll fly through the basics of variables, operators, and control structures. These will get you well on your way to writing PHP scripts, especially if you have any familiarity with programming languages in general.

Variables and Types in PHP

Variables in PHP are not vastly different from variables in any other programming language.

- They cannot begin with a numeric character.
- They can contain numbers and the underscore character (_).
- They are case sensitive.

Types in PHP include arrays, integers, and floating-point numbers and strings, as well as a few others not explained here, such as objects. The type of a variable is usually not explicitly set. Rather, it is decided at runtime by PHP, depending on the context in which that variable is used. You can force a variable to be converted to a specific type by using the settype() function, if you like. Visit the PHP Manual for significantly more information on forced types and type juggling.

Arrays

In PHP, arrays can be single or multidimensional. All arrays are zero based, meaning that if you have three elements in an array, the index of the first element is 0, the second element is 1, and the third element is 2.

You can create an array using the array() function:

```
$myArray = array("apple", "orange");
```

or you can assign a value to an array variable using empty brackets:

```
$myOtherArray[] = "banana";
$myOtherArray[] = "pear";
```

There are numerous built-in functions to work with arrays; see the Array chapter of the PHP Manual for functions to help you sort, count, traverse, or otherwise work with arrays.

Integers and Floating-Point Numbers

Integers can be indicated a number of ways, depending on the type of integer you're using:

```
$myInt = 1234; # $myInt is a decimal number
$myInt = -123; # $myInt is a negative number
$myInt = 0123; # $myInt is an octal number
$myInt = 0x12; # $myInt is a hexadecimal number
```

The size of an integer is platform-dependent, although a maximum value of about 2 billion is the usual value, or 32 bits signed.

Floating-point numbers can be indicated in either of the following ways:

```
$a = 1.234;
$a = 1.2e3;
```

The size of a floating-point number is also platform-dependent, although a maximum of ~1.8e308 with a precision of roughly 14 decimal digits is common (that's 64-bit IEEE format).

Strings

Strings are enclosed in either single or double quotes. You can use the backslash to escape special characters within your string, such as linefeeds (\n), tabs (\t), or other quotes (\"). If your strings are enclosed in single quotes, the only escaped characters that will be understood are "\\" and "\'".

Here are some string examples:

```
$myString = "This is a string with a linefeed.\n";
$mySingleString = 'Single-quoted string';
$mySpecialString = "Fancy \"escaping\" is needed\n!";
```

Variables within a double-quoted string are parsed accordingly. For example, this code

```
$color = "blue";
$string = "My favorite color is $color";
echo "$string";
```

produces the following output:

```
My favorite color is blue.
```

Variables from HTML Forms

Depending on the method of your HTML form (GET or POST), the variables are part of the $HTTP_POST_VARS or $HTTP_GET_VARS global array. The name of the input field becomes the name of the variable. For example, the following input field produces the variable $firstname:

```
<input type="text" name="firstname" size="20">
```

If the method of this form were POST, this variable could also be referenced as $HTTP_POST_VARS["firstname"]. If the method were GET, you could also use $HTTP_GET_VARS["firstname"].

Variables from Cookies

Like variables from forms, variables from cookies are kept in a global array. In this case, the array is named $HTTP_COOKIE_VARS. If you set a cookie named *"user"* with a value of "Joe Smith", like so:

```
setcookie ("user", "Joe Smith", time()+3600);
```

then $HTTP_COOKIE_VARS['user'] will have a value of "Joe Smith". You can refer to $user or $HTTP_COOKIE_VARS['user'] to get that value.

Environment Variables

When a Web browser makes a request of a Web server, it sends along with the request a list of extra variables called *environment variables*. They are very useful for displaying dynamic content or authorizing users.

By default, environment variables are available to PHP scripts as $VARNAME. However, to be absolutely sure that you're reading the correct value, you can use the getenv() function to assign a value to a variable of your choice. Following are two common environment variables:

- REMOTE_ADDR gets the IP address of the machine making the request—for example:

```
<?
        $remoteaddress = getenv("REMOTE_ADDR");
        echo "Your IP address is $remoteaddress.";
?>
```

- HTTP_USER_AGENT gets the browser type, browser version, language encoding, and platform—for example:

```
<?
        $browsertype = getenv("HTTP_USER_AGENT");
        echo "You are using $browser~type.";
?>
```

For a list of HTTP environment variables and their descriptions, visit http://hoohoo.ncsa.uiuc.edu/cgi/env.html.

Operators in PHP

An *operator* is a symbol that represents a specific action. For example, the + arithmetic operator adds two values, and the = assignment operator assigns a value to a variable. PHP doesn't have any funky operators; if you're familiar with any programming language, you've got the bases covered.

- **Arithmetic Operators.** These operators bear a striking resemblance to simple math and include the addition (+), subtraction (-), multiplication (*), division (/), and modulus (%) operators.
- **Assignment Operators.** The = is the basic assignment operator, but other assignment operators include binary arithmetic and string operators such as +=, -=, and .=, which are quite useful.
- **Comparison Operators.** Not surprisingly, these operators compare two values and return true or false. You have equal to (==), not equal to (!=),

greater than (>), less than (<), greater than or equal to (>=), and less than or equal to (<=).

- **Increment/Decrement Operators.** These operators add or subtract from a variable. For example, ++$a increments $a by 1 and returns $a; $a++ returns $a and then increments $a by 1. Use --$a and $a-- to decrement $a.

- **Logical Operators.** These operators determine the status of conditions and, in the context of control structures such as if or while statements, execute certain code based on which conditions are true and which are false. The logical operators are not (!), and (&&), and or (||).

Control Structures in PHP

PHP *scripts* are essentially a series of statements, and control structures determine how those statements are executed. Control structures are usually built around a series of conditions, such as "If it is raining, carry an umbrella." Braces ({ and }) are used to separate the groups of statements from the remainder of the program.

As with operators and variable types, there's nothing new in PHP, if you're familiar with programming languages in general.

if...else if...else

The if...else if...else construct executes a statement based on the value of the expression being tested. In the following sample if statement, the expression being tested is "$a is equal to 10."

```
if ($a == "10") {
    // execute some code
}
```

To offer an alternative series of statements, should $a not have a value of 10, add an else statement to the structure, to execute a section of code when the condition is FALSE:

```
if ($a == "10") {
    echo "a equals 10";
} else {
    echo "a does not equal 10";
}
```

The else if statement can be added to the structure to evaluate an alternative expression before heading to the final else statement. For example, the following structure first evaluates whether $a is equal to 10. If that condition is FALSE, the else if statement is evaluated. If it is found to be TRUE, the code within its braces executes. Otherwise, the program continues to the final else statement.

```
if ($a == "10") {
      echo "a equals 10";
} else if ($b == "8") {
      echo "b equals 8";
} else {
      echo "a does not equal 10 and b does not equal 8.";
}
```

You can use if statements alone or as part of an if...else or if...else if...else statement.

while

A while statement continues to loop until an expression evaluates as FALSE. In other words, the while loop continues for as long as the expression is TRUE. In the following while loop, the value of $a is printed on the screen and is incremented by 1 for as long as the value of $a is less than or equal to 5.

```
$a = 0 // set a starting point
while ($a <= "5") {
      echo "a equals $a<br>";
      $a++;
}
```

Here is the output of this loop:

```
a equals 0
a equals 1
a equals 2
a equals 3
a equals 4
a equals 5
```

for

Like while loops, for loops evaluate the set of conditional expressions at the beginning of each loop. Take the counting example used in the while loop, and rewrite it using a for loop:

```
for ($a = 0; $a <= "5"; $a++) {
      echo "a equals $a<br>";
}
```

At the beginning of the loop, the first expression is evaluated, followed by the second expression. If the second expression is TRUE, the loop continues by executing the code and then evaluating the third expression. If the second expression is FALSE, the loop does not continue, and the third expression is never evaluated.

The output is the same as the `while` loop's:

```
a equals 0
a equals 1
a equals 2
a equals 3
a equals 4
a equals 5
```

switch

The `switch` statement is similar to a series of `if` statements on the same expression. If you want to compare the same variable against many values and execute a different piece of code, depending on which value it equals, use `switch`.

Take this series of `if` statements:

```
if ($i == 0) {
    print "i equals 0";
}
if ($i == 1) {
    print "i equals 1";
}
```

You could instead use `switch`:

```
switch ($i) {
    case 0:
        print "i equals 0";
        break;
    case 1:
        print "i equals 1";
        break;
}
```

If you don't write a `break` statement at the end of a case's statement list, PHP will go on executing the statements of the following case.

foreach

The foreach construct is pretty cool. It's a shortcut of sorts for iterating through an array. For example:

```
foreach($somearray as $somevalue) {
     // do something
}
```

As the construct iterates through the $somearray array, the value of the current element is assigned to $somevalue, and the internal array pointer is advanced by one.

This piece of code:

```
$somearray = array ("apple", "orange", "peach");
foreach ($somearray as $somevalue) {
   echo "current: $somevalue <br>";
}
```

produces this output:

```
current: apple
current: orange
current: peach
```

For More Information

This section gives only a smattering of PHP basics. For the best reference book out there, visit the PHP Web site and immediately bookmark the PHP Manual, at http://www.php.net/.

Moving forward, you will learn about the PostgreSQL functions built in to PHP and how to connect to and query the database, retrieve your results, and generally make your Web site dynamic and database driven.

Connecting to PostgreSQL

The PHP functions for talking to PostgreSQL simply require that PostgreSQL run somewhere to which your Web server can connect—not necessarily the same machine as your Web server. You also must have a user created (with a password), and you must know the database name to which you want to connect.

When you know all these things, you're ready to make that first simple connection. Connections stay alive for as long as a PHP script executes; then they are automatically shut down. You can also create a persistent connection, but that leaves the door open for connections to run wild and potentially crash your database if not managed properly.

The examples in this chapter all utilize single, per-script connections. In all instances in this chapter, the sample database name is *testdb*, the sample user is *testuser*, and the sample password is *testuser*. Substitute your own information when you try this out.

> If you want to use persistent connections, look up the `pg_pconnect()` function in the PHP Manual.

Using pg_connect()

The `pg_connect()` function is the first function you must call when utilizing a PHP script to work with PostgreSQL. Without an open connection to PostgreSQL, you won't get very far. The basic syntax for the connection is

```
pg_connect (host="hostname" port="port" dbname="database name" user="username"
password="password");
```

This function returns a connection index upon a successful connection or returns `false` if there is an issue with the connection.

A working example of a connection script follows, showing the value of the connection index as proof of a connection:

```
<?
$conn = pg_connect("host=localhost port=5432 dbname=testdb user=testuser
password=testuser");
echo "$conn";
?>
```

If successful, the result of this script is something like

```
Resource id #1
```

Now, if you change the script to attempt to connect with an incorrect user:

```
<?
$conn = pg_connect("host=localhost port=5432 dbname=testdb user=testuser2
password=testuser");
echo "$conn";
?>
```

you get a warning such as:

```
Warning: Unable to connect to PostgreSQL server: FATAL 1: user "testuser2" does not
exist in /usr/local/bin/apache_1.3.12/htdocs/test/index_fail.html on line 2
```

Connecting to PostgreSQL using the `pg_connect()` function is straightforward. The connection closes when the script finishes its execution, but if you want to explicitly close the connection, simply add the `pg_close()` function at the end of the script.

```
<?
$conn = pg_connect("host=localhost port=5432 dbname=testdb user=testuser2
password=testuser");
echo "$conn";
pg_close($conn);
?>
```

That's all there is to it. The next section covers the query execution functions, which are far more interesting than simply opening a connection and letting it sit there.

Executing Queries

If you know how to write a valid SQL statement, you're halfway to knowing how to execute queries against PostgreSQL using PHP. The `pg_exec()` function in PHP is used to send a SQL query to PostgreSQL. If successful, a result index is returned. If a failure occurs, the function returns `false`.

The syntax of `pg_exec()` is

```
pg_exec (connection, query);
```

In your script, you'd first open the connection and then execute a query. For example, create a simple table named *Contacts* that you can use later in this chapter:

```
<?
// open the connection
$conn = pg_connect("host=localhost port=5432 dbname=testdb user=testuser
password=testuser");
// create the SQL statement
$sql = "CREATE TABLE contacts (name CHAR(75), emailaddress CHAR (75))";
// execute the SQL statement
$result = pg_exec($conn, $sql);
// echo the result identifier
echo $result;
?>
```

Because only a result index is being returned upon success, the boring output of this script is

```
Resource id #2
```

This is actually very exciting because, you realize, you now have created a table in your PostgreSQL database, using PHP.

Retrieving Error Messages

Now that you're creating "complicated" database connection scripts, take the time to learn the usage of the `pg_errormessage()` function because it will become your friend. When used in conjunction with the `die()` function, `pg_errormessage()` returns a helpful error when you make a mistake.

For example, now that you have created a table named *Contacts*, you won't be able to execute that script again without an error—so make it do just that, but modify it first to utilize the `pg_errormessage()` function:

```
<?
// open the connection
$conn = pg_connect("host=localhost port=5432 dbname=testdb user=testuser
password=testuser");
// create the SQL statement
$sql = "CREATE TABLE contacts (name CHAR(75), emailaddress CHAR (75))";
// execute the SQL statement
$result = pg_exec($conn, $sql) or die(pg_errormessage());
// echo the result identifier
echo $result;
?>
```

You should now see something like this message:

```
Warning: PostgreSQL query failed: ERROR: Relation 'contacts' already exists in /
usr/local/bin/apache_1.3.12/htdocs/test/exec_error.html on line 7
ERROR: Relation 'contacts' already exists
```

Looks like two messages to me. The first message is from PHP. The second is the output of `pg_errormessage()`. To suppress the ugly first message and just go with the output of `pg_errormessage()`, use the @ symbol to suppress the PHP-generated warning. Modify the line in your script containing the `pg_exec()` function so that it looks like this:

```
$result = @pg_exec($conn, $sql) or die(pg_errormessage());
```

Now run the script again. You should see only one error message:

```
ERROR: Relation 'contacts' already exists
```

How exciting! Move on to the next section to start inserting data into your table. Soon you will be retrieving it via PHP.

Working with Basic Data

Inserting, updating, deleting, and retrieving data all revolve around the use of the `pg_exec()` function to execute the basic SQL queries. For INSERTS, UPDATES, and DELETES, you're done after the query has been executed. For SELECTS, you have a few options for data retrieval. Start with the basics, and insert some data. You will need the data to retrieve something later.

Inserting Data

The easiest method for inserting data is to hard-code the INSERT statement—for example:

```
<?
// open the connection
$conn = pg_connect("host=localhost port=5432 dbname=testdb user=testuser
password=testuser");
// create the SQL statement
$sql = "INSERT INTO contacts VALUES ('John Doe', 'john@doe.com')";
// execute the SQL statement
$result = pg_exec($conn, $sql) or die(pg_errormessage());
// echo the result identifier
echo $result;
?>
```

Wait a moment. Why do you need to echo the result identifier if you're just inserting data? Well, you don't have to. You can clean up this script by replacing the query execution line and making the echo statement something relevant to you:

```
<?
// open the connection
$conn = pg_connect("host=localhost port=5432 dbname=testdb user=testuser
password=testuser");
// create the SQL statement
$sql = "INSERT INTO contacts VALUES ('John Doe', 'john@doe.com')";
// execute the SQL statement
```

```
@pg_exec($conn, $sql) or die(pg_errormessage());
echo "record added!";
?>
```

Running this script results in a row being added for *John Doe*, in your Contacts table. If you have more contacts than just John Doe, the method of hard-coding your SQL query will get old quickly. Why not make a form-based interface to this script? It's simple.

First, create the HTML form. You know that you will have two fields: one for the name and one for the email address. The action of the form will be the name of the script. Call it *insert2.php*. Your HTML form might look something like this:

```
<HTML>
<HEAD>
<TITLE>Insert Form</TITLE>
</HEAD>
<BODY>
<FORM ACTION="insert2.php" METHOD=POST>
<P>Name:<br>
<input type=text name="name" size=30>
<P>E-Mail Address:<br>
<input type=text name="emailaddress" size=30>
<br>
<input type=submit name="submit" value="Insert Record">
</FORM>
</BODY>
</HTML>
```

In your script, insert2.php, replace the hard-coded values in the SQL query with variables named $name and $emailaddress. These variables will be replaced with the values from the form.

```
<?
// open the connection
$conn = pg_connect("host=localhost port=5432 dbname=testdb user=testuser
password=testuser");
// create the SQL statement
$sql = "INSERT INTO contacts VALUES ('$name', '$emailaddress')";
// execute the SQL statement
@pg_exec($conn, $sql) or die(pg_errormessage());
echo "record added!";
?>
```

In your Web browser, access the HTML form you created, and enter some values in the fields for Name and E-Mail Address. Click the Submit button, and the PHP script should execute, insert the data, and return the *record added!* message.

Retrieving Data

Now the fun begins. Because you have a few rows in your Contacts table, you can write a little script to retrieve that data. Starting with the basics, write a script that issues a SELECT query but doesn't overwhelm you with result data; just get the number of rows. To do this, use the `pg_numrows()` function. This function requires a result, so when you execute the query, put the result index in `$result`.

```
<?
// open the connection
$conn = pg_connect("host=localhost port=5432 dbname=testdb user=testuser
password=testuser");
// create the SQL statement
$sql = "SELECT * FROM contacts";
// execute the SQL statement
$result = @pg_exec($conn, $sql) or die(pg_errormessage());
$number_of_rows = @pg_numrows($result);
echo "the number of rows is $number_of_rows";
?>
```

When you run this script, you should see a result such as

```
the number of rows is 2
```

The number should be equal to the number of records you recall inserting during testing. Now that you know some records are in the table, it's time to get all fancy and fetch the actual contents of those records. You can do this a few ways, but the easiest by far is to retrieve each row as an array.

What you will be doing is placing the `pg_fetch_array()` function inside a for statement and using the value of `pg_numrows()` as a baseline. For as long as there are rows, you will grab the values out of each one and display the data on-screen. The syntax of `pg_fetch_array()` is

```
$newArray = pg_fetch_array($result, rownumber);
```

Try it out:

```
<?
// open the connection
$conn = pg_connect("host=localhost port=5432 dbname=testdb user=testuser
```

```
password=testuser");
// create the SQL statement
$sql = "SELECT * FROM contacts";
// execute the SQL statement
$result = @pg_exec($conn, $sql) or die(pg_errormessage());
$number_of_rows = @pg_numrows($result);
for ($i = 0; $i<$number_of_rows; $i++) {
//retrieve row as an array
$row = pg_fetch_array($result,$i);
// give a name to the fields
$name_field  = $row['name'];
$email_field = $row['emailaddress'];
echo "Name: $name_field, E-Mail Address: $email_field<br>";
}
?>
```

In this example, $i is replaced each time through the loop. Within the loop, you're echoing the value of the variables to the screen, for each row. Because I entered two rows into my Contacts table, the result I see is

```
Name: John Doe, E-Mail Address: john@doe.com
Name: Jane Smith, E-Mail Address: jane@smith.com
```

Essentially, you can create an entire database-driven application (albeit a simple one) using just four or five PostgreSQL-specific functions. Sure lessens the learning curve!

Additional PostgreSQL Functions in PHP

Approximately 40 functions in PHP are specific to PostgreSQL. Most of these functions are simply alternative methods of retrieving data or are used to gather information about the table structure in question. Some of the more popular functions are listed here, with brief examples of their usage.

- **pg cmdtuples().** This function returns the number of affected tuples after an INSERT, UPDATE, or DELETE query is executed. Usage is

  ```
  $affected = pg_cmdtuples([result index]);
  ```

  If no tuple is affected, the function returns 0.

- **pg end_copy().** This function ensures that PostgreSQL is in sync after a copy. Usage is

  ```
  pg_end_copy([connection]);
  ```

- **pg_fieldisnull().** Use this function to determine whether a given field is NULL. Usage is

```
pg_fieldisnull([result index], [rownumber], [fieldname]);
```

To find out whether emailaddress is NULL in row 3 of your result set ($result), use

```
$test = pg_fieldisnull($result, 3, "emailaddress");
```

If $test is 1, emailaddress is NULL.

- **pg_getlastoid().** Use this function to retrieve the last object identifier used after an INSERT STATEMENT. Usage is

```
$oid = pg_lastoid([result index]);
```

This function returns -1 if an error occurred or the last query was not an INSERT.

- **pg_result().** Returns a value from a single field within a given row in your result set. Usage is

```
$value = pg_result([result index], [rownumber], [fieldname]);
```

For example, to extract just emailaddress from row 2 of your result set ($result), use

```
$value = pg_result($result, 2, "emailaddress");
```

Obviously, these are just a few of the many PostgreSQL functions in PHP but, for the most part, all you need for normal database activity. For a complete list, visit the PostgreSQL section of the PHP Manual at http://uk.php.net/manual/en/ref.pgsql.php.

Summary

Using PHP and PostgreSQL to create dynamic, database-driven Web sites is a breeze. All you have to remember is that the PHP functions are essentially a gateway to pgsql; anything you enter on the pgsql command line, you can do through pg_exec()!

Chapter 15: Programming with Perl

by Julie Meloni

During the first years of the World Wide Web, Perl was the be-all and end-all of programming languages used for CGI (*Common Gateway Interface*) programs on the Web. It has been surpassed in popularity by languages such as PHP, ASP, and Cold Fusion, but is still a powerful language used for a variety of tasks on and off the Web.

Perl is an *interpreted* language (not compiled), which requires more CPU time than a program written in C. It's a more compact language than C, relatively easy to pick up and useful for tasks both big and small. If you have used shell scripts of any sort, you can probably replace those scripts with a little bit of Perl.

You can use Perl to manipulate your PostgreSQL database, in both shell scripts and CGI programs that are part of your Web site. The Perl DBI (*Database Interface*) module is a simple interface used to send SQL queries and retrieve results. You can use DBI for connecting not only to PostgreSQL but also numerous other databases. For our purposes, we'll just focus on PostgreSQL.

This chapter gives you a brief overview of installing Perl and DBI and then familiarizes you with the Perl language and how to write simple scripts. Ultimately, you will learn how to access a PostgreSQL database, using Perl's DBI.

Installing Perl and DBI

If you are hosting your Web site with an Internet service provider (ISP) that already allows access to Perl and DBI, feel free to skip this section. If you want to use Perl on a development machine in-house, or at a colocation facility, or you have some other arrangement that allows you to manage your own development environment, you can get an overview here of how to install these things.

Downloading and Compiling the Perl Source

To install the latest version of Perl, go to the Perl Web site at http://www.perl.com/ and head to the Downloads section. You want the latest version of the source code, which is 5.6.1. (as of this writing). Download the source code to somewhere on your hard drive, such as /usr/local/.

> If you already have a version of Perl installed or need to verify its location, type `which perl`. If the system finds Perl, type `perl -v` to determine the version number.

Now that you have the source, extract the source code and build Perl. Just follow these simple steps:

1. gunzip or uncompress the file so that you're left with the *.tar file.

2. Type the following to untar the archive:

   ```
   tar -xvf stable.tar
   ```

3. Untarring the archive creates a perl-5.6.1 directory for you. Enter the directory:

   ```
   cd /usr/local/perl-5.6.1
   ```

If you list the contents of the perl-5.6.1 directory, you will see about a billion READMEs, for different platforms. If you get into trouble, check one of those READMEs first. Otherwise, the first entry in the INSTALL file gives you the instructions for installing Perl on your UNIX-like system:

1. Type `rm -f config.sh Policy.sh`.

2. Type `sh Configure`. You will see a message that starts with *This installation shell script will examine your system and ask you questions to determine how the perl5 package should be installed*. This script is very timesaving. On a standard system, you sit around and press Enter a lot to accept all the defaults and create the configuration file.

3. When you're back at the prompt, type `make`.

4. Type `make test`.

5. Type make install.

If an error occurs after any of these steps, stop and read the INSTALL file and the README, or visit the Perl FAQ at http://www.perl.com/perl/faq/. Next, download and install the DBI module.

Downloading and Compiling the DBI Source

To install the latest version of the Perl DBI module, go to the CPAN (*Comprehensive Perl Archive Network*) Web site at http://www.perl.com/CPAN-local/modules/ and navigate until you get to the DBI section. You want the latest version of the source code, which is 1.15 (as of this writing). Download the source code to somewhere on your hard drive, such as /usr/local/.

Now that you have the source, extract the source code and build the DBI module. Follow these steps:

1. gunzip or uncompress the file so that you're left with the *.tar file.
2. Type the following to untar the file:

```
tar -xvf DBI-1.15.tar
```

3. Untarring the archive creates a DBI-1.15 directory for you. Enter the directory:

```
cd /usr/local/DBI-1.15
```

4. Type `perl Makefile.PL.`
5. This script checks for requirements and then puts you back at the prompt. At the prompt, type `make.`
6. When the make process finishes, type `make test` to ensure that everything compiled correctly.
7. After a successful test, type `make install.`

The DBI module should now be installed on your system. If an error occurs after any of these steps, stop and read the INSTALL and README files, or visit the Perl FAQ at http://www.perl.com/perl/faq/. Next, you download and install the DBD (*Database Definition*) module so that your Perl scripts can connect to PostgreSQL.

Downloading and Compiling the DBD Source

There's one more piece to the puzzle, besides Perl and the DBI module: the DBD module for PostgreSQL, DBD:Pg. Although DBI lets Perl talk to databases, it relies on the specific DBD module to help it along for the specific target database.

To install the latest version of the Perl DBD:Pg module, go to the CPAN Web site at http://www.perl.com/CPAN-local/modules/, and navigate until you get to the DBD section. You want the latest version of the DBD:Pg source code, which is 1.00 (as of this writing). Download the source code to somewhere on your hard drive, such as /usr/local/.

Now that you have the source, extract the source code and build the DBD:Pg module. These are the steps:

1. gunzip or uncompress the file so that you're left with the *.tar file.
2. Type the following to untar the file:

```
tar -xvf DBD-Pg-1.00.tar
```

3. Untarring the archive creates a DBD-Pg-1.00 directory for you. Enter the directory:

```
cd /usr/local/DBD-Pg-1.00
```

4. Before going any further, you must set some environment variables (POSTGRES_INCLUDE and POSTGRES_LIB) regarding PostgreSQL file locations. At the prompt, type

```
POSTGRES_INCLUDE=/usr/local/pgsql/include; export POSTGRES_INCLUDE

POSTGRES_LIB=/usr/local/pgsql/lib; export POSTGRES_LIB
```

> If your files are not in /usr/local/pgsql/, simply substitute the file locations in the preceding sample code.

5. Type `perl Makefile.PL`.

6. This script checks for requirements and then puts you back at the prompt. At the prompt, type `make`.

7. When the make process finishes, type `make test` to ensure that everything compiled correctly.

8. After a successful test, type `make install`.

DBI should now be installed on your system. If an error occurs after any of these steps, stop and read the INSTALL and README files, or visit the Perl FAQ at **http://www.perl.com/perl/faq/**.

Testing Your Installation

When you get through the build process for Perl and the DBI and DBD:Pg modules, there's one good way to test your installation of Perl—the infamous Hello World script!

First, go to your home directory and make a subdirectory named *perltest* to keep the sample files for this chapter. Of course, you can put your sample files anywhere you please, but I like to keep things tidy.

1. Type `which perl` to verify that Perl is installed and is accessible to you. Remember the result of `which perl` because you will need it in a moment.

2. Open a text editor, and type the following as the first line:

```
#!/usr/local/bin/perl
```

The /usr/local/bin/perl path should be replaced with the result of `which perl`, if it's not /usr/local/bin/perl. This line indicates the location of the Perl interpreter, which is crucial to running a Perl script.

3. Type the next line of the script, which simply tells Perl to print a little message:

```
print "Hello World!\n";
```

4. Save this file as *helloworld.pl*, and make sure that the proper executable permissions are set, by typing the following at the prompt:

```
chmod +x helloworld.pl
```

5. Now test your script by typing the following at the prompt:

```
perl helloworld.pl
```

Your screen should look something like this, with your own shell prompt replacing mine, of course:

```
julie@wiley:~/perltest > perl helloworld.pl
Hello World!
julie@wiley:~/perltest >
```

Next, you will look at the basic structure and syntax of the Perl language. After that, you will write a few connection routines so that you can have Perl and PostgreSQL playing together nicely in your development environment.

General Perl Syntax

Perl is an interpreted language. First, you create a simple text file full of commands, make the file executable, and then run the script. The Perl interpreter does its thing and produces whatever you tell it to output. The first line of a Perl script is crucial because it's the full path to the Perl interpreter. You used this line in the Hello World program earlier:

```
#!/usr/local/bin/perl
```

The first line could be `#!/usr/bin/perl` or `#!/opt/perl`, or anywhere on your system, as long as it's where the Perl interpreter lives.

Perl is not a difficult language; when you want to produce output, you use the print statement. In your Hello World example, the line is

```
print "Hello World\n";
```

That \n is an indicator of a new line. The instruction terminator (a.k.a the semicolon) is key. It tells the interpreter that the instruction is over and that it needs to move on to the next one.

In the next section, you will fly through the basics of variables, operators, and control structures. These will get you well on your way to writing Perl scripts, especially if you have any familiarity with programming languages in general.

Data Structures in Perl

There are three basic data structures in Perl: scalars, arrays, and hashes. An *array* is basically a bunch of scalars, and a *hash* is an associative array of scalars. In Perl, everything's a scalar of some sort.

Scalar variables may contain numbers or strings, or references to arrays or hashes. You will look briefly at each of these structures in the next few sections.

Scalar Variables

Because everything in Perl is a scalar or relative thereof, you don't have to declare your scalar variables to be of any particular type. Type conversion occurs transparently to the user and happens automatically through the interpreter.

You can name a scalar variable using any alphanumeric characters and underscores. The limit on the length of the name of a scalar variable is 255 characters. Scalar variable names are case-sensitive: $string and $String would be considered two different variables.

The first character in the name of a scalar variable is always $. Here are some examples of scalar variables:

```
$a = 1;        #a number
$b = "string"; #a string
$c = $a + 9;   #a new number
```

When you use scalar variables in your Perl program, it's good practice to declare your variables as local, using the my function. If you were to use the sample variables in a script, you'd do something like this the first time around:

```
my $a = 1;        #a number
my $b = "string"; #a string
my $c = $a + 9;   #a new number
```

In the next section, you will look at arrays.

Arrays

In Perl, arrays are single-dimensional, and multidimensional (or *associative*) arrays are referred to as *hashes*. Arrays are *zero-based*, meaning that if you have three elements in an array, the index of the first element is 0, the second element is 1, and the third element is 2.

Just as all scalars start with $ in Perl, all arrays start with @. Similarly, you use the my function to declare your arrays as local and initialized:

```
my @new_array = (1, 2, 3, 4) # includes 4 elements
```

You now have an array that contains the following scalars: `$new_array[0]`, `$new_array[1]`, `$new_array[2]`, and `$new_array[3]`.

There are numerous ways to manipulate arrays and work with their values. See the Perl Manual or FAQ for information on slicing and dicing arrays, such as the `push`, `pop`, `shift`, and `unshift` functions.

Hashes

Hashes is the cool-sounding term that Perl developers use for associative arrays. In a hash, each element has a key (identifier) and a value (associated with a given key). Keys are always unique, can be of any length, and can contain strings, numbers, you name it.

Just as all scalars start with $ and all arrays start with @, all hashes start with %. Similarly, you use the my function to declare your hashes as local and initialized:

```
my %fruit_hash;
$fruit_hash{'fave_fruit} = 'apple';
$fruit_hash{'gross_fruit} = 'banana';
```

You now have a hash that contains two keys: `fave_fruit` and `gross_fruit`. Those keys have the values of `apple` and `banana`, respectively.

You can manipulate hashes and work with their keys and values in numerous ways. See the Perl Manual or FAQ for information on working with hashes, such as the `keys`, `values`, `exists`, and `remove` functions.

Operators in Perl

An *operator* is a symbol representing a specific action that can be used on scalar variables and values. For example, the + arithmetic operator adds two values, and the = assignment operator assigns a value to a variable. If you're familiar with any programming language, your bases are covered.

- **Assignment and string operators.** The `=` is the basic assignment operator, and the string operators, such as `+=`, `-=`, and `.=`, are quite useful for string concatenation.

- **Numerical operators.** These operators bear a striking resemblance to simple math and include the addition (`+`), subtraction (`-`), multiplication (`*`), division (`/`), exponentiation (`**`), and modulus (`%`) operators.

- **Comparison operators.** Not surprisingly, these operators compare two values and return true or false. You have equal to (`==`), not equal to (`!=`), greater than (`>`), less than (`<`), greater than or equal to (`>=`), less than or equal to (`<=`), and compare (`<=>`).

- **Increment/decrement operators.** These operators add or subtract from a variable. For example, `++$a` increments `$a` by 1 and returns `$a`; `$a++` returns `$a` and then increments `$a` by 1. Use `--$a` and `$a--` to decrement `$a`.

Control Structures in Perl

As in most programs, Perl scripts are essentially a series of statements. Control structures determine how those statements are executed and are usually built around a series of conditions, such as "If you are hungry, eat." Braces (`{` and `}`) are used to separate the groups of statements from the remainder of the program.

If you're familiar with programming languages in general, control structures in Perl will not throw you for a loop.

Plain Ol' Blocks

You might be accustomed to seeing blocks with conditions attached to them, such as this pseudo-code:

```
if (something) {
    do something else;
}
```

In Perl, you can have a code block that is not associated with any particular control structure, like this:

```
{
my $var;
some_statement;
some_other_statement;
}
```

Any variable declared in the block lives only until the end of that block.

if...elsif...else and unless

The if...elsif...else construct executes a statement based on the value of the expression being tested. In the following sample if statement, the expression being tested is $a *is equal to 10.*

```
if ($a == "10") {
        // execute some code
}
```

To offer an alternative series of statements, should $a not have a value of 10, add an else statement to the structure, to execute a section of code when the condition is false:

```
if ($a == "10") {
        echo "a equals 10";
} else {
        echo "a does not equal 10";
}
```

The elsif statement can be added to the structure to evaluate an alternative expression before heading to the final else statement. For example, the following structure first evaluates whether $a is equal to 10. If that condition is false, the elsif statement is evaluated. If it is found to be true, the code within its braces executes. Otherwise, the program continues to the final else statement:

```
if ($a == "10") {
        echo "a equals 10";
} elsif ($b == "8") {
        echo "b equals 8";
} else {
        echo "a does not equal 10 and b does not equal 8.";
}
```

You can use if statements alone or as part of an if...else or if...elsif...else statement.

The unless statement works just like an if statement, except that the code block is executed only if the expression is false—for example:

```
unless ($a == 1) {
        do something;
}
```

This is functionally equivalent to

```
if ($a != 1) {
        do something;
}
```

while and until

A while statement continues to loop until an expression evaluates as false. In other words, the while loop continues for as long as the expression is true. In the following while loop, the value of $a is printed on the screen and is incremented by 1 for as long as the value of $a is less than or equal to 5:

```
$a = 0 // set a starting point
while ($a <= "5") {
        echo "a equals $a<br>";
        $a++;
}
```

Here is the output of this loop:

```
a equals 0
a equals 1
a equals 2
a equals 3
a equals 4
a equals 5
```

The until statement works just like a while statement, except that the code block is executed only if the expression is false—for example:

```
until ($a == 6) {
      do something;
}
```

This is functionally equivalent to

```
while ($a != 6) {
      do something;
}
```

for

Like while loops, for loops evaluate the set of conditional expressions at the beginning of each loop. Take the counting example used in the while loop, and rewrite it using a for loop:

```
for ($a = 0; $a <= "5"; $a++) {
      echo "a equals $a<br>";
}
```

At the beginning of the loop, the first expression is evaluated, followed by the second expression. If the second expression is true, the loop continues by executing the code and then evaluating the third expression. If the second expression is false, the loop does not continue, and the third expression is never evaluated.

The output is the same as the `while` loop's:

```
a equals 0
a equals 1
a equals 2
a equals 3
a equals 4
a equals 5
```

foreach

Given an array, the `foreach` structure grabs each value in the list, one at a time—for example:

```
my @friends = ("Joe", "Jane", "Jerry", "Jim Bob");
foreach my $name(@friends) {
    print "$name\n";
}
```

which results in

```
Joe
Jane
Jerry
Jim Bob
```

For More Information

This section explains only a smattering of the basics of Perl. You will want to spend some time learning Perl through the Perl Web site at http://www.perl.com/ and the numerous FAQs, mailing lists, and tutorials available to you.

Moving forward, you will learn how to connect to and query your PostgreSQL database using the Perl DBI and to do something with the results that are returned to you.

Connecting to PostgreSQL

You took care of two requirements earlier in this chapter: installing the DBI and the DBD for PostgreSQL. To make these things work in your Perl script, the last piece of the puzzle is that PostgreSQL must be running on your machine. You also must have a user created (with a password), and you must know the database name to which you want to connect.

When you know all these things, you're ready to make that first simple connection. The examples in this chapter utilize single, per-script connections. In all instances in this chapter, the sample database name is *testdb*, the sample user is *testuser*, and the sample password is *testuser*. Substitute your own information when you try this out!

Making the Initial Connection

The DBI is used, in conjunction with the DBD::Pg module, to provide access to PostgreSQL databases. In your script, you must first tell Perl that you want to use the DBI. If you have DBD::Pg installed, the DBI will know about it, so you don't need to tell it explicitly that you want to use it—not yet. This section creates a simple little script that logs on and logs off your PostgreSQL database:

1. Create a text file starting with the path to Perl:

   ```
   #!/usr/local/bin/perl
   ```

2. Tell the Perl interpreter that you want to use the DBI:

   ```
   use DBI;
   ```

3. Make the initial connection:

   ```
   $database_handler = DBI-> connect("dbi:Pg:dbname=testdb", "testuser",
   "testuser");
   ```

   When the connection is made, values are placed in the object `$database_handler`. You will reference the `$database_handler` object throughout your script.

4. Add some conditions to test the validity of the `$database_handler` object:

   ```
   if (!$database_handler) {
           die "Cannot connect to database!\n";
   } else {
           print "database_handler value is $database_handler\n";
   }
   ```

5. Save the file as *testdbi.pl*, and change its permissions to executable.

6. At the prompt, type **perl testdbi.pl**.

Now you get to see whether it worked! If the connection was successful, you should see something like this:

```
julie@wiley:~/perltest > perl testdbi.pl
database_handler value is DBI::db=HASH(0x8230260)
```

If you change the script to attempt to connect to a database that doesn't exist:

```
$database_handler = DBI-> connect("dbi:Pg:dbname=mydb", "testuser", "testuser");
```

you will get a warning and a message, such as

```
julie@wiley:~/perltest > perl testdbi_bad.pl
DBI->connect(dbname=mydb) failed: FATAL 1:  Database "mydb" does not exist in the
system catalog. at testdbi_bad.pl line 5
Cannot connect to database!
```

You're missing one thing in your connection script—disconnecting! To close the connection explicitly at the end of the script, use the `disconnect()` function:

```
$database_handler -> disconnect();
```

Your new script, including the `disconnect` function, looks something like this:

```
#!/usr/local/bin/perl
use DBI;

$database_handler = DBI-> connect("dbi:Pg:dbname=testdb", "testuser", "testuser");

if (!$database_handler) {
        die "Cannot connect to database!\n";
} else {
        print "database_handler value is $database_handler\n";
}
$database_handler -> disconnect();
```

In the next section, you will extend this simple script to make a query against your PostgreSQL database.

Executing Queries

If you know how to write a valid SQL statement, you're halfway to knowing how to execute PostgreSQL queries using Perl. There are three basic steps to executing a SQL statement after a connection is made: preparing the statement, executing the statement, and (optionally) retrieving the results.

In this section, you will issue a table creation query to create a table named *friends* containing two fields: friend_name and email. First, create a text file, and open a connection to your PostgreSQL database, as shown previously:

```
#!/usr/local/bin/perl
use DBI;
$database_handler = DBI-> connect("dbi:Pg:dbname=testdb", "testuser", "testuser");
```

Next, prepare the statement:

```
$statement_handler = $database_handler->prepare("CREATE TABLE friends (friend_name
CHAR(75), email CHAR (75))");
```

Test whether the statement handler is defined. If it's not defined, use the `errstr` function in DBI to print an error message:

```
if (!defined $statement_handler) {
die "$DBI::errstr\n";
}
```

Now execute the statement:

```
else {
$statement_handler->execute;
}
```

Now stop to see how far you get with this script. So far, the code should look like this:

```
#!/usr/local/bin/perl
use DBI;
$database_handler = DBI-> connect("dbi:Pg:dbname=testdb", "testuser", "testuser");
$statement_handler = $database_handler->prepare("CREATE TABLE friends (friend_name
CHAR(75), email CHAR (75))");
if (!defined $statement_handler) {
die "$DBI::errstr\n";
} else {
$statement_handler->execute;
}
```

Save this file as *testdbi_statement.pl*, and change its permissions to be executable. Run the script by typing **perl testdbi_statement.pl** at the prompt. If the query was successful, you should see absolutely nothing as output.

```
julie@wiley:~/perltest > perl testdbi_statement.pl
julie@wiley:~/perltest >
```

This is because you told the script to output something only if an error occurs.

Try to run the script again. You should get an error because the friends table should already exist if the first execution of the script was successful:

```
julie@wiley:~/perltest > perl testdbi_statement.pl
julie@wiley:~/perltest >
julie@wiley:~/perltest > perl testdbi_statement.pl
DBD::Pg::st execute failed: ERROR:  Relation 'friends' already exists at
testdbi_statement.pl line 12.
```

Perfect! Everything seems to be working as planned. Now clean up the script a little before moving on. You want to free the statement handler when you're through using it and also close the connection to the database. At the end of your script, add these two lines:

```
$statement_handler -> finish;
$database_handler -> disconnect;
```

Your script now looks like this:

```
#!/usr/local/bin/perl
use DBI;
$database_handler = DBI-> connect("dbi:Pg:dbname=testdb", "testuser", "testuser");
$statement_handler = $database_handler->prepare("CREATE TABLE friends (friend_name
CHAR(75), email CHAR (75))");
if (!defined $statement_handler) {
die "$DBI::errstr\n";
} else {
$statement_handler->execute;
}
$statement_handler -> finish;
$database_handler -> disconnect;
```

Now that you have a table with which to work, move on to the next section to insert some data.

Working with Basic Data

Inserting, updating, deleting, and retrieving data all revolve around the use of the prepare and execute functions. For INSERTS, UPDATES, and DELETES, you're done after the query has been executed. For SELECTS, you have a few options for data retrieval. You will start with the basics and insert some data. You need the data in order to retrieve something later!

Inserting Data

The easiest method for inserting data is simply to hard-code the INSERT statement—for example:

```perl
#!/usr/local/bin/perl

use DBI;

$database_handler = DBI-> connect("dbi:Pg:dbname=testdb", "testuser", "testuser");


# create the SQL statement
$sql = "INSERT INTO friends VALUES ('John Doe', 'john@doe.com')";


#prepare the statement
$statement_handler = $database_handler->prepare($sql);


#test and execute the statement
if (!defined $statement_handler) {
        die "$DBI::errstr\n";
} else {
        $statement_handler->execute;
}


$statement_handler -> finish;
$database_handler -> disconnect;
```

Call this script *testdbi_insert.pl*, make it executable, and execute it. The result should be a row added for *John Doe* in your friends table and no error output to the screen. Add a few more rows so that there's some data to work with in the next section.

Retrieving Data

Now the fun begins. Because you have a few rows in your friends table (I have three in mine), you can write a little script to retrieve that data. The only addition you will make to the preceding script is the use of the fetchrow function. You start slowly:

```perl
#!/usr/local/bin/perl
use DBI;
$database_handler = DBI-> connect("dbi:Pg:dbname=testdb", "testuser", "testuser");


# create the SQL statement
```

```
$sql = "SELECT friend_name, email FROM friends";


#prepare the statement
$statement_handler = $database_handler->prepare($sql);


#test and execute the statement
if (!defined $statement_handler) {
        die "$DBI::errstr\n";
} else {
        $statement_handler->execute;
}
#fetch values and print that you did it
while ($statement_handler->fetchrow) {
    print "fetched something\n";
}
$statement_handler -> finish;
$database_handler -> disconnect;
```

Call this script *testdbi_select.pl*, make it executable, and execute it. The result should be a message of *fetched something* for each row in your table. Because I have three rows in my table, the resulting output is

```
julie@wiley:~/perltest > perl testdbi_select.pl
fetched something
fetched something
fetched something
```

I'm assuming that you want to use the data you fetched, so change the *fetched something* message into an actual display of the values fetched.

Modify the `while` statement so that it names the slots fetched from your table:

```
while (($friend_name, $email) = $statement_handler ->fetchrow()) {
```

Next, use the print statement to print a display you'd like to see. Then, close the `while` statement:

```
print "Name: $friend_name\tEmail:$email\n";
}
```

Your new code should look like this:

```
#!/usr/local/bin/perl
use DBI;
```

```
$database_handler = DBI-> connect("dbi:Pg:dbname=testdb", "testuser", "testuser");


# create the SQL statement
$sql = "SELECT friend_name, email FROM friends";


#prepare the statement
$statement_handler = $database_handler->prepare($sql);


#test and execute the statement
if (!defined $statement_handler) {
        die "$DBI::errstr\n";
} else {
        $statement_handler->execute;
}
#fetch values and print that you did it
while (($friend_name, $email) = $statement_handler ->fetchrow()) {
print "Name: $friend_name\tEmail:$email\n";
}
$statement_handler -> finish;
$database_handler -> disconnect;
```

Save this new script as *testdbi_select_cool.pl*, make it executable, and execute it. You should see the output from each row in your table—for example:

```
julie@wiley:~/perltest > perl testdbi_select_cool.pl
Name: John Doe          Email:john.com
Name: Jane Doe          Email:jane.com
Name: Mary Smith        Email:mary.com
```

That's all there is to the three very basic steps to working with DBI and PostgreSQL.

More Information on DBI

The man page for DBI is nearly 4,100 lines long, so you can imagine how many more functions are available to you than those described in this chapter.

Most DBI functions are alternative methods of retrieving data or are used to gather information about the table structure in question.

Connecting Perl and PostgreSQL isn't all that difficult. Just remember that the DBI functions are there as a gateway to pgsql. If there's something you want to do on the pgsql command line, you can probably find a corresponding function for it in DBI.

Chapter 16: Programming with Java

ava is an object-oriented language developed by Sun. Currently, it is used primarily in client-server and Web-based applications on both the front end, in the form of Java Applets and Java Server Pages (JSP), and the back end, in application servers such as Enhydra and Bea Weblogic. A very common use of Java is data manipulation. PostgreSQL provides a set of Java libraries, built to the information technology industry's Java Database Connectivity (JDBC) standard.

This chapter gives you a brief overview of the Java language and the JDBC libraries. Then you will learn how to access a PostgreSQL database using Java.

Java Setup

To program in Java, you need the Java Development Kit (JDK) from either Sun (http://www.javasoft.com) or IBM (http://www.alphaworks.ibm.com/tech/linuxjdk). The Javasoft site contains JDKs for most hardware platforms. The IBM site is a favorite of Linux users. Either site can provide you with what you need to get started. Java is not yet included as a stored-procedure language in PostgreSQL. I expect that in the future Java will be included as an optional stored-procedure language, like Tcl or Perl. Until then, Java programs will remain external to PostgreSQL and access data via JDBC.

JDBC is a Java standard for database drivers. Using this standard, Java programmers have written database drivers for every modern database, including PostgreSQL. The normal installation of PostgreSQL on Red Hat Linux puts the database drivers in a file named *jdbc7.0-1.2.jar* in the /usr/lib/pgsql directory. A *jar* file is a Java archive. Like a zip or tar file, a jar is a collection of files under one file name. Now that you have all the pieces, let's see how to make Java work.

To write a Java program, you need the following three things:

- A source file
- The Java compiler, javac
- The Java interpreter, java

A *source file* contains a program written in Java. The Hello World example saved in the file HelloWorld.java would look like this:

```
package chapter16;


/**

 * Title:        Hello World Project for Chapter 16
 * Description:
 * Copyright:    Copyright (c) 2000
```

```
 * Company:
 * @author Jeff Perkins
 * @version 1.0
 */

public class HelloWorld
{

  public HelloWorld()
  {
    System.out.println("Hello World from Java");
  }
  public static void main(String[] args)
  {
    HelloWorld helloWorld1 = new HelloWorld();
  }
}
```

Don't worry about the syntax—I will cover that next. After the program is written, javac (the Java compiler) is used to change your file into a class file. This compiles HelloWorld.java:

```
[root@laura java]# javac ./chapter16/HelloWorld.java
```

After the program becomes a class file, you can run it by typing

```
[root@laura java]# java chapter16.HelloWorld
Hello World from Java
```

There is your first Java program! Now look at some details.

Java General Syntax

Those of you familiar with C and C++ syntax will note that basic Java syntax is very similar. For example, statements in Java, C, and C++ are terminated by a semicolon (;). You can stack multiple statements on a single line. The entire HelloWorld class from the preceding example could look like this:

```
public class HelloWorld{public HelloWorld(){System.out.println("Hello World from Java");}}
```

Java would still compile and run this line, but personally, I wouldn't want to maintain it. I recommend one statement per line. It makes your code more readable. Code is even more readable when you use comments.

Java Commenting

There are three types of comments in Java. The first type starts with a `/*` and ends with a `*/`:

```
/*This is my first Java function*/
```

Comments can come after a semicolon. You can write something like this:

```
return retval; /*Glad this is done*/
```

The second type of comments in Java is the double forward slash (`//`). Everything from the double forward slash to the end of the line is considered a comment. In its basic form, the second type looks like this:

```
//This is a comment
```

This type can be used at the end of a line, also:

```
For(I = 0;I < count; I++)//This is the start of a for loop
```

If you mix and match these comments, be sure that you don't lose the last `*/` behind a `//`. Otherwise, everything past the beginning `/*` will be considered a remark, which can make for a very short program.

The third type of comment in Java is a variation of the multiline (`/*`, `/*`). In this form, you start the comment with a `/**` and end it with a `*/`. The sample program contains this sort of comment:

```
/**
 * Title:       Hello World Project for Chapter 16
 * Description:
 * Copyright:   Copyright (c) 2000
 * Company:
 * @author Jeff Perkins
 * @version 1.0
 */
```

A Java program named *javadoc* uses this comment type to generate an HTML page documenting the details of a class. Running javadoc on the HelloWorld example looks like this:

```
[root@laura java]# javadoc chapter16.HelloWorld
Loading source file for class chapter16.HelloWorld...
Constructing Javadoc information...
Building tree for all the packages and classes...
```

```
Building index for all the packages and classes...
Generating overview-tree.html...
Generating index-all.html...
Generating deprecated-list.html...
Building index for all classes...
Generating allclasses-frame.html...
Generating index.html...
Generating packages.html...
Generating chapter16/HelloWorld.html...
Generating serialized-form.html...
Generating package-list...
Generating help-doc.html...
Generating stylesheet.css...
```

The first page of the generated code appears in Figure 16.1.

I have programmed in a dozen languages and used many documentation tools. In my opinion, javadoc and the comments embedded using the /** and */ comment tags are among the most useful documentation tools available at any price. The details of javadoc are beyond the scope of this book, but if you wind up using Java, remember javadoc.

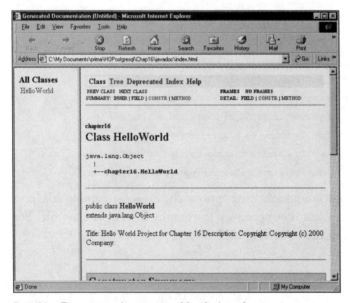

Figure 16.1 *Documentation generated by the javadoc program*

Java is case sensitive; for example, the class name *System* cannot be typed as *system*. If you change the HelloWorld code thus:

```
system.out.println("Hello World from Java");
```

and then compile it, the result is

```
[root@laura java]# java chapter16/HelloWorld.java
Exception in thread "main" java.lang.NoClassDefFoundError: chapter16/HelloWorld/
java
```

Notice that the error is caught in the Java compiler. You will not get a class file to run using Java unless your Java code gets past the compiler.

Look more closely at the Java compiler. If you ask it, javac itself will show you how it is used:

```
 [root@laura /root]# javac
Usage: javac <options> <source files>

where <options> includes:
  -g                       Generate all debugging info
  -g:none                  Generate no debugging info
  -g:{lines,vars,source}   Generate only some debugging info
  -O                       Optimize; may hinder debugging or enlarge class files
  -nowarn                  Generate no warnings
  -verbose                 Output messages about what the compiler is doing
  -deprecation             Output source locations where deprecated APIs are used
  -classpath <path>        Specify where to find user class files
  -sourcepath <path>       Specify where to find input source files
  -bootclasspath <path>    Override location of bootstrap class files
  -extdirs <dirs>          Override location of installed extensions
  -d <directory>           Specify where to place generated class files
  -encoding <encoding>     Specify character encoding used by source files
  -target <release>        Generate class files for specific VM version
```

The `classpath` is the most commonly used option. The `classpath` option tells Java where to find any other class files necessary to compile the target class file. For example, change the class declaration of HelloWorld to this:

```
public HelloWorld()
  {
    SayHello sayHello = new SayHello();
    System.out.println(sayHello.sayIt());
  }
```

Notice that this refers to another class, named *SayHello*. Create a SayHello class that looks like this:

```
package chapter16;

/**
 * Title:        Hello World Project for Chapter 16
 * Description:
 * Copyright:    Copyright (c) 2000
 * Company:
 * @author Jeff Perkins
 * @version 1.0
 */
public class SayHello
{
  public SayHello()
  {
  }
  public String sayIt()
  {
    return "Hello World from SayHello";
  }
}
```

Compile each program using the `classpath` option to clarify the location of the source files:

```
[root@laura java]# javac -classpath /tmp/examples/java ./chapter16/HelloWorld.java
```

Notice that you have to compile only the main program, HelloWorld. The javac program automatically compiles any other classes you need to run the main program, provided that the `classpath` option contains paths to all the required classes.

The java program is an interpreter. Javac compiles your source files into a class file. The class file is called *byte code*. The java program takes the byte code and runs on a particular software platform. For example, there are java programs for Linux, Windows, and Solaris. The byte code compiled on any one of these platforms can be run using the platform-specific java program. This is where the Java slogan "Write once, run anywhere" comes from.

There is one more important general feature of Java, the garbage collector. When a variable or class is initialized in Java, such as the new HelloWorld declaration in the example, it doesn't have to be specifically destroyed to reclaim its memory. The Java garbage collector runs from time to time and frees up the memory used by variables that have fallen out of scope. In a language such as C or C++, memory allocation and deallocation are a major concern. In Java, it is a background process.

Java Variables

The Java language supports the following basic data types:

- **int.** An integer (32 bits, signed, ranging from -2.14e+9 to 2.14e+9)
- **long.** A long integer (64 bits, signed, ranging from -9.22e+18 to 9.22e+18)
- **float.** A floating-point number (32 bits, signed, ranging from 1.402e-45 to 3.402e+38)
- **double.** A decimal number (64 bits, signed, ranging from 1.402e-45 to 3.402e+38)
- **byte.** A small integer (8 bits, ranging from -128 to 127)
- **short.** A short integer (16 bits, ranging from -32768 to 32767)
- **char.** A character, 16 bits wide
- **boolean.** The value true or false

Unlike C and C++, where data type precision varies from platform to platform, Java variable precision is independent of platform.

Classes and Packages

All programs in Java are composed of classes. Recall the HelloWorld example from earlier in the chapter. It is composed of two classes, HelloWorld and SayHello. Each class contains its own variables and methods. For example, the SayHello class has a `sayIt` method:

```
public class SayHello
{
  public SayHello()
  {
  }
  public String sayIt()
  {
    return "Hello World from SayHello";
  }
}
```

The `sayIt` method returns another class, `String`. `String` is one of the classes included with Java. (See the Java documentation for details.) A class can have a special method named `main`. This `main` class is what the java program looks for to start a program running. Look at the HelloWorld code:

```
package chapter16;
import chapter16.SayHello;


public class HelloWorld
{

  public HelloWorld()
  {
    SayHello sayHello = new SayHello();
    System.out.println(sayHello.sayIt());
  }
  public static void main(String[] args)
  {
    HelloWorld helloWorld1 = new HelloWorld();
  }
}
```

Notice the `main` function. When you use java to run this program, the `main` function creates an instance of HelloWorld. A class doesn't need a `main`—SayHello doesn't have one—unless the class will be used to launch a program. This makes the code in Java more prone to reuse, because each individual class compiles independently of the other classes. You can build and test a class like SayHello and use it from any number of other classes. Once built and tested, SayHello doesn't have to be recompiled when the calling classes change.

Java also allows you to group code into packages. Note the package statements at the top of both the sample classes. This creates a package named *chapter16* that contains both classes. This also enables you to have a different class with the same name as HelloWorld in a different package. To reach one, you would type **chapter16.HelloWorld,** and the other could be `chapter17.HelloWorld`. If you wind up using Java on a large project, you will find packages a useful concept.

Java Arrays

Java arrays are an 'N' dimensional collection of variables. An array is declared like this:

```
int myArray[] = new int[20];
```

Notice how the new keyword is used to allocate space for the new array. The elements of an array are accessed using brackets ([ ]):

```
myarray[1] = 1;
```

Multidimensional arrays are allowed:

```
int myarray[][][] = new int[5][5][5];
myarray[1][1][1] = 3;
```

Arrays in Java are zero based. This means that if you declare an integer array with a size of 10, the first value is accessed using

```
myarray[0]
```

The last element is accessed with this:

```
myarray[9]
```

Unlike C, Java doesn't let you put more into your array than it can hold. If, in the preceding array, you did something like this:

```
myarray[10] = 4;
```

the compiler would create the class file, but your program would throw an error saying that the array is out of bounds:

```
java.lang.ArrayIndexOutOfBoundsException
        at chapter16.HelloWorld.<init>(HelloWorld.java:19)
        at chapter16.HelloWorld.main(HelloWorld.java:25)
Exception in thread "main"
```

Java Vectors and Hashtables

I don't often use arrays when I program in Java because two classes in Java, named *Vector* and *Hashtable*, are easier to work with and provide more functions. When you use an array, you have to declare its size, and as you have just learned, if you exceed the size, an error is thrown. Often you don't know how big something is until the program is running. The Vector class gives you array-like functions without array-like problems.

A Vector is created with a line like this:

```
Vector myVector = new Vector();
```

New members are added using the Vector's `addElement` and are fetched using the get command. As elements are added to and deleted from a Vector, it allocates and deallocates its own memory, freeing you from having to know how many things will need to be in your Vector.

The Hashtable class takes the vector concept and expands it to include a key value. This is very much like the associative array in Tcl.

Methods and Variable Scope

Writing a method in Java is straightforward. You have already seen an example of a method, `sayIt`, in the SayHello class. In Java, methods must be part of a class and have the following general syntax:

```
Visibility Returnvalue procedurename(variabletype variable name,
                              variabletype variablename...)
{ Statement;
Statement;
}
```

The visibility tag determines whether the method is available outside the class. Declaring a method as *public* makes that method available to anyone creating an instance of that class. Refer to the SayHello class for an example of a public method. A *private* method is available only inside a class—for example:

```
package chapter16;

/**
 * Title:        Hello World Project for Chapter 16
 * Description:
 * Copyright:    Copyright (c) 2000
 * Company:
 * @author Jeff Perkins
 * @version 1.0
 */

public class PrivatePublic
{

  public PrivatePublic()
  {
  }
  public static void main(String[] args)
  {
    PrivatePublic privatePublic = new PrivatePublic();
    System.out.println(privatePublic.doubleMe(4));
```

```
  }
  private int addTwo(int arg1, int arg2)
  {
    return arg1 + arg2;
  }
  public int doubleMe(int arg1)
  {
    return addTwo(arg1, arg1);
  }
}
```

Here the public method, doubleMe, calls the private method, addTwo. Running the program will print out *8*. Any other class trying to call the addTwo method will generate an error.

The Java language mandates that all variables be declared. You cannot get past the compile stage without declaring all the variables used in your program or function. Variables declared inside a function are visible only inside that function. Here is an example:

```
package chapter16;


/**
 * Title:        Hello World Project for Chapter 16
 * Description:
 * Copyright:    Copyright (c) 2000
 * Company:
 * @author Jeff Perkins
 * @version 1.0
 */


public class PrivatePublic
{
  static String PackageName = new String("chapter16");
  public PrivatePublic()
  {
  }
  public static void main(String[] args)
  {
    String myLocation = new String("In main");
    System.out.println(PackageName + myLocation);
```

```
    System.out.println(firstFunction());
    System.out.println(secondFunction());
  }
  static private String firstFunction()
  {
    String myLocation = new String("In firstFunction");
    return PackageName + myLocation;
  }
  static public String secondFunction()
  {
    String myLocation = new String("In secondFunction");
    return PackageName + myLocation;
  }
}
```

In this program, the same variable name, myLocation, is used in three functions. In addition, the variable PackageName is declared in the class but outside the functions. This makes PackageName global to the functions in PrivatePublic. Running the program produces

```
[root@laura java]# javac ./chapter16/PrivatePublic.java
[root@laura java]# java chapter16.PrivatePublic
[root@laura java]# chapter16In main
[root@laura java]# chapter16In firstFunction
[root@laura java]# chapter16In secondFunction
```

This shows that the variable PackageName is visible in all three functions, whereas the String myLocation, even though it has the same name, is unique to each function.

Control Structures

The Java language has five types of control structures: if, for, do, while, and switch.

The if Statement

The if statement has three forms:

```
if ( <condition> )
{
  <statement1>;
}
```

or

```
if ( <condition> )
{
  <statement1>;
}
else
{
<statement2>;
}
```

or

```
if ( <condition> )
{
  <statement1>;
}
else if
{
<statement2>;
}
```

The if statement is straightforward. It must have an expression to evaluate and statements to execute if the expression is true. An if statement can also contain an else clause. If the expression evaluates to true, the statements contained in the braces after the then keywork are executed. If there are no braces, only the next statement is executed.

Forgetting to use the braces to enclose all the statements you want to run if the condition is true is a common cause of logic errors in Java. I recommend using braces to enclose every if and else clause. Your code will be more readable, and you will avoid this class of logic errors.

If the expression evaluates to false, and there is an else clause, the statements between the braces after the else are executed. Here is a simple example.

The third form of if shows that an if statement can be embedded in an else. In this case, only one of the clauses is evaluated, and the rest are skipped. Here is an example:

```
String testif (int x
{
```

```
String retval = new String(;
if (x > 0)
{
   retval = "Positive";
}
else if(x < 0)
{
   retval = "Negative";
}
else
{
   retval = "Zero";
}
return retval;
}
```

This function returns the value "Positive" if the given number is greater than zero and "Negative" if the value is less than zero. Otherwise, it returns "Zero".

The for Statement

The syntax of the for in the Java language is

```
for ( [<initialization>] ; [<condition>] ; [<increment>] )
{
   <statement>
}
```

The following example shows how this works:

```
void testfor(int x)
{
   int i;
   for (i=0;i <= x; i=i+1)
{
      System.out.println( "The variable i is %d" + i);
}
}
```

When this function is called, it prints out the value of i as it moves from 0 to the value of x. If x is negative, nothing is printed.

The do's and while's

The keywords `do` and `while` can be combined two different ways. The first is

```
Do
{
 statement
}while ( condition );
```

This results in a loop that will be executed at least once and until the condition is true. The second way, the while on top without a do, results in a loop that may not be executed if the expression is false upon the first evaluation:

```
While( expression)
{
 statement;
}
```

In this second form, if the expression is true upon its first evaluation, it will execute until the statement becomes false. Be careful with these statements. A logic error, such as using `i++` instead of `i--`, can result in an ending condition that is never reached. Here is an example of the `while`:

```
int i = 5;
    while(i > 0)
    {
      System.out.println(i);
      i--;
    }
```

The switch Statement

The Java language contains a very straightforward switch control structure. The Tcl switch control structure allows you to take actions based on an exact character match. The syntax is

```
switch (variable ){
  case varvalue :
    statement;
  break;
  case varvalue :
    statement;
```

```
    break;
  default:
    statement;
}
```

This `switch` statement is not as flexible as the Tcl switch. Remember, the Tcl `switch` statement can use strings and pieces of strings to route execution to a particular case. (Review Chapter 11, "Programming with PL/Tcl and Tcl," for details.) The C `switch` statement routes execution based on the value of a single character. If no cases match, execution is routed to the optional default statement. Here is an example:

```
void testswitch(char x)
{
  switch x
{
    case 'M':
    case 'W':
    case 'F':
      System.out.println("English and History" );
      break;
    case 'T':
      System.out.println ("Tennis and Golf");
    break;
    default :
     System.out.println ("nothing scheduled");
  }/* end switch x */
}
```

This function prints *"English and History"* if passed the characters M, W, or F. Notice how the `break` statement is absent from the M and W cases. A case that matches the `switch` without a `break` will execute its own statement and every subsequent statement until a `break`, the default case, or the end of the `switch` statement is encountered.

Dealing with Data: JDBC Classes

Because Java is not one of the languages currently enabled by PostgreSQL for stored procedures, there is only one way to interface with data, via the JDBC. These classes are provided with your PostgreSQL setup. On a Red Hat system, they are normally found in the /usr/lib/pgsql/ directory. The JDBC classes are stored in a jar file (named *jdbcX.X-X.jar*, where the *X*'s represent the version of

PostgreSQL). For your example, you will use jdbc7.0-1.2.jar, the most current JDBC classes as of this writing. The JDBC classes allow you to:

- Connect to the database
- Execute a query
- Manipulate data
- Close the database

Here is a program that shows the basics:

```java
package chapter16;


/**
 * Title:        Hello World Project for Chapter 16
 * Description:
 * Copyright:    Copyright (c) 2000
 * Company:
 * @author Jeff Perkins
 * @version 1.0
 */
import java.sql.*;
public class DataBase
{
  static private Connection conn = null;
  private String usr = new String();//User Name
  private String pwd = new String();//Password
  private String url = new String();//URL
  private String query = new String();//Query

  public DataBase(String theUrl, String theUser, String thePwd, String theQuery)
  {
    //Register the database class
    try
    {
      Class.forName("org.postgresql.Driver");
      usr = theUser;
      pwd = thePwd;
      url = theUrl;
      query = theQuery;

    }
```

```
  catch(Exception e)
  {
    System.out.println(e.toString());
  }


}
public static void main(String[] args)
{
  if(args.length == 4)
  {
    DataBase db = new DataBase(args[0], args[1], args[2], args[3]);
    db.dbInit();
    if(isConnected())//We have a connection
    {
      db.manipulateData();
    }
    db.dbClose();
  }
  else //Not enough arguments
  {
    System.out.println("Usage:  URL usr pwd query");
  }
}
//Connect to the Database
private void dbInit()
{
  //URL is jdbc:postgresql://host/database or
  //jdbc:postgresql:database or
  //jdbc:postgresql://hostport/database
  try
  {
    if(conn != null)//If we have a connection, close it
    {
      conn.close();
      conn = null;
    }
    //Make the connection
    conn = DriverManager.getConnection(url,usr,pwd);
  }
```

```java
    catch(Exception e)//Oops, something happened
  {
    System.out.println(e.toString());
    //Set database back to null so that we know we have no connection
    conn = null;
  }
}
//Close the connection
private void dbClose()
{
  try
  {
    if(conn == null)//If we have a connection, close it
    {
      conn.close();
      conn = null;
    }
  }
  catch(Exception e)//Oops, something happened
  {
    System.out.println(e.toString());
    //Set database back to null so that we know we have no connection
    conn = null;
  }
}
//Manipulate the Data
private void manipulateData()
{
  try
  {
    DatabaseMetaData metaData = conn.getMetaData();
    System.out.println("Database Product is "
      + metaData.getDatabaseProductName());
    Statement statement = conn.createStatement();
    ResultSet result = statement.executeQuery(query);
    ResultSetMetaData rMetaData = result.getMetaData();
    int numOfColumns = rMetaData.getColumnCount();
    for(int i = 1;i < numOfColumns;i++)
    {//Print column names
      System.out.print(rMetaData.getColumnName(i) + " |");
```

```
      }
      System.out.println();//Line Feed
      //Print out Data
      while(result.next())
      {
        for(int i = 1;i < numOfColumns;i++)
        {//Print column values
          System.out.print(result.getString(i) + " |");
        }
        System.out.println();//Line Feed
      }
    }
    catch(Exception e)
    {
      System.out.println(e.toString());
    }
  }
  //Test to see if the database is connected
  static private boolean isConnected()
  {
    boolean retval = false;
    if(conn != null)
    {
      retval = true;
    }
    return retval;
  }
}
```

Now compile it:

```
[perkins@laura java]$ javac ./chapter16/Database.java
```

Now run it:

```
[perkins@laura java]$ java chapter16.Database
-classpath /usr/lib/pgsql/ jdbc7.0-1.2.jar jdbc:postgresql://laura.perkinsfamily/
perkins perkins *******
"select * from address"
Database Product is PostgreSQL
nickname |street |state |zipcode |
Tyler |567 Doggy Heave |FL |34444 |
```

```
Leslie |1313 MBird Lane |CA |95555 |
Laura |Rt 66 |AZ |55555 |
Kelly |1010 Pudder Ln |FL |77555 |
Ruth |4624 Minn |CA |88888 |
Alton |1872 Waco |TX |45454 |
Valerie |555 Dodah Dr |FL |99955 |
Jeff |555 Dodah Dr |FL |99955 |
Jeff |1600 Penn |FL |55599 |
Puder |1456 Old Rd |FL |8990 |
```

First, the function initDB checks whether it can find org.postgresql.Driver. This class is contained in the JDBC jar file and referenced by the `-classpath` option used with the java program. When the class is found, a connection is attempted using the arguments passed in on the command line via the args array in the main function. If the connection is successful, `manipulateData` is called. In `manipulateData`, you first get some general database information by creating a `DatabaseMetaData` instance. `DatabaseMetaData` contains dozens of potential useful functions for extracting data about the database. In this example, you get the database type, PostgreSQL, and print it out. Then the query is executed and the results placed in a `ResultSet` object. From the `ResultSet` object, you get a `ResultSetMetaData` object that is used to print out the column names from the query. `ResultSetMetaData` also has dozens of useful functions for data about the results of the query. Then the ResultSet is used to print out the data values.

After you are done manipulating the data, the connection is closed.

This example covers about 95 percent of the data needs of your average stand-alone Java program.

Summary

Thousands of pages in hardcopy books and online articles cover the topics of object-oriented programming and Java. I don't have enough space and time here to cover either topic in sufficient detail to make you proficient. This chapter is intended as an introduction to Java in the PostgreSQL environment. The information here is enough for experienced Java programmers to find a starting point for using PostgreSQL in Java-based applications. Those new to Java should now understand the basic structure of Java and what it brings to the PostgreSQL arena.

Aside from the basics of Java, this chapter shows by example how to connect to the database from a stand-alone Java program. There are several Java resources you can pursue, starting with javasoft.com, Sun's Java site. If you want to try programming in Java and don't want to spend any money for tools, download JBuilder Foundation from http://www.borland.com or NetBeans, an open-source Java programming environment found at http://www.netbeans.org. Both programs are free, and both contain tutorials and help files enough to get you started.

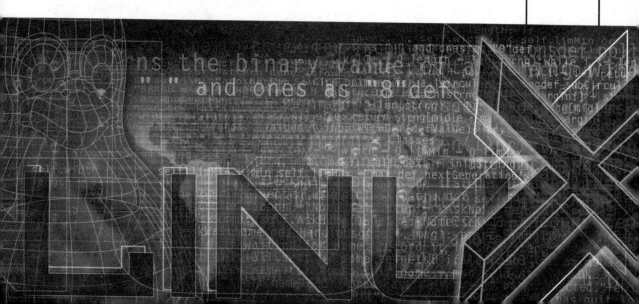

Chapter 17: Advanced PostgreSQL Data Types

his chapter covers the advanced data types found in PostgreSQL. What is an advanced data type? One definition would be anything not covered in Chapter 9, "Basic PostgreSQL Data Types and SQL Functions." Another would be those data types that are not normally used in day-to-day work but have definite value for certain applications. In this chapter, I cover date and time, geometric, and IP data types. For each type, there is an example of a table created using the selected data type, followed by an example of inserting the various data type values into the table, topped off by examples of the data type–specific functions. This will give you enough to understand how these advanced data types can be use to solve your programming problems.

Date and Time Data Types, Variables, and Functions

In Tables 17.1 through 17.3, you can examine PostgreSQL date and time data types, variables, and functions.

Creating a Table

Create a table, with two of each data type:

```
create table "timetest" ("date1" date,"date2" date,"interval1" interval,"interval2"
interval,"timespan1" timespan,"timespan2" timespan,"time1" time,"time2" time)
```

Put another way, the table looks like this:

```
perkins=# \d timetest
        Table "timetest"
 Attribute |   Type   | Modifier
-----------+----------+----------
 date1     | date     |
 date2     | date     |
 interval1 | interval |
 interval2 | interval |
 timespan1 | interval |
 timespan2 | interval |
 time1     | time     |
 time2     | time     |
```

Table 17.1   PostgreSQL Date and Time Data Types

Type	Function
timestamp	Stores date and time information for dates between 4713 B.C. and 1465001 A.D. If the time zone is included, the dates are between 1903 A.D. and 2037 A.D.
interval	Represents the time elapsed between two points in time. Can be between -178,000,000 and 178,000,000 years.
date	Stores date information without time-of-day information, from 4713 B.C. to 32727 A.D
time	Stores the time of day from 00hr 00min 00.00sec to 23hr 59min 59.99sec, with or without a time zone

Table 17.2   PostgreSQL Built-in Time Variables

Variable	Description
current	The current date and time
epoch	The date 1970-01-01 00:00:00+00, the first of January, 1970, Greenwich Mean Time (GMT)
infinity	A date and time later than any other time, useful for comparisons
-infinity	A date and time earlier than any other time, useful for comparisons
now	The current date and time, same as *current*
today	Midnight of the current day
tomorrow	Midnight of the day after the current day
yesterday	Midnight of the day before the current day

Table 17.3   Time-Related PostgreSQL Functions

Function	Description
abstime(timestamp)	Returns an internal data type of absvalue from the given timestamp object. The PostgreSQL documentation warns against using the internal data types because they are subject to change and can even disappear.
age(timestamp)	Returns an interval object representing the time between the current day and the epoch constant
age(timestamp,timestamp)	Returns an interval object representing the time between the given timestamps
date_part(text,timestamp)	Returns a float8 representing the part of the timestamp given in text. For example, `'hour' now,` would return the hour.
date_part(text,interval)	Same as above, only it operates on interval objects
date_trunc(text,timestamp)	Returns a timestamp object accurate to the element given in the text variable. If the year is specified, the year will be accurate, but all elements after the year will be zero.
interval(reltime)	Creates an interval object from the internal data type reltime. A reltime data type expresses time in relative terms, such as `'5 min'` or `'6 hours'`. The PostgreSQL documentation warns against using the internal data types; they are subject to change and can even disappear.
isfinite(timestamp)	Returns boolean true if the given timestamp is not infinite
isfinite(interval)	Returns boolean true if the given interval is not infinite
reltime(interval)	Converts an interval object to the internal data type reltime. The PostgreSQL documentation warns against using the internal data types because they are subject to change and can even disappear.
timestamp(date)	Converts a date object to a timestamp object
timestamp(date,time)	Combines the given date and time into a timestamp object
to_char(timestamp,text)	Converts the given timestamp object to a text data type, using the format contained in the text variable

Now, populate the table:

```
insert into "timetest"
("date2","date1","interval1","interval2","time1","time2","timespan1","timespan2")
values ('17 Jan 1979','30 May 1982','5 Days 4 Hours','7
Days','16:00:45.99','23:34:55.34','March 21, 1921 07:00:01.30','19230219 08:09:00')
```

Write a new function, also named chartypes, as

```
perkins=# select abstime(timestamp 'current');
        abstime
------------------------
 2001-05-08 00:44:45-05
(1 row)


perkins=# select abstime(timestamp 'now');
        abstime
------------------------
 2001-05-08 00:44:58-05
(1 row)
perkins=# select age(timestamp 'epoch');
          age
------------------------
 31 years 4 mons 7 05:00
(1 row)
```

Notice how the 'now' and 'current' functions do the same thing. Let's see how old I am right now:

```
perkins=# select age(timestamp 'now', timestamp '15 May 1955');
            age
-----------------------------
 45 years 11 mons 24 00:57:44
(1 row)
```

Could be worse. Now, try the date_trunc function:

```
perkins=# select date_trunc('year', timestamp 'now');
      date_trunc
------------------------
 2001-01-01 00:00:00-06
(1 row)


perkins=# select date_trunc('day', timestamp 'now');
```

```
        date_trunc
------------------------
 2001-05-08 00:00:00-05
(1 row)


perkins=# select date_trunc('min', timestamp 'now');
        date_trunc
------------------------
 2001-05-08 01:04:00-05
(1 row)
```

Notice that the time zone indication (-5) at the end of the timestamp isn't zeroed out. Finally, combine some data from the table:

```
perkins=# select timestamp(date1, time1) from timetest;
        timestamp
-------------------------
 1982-05-30 16:00:45.99-05
(1 row)
```

See how the `timestamp` function combines the data. This table has only one row. If there were multiple rows of data, there would be multiple returns.

Geometric Data Types and Functions

Geometric data types are built to hold descriptions of several basic geometric shapes. Table 17.4 lists the PostgreSQL geometric data types.

PostgreSQL has built in Geometric functions, listed in Table 17.5. These functions keep you from reinventing the wheel if your problem set involves geometry.

Creating a Table with Geometric Data Types

Create a Noah's Ark table, with two of each data type:

```
create table "geotest" ("point1" point,"point2" point,"box1" box,"box2"
box,"circle1" circle,"circle2" circle,"line1" line,"line2" line,"lseg1"
lseg,"lseg2" lseg,"path1" path,"path2" path,"polygon1" polygon,"polygon2" polygon)
```

Put another way, the table looks like this:

```
perkins=# \d geotest
        Table "geotest"
```

Table 17.4   PostgreSQL Geometric Data Types

Type	Description
point	`(x,y)`. Single point.
line	`((x1,y1),(x2,y2))`. A line passing through the given points, not yet implemented as of PostgreSQL version 7.03.
lseg	`((x1,y1),(x2,y2))`. Same syntax as *line*, but represents the segment between the first and last point.
box	`((x1,y1),(x2,y2))`. Again, the same syntax as *line* and *lseg*, but with a box, each pair is an opposite corner. Any two opposite corners can be entered, but when the box type is printed out, the order is lower-left corner followed by upper-right corner.
ath	`((x1,y1),...(xn, yn))`. This syntax forms a closed path, where the first and last points are connected. If outer brackets are used, as in `[(x1,y1),...(xn, yn)]`, the path is open—the start and end points are not connected.
polygon	`((x1,y1),...(xn, yn))`. Same syntax and same result as a closed path.
circle	`((x1,y1),r)`. The center and radius of a circle.

```
Attribute | Type   | Modifier
----------+--------+----------
point1    | point  |
point2    | point  |
box1      | box    |
box2      | box    |
circle1   | circle |
circle2   | circle |
line1     | line   |
line2     | line   |
lseg1     | lseg   |
lseg2     | lseg   |
path1     | path   |
path2     | path   |
polygon1  | polygon |
polygon2  | polygon |
```

Table 17.5   Geometric Functions

Function	Description
area(object)	Returns a float8 representing the area of a given shape (box, circle, polygon). (I would like to have had this function in my high school geometry class.)
box(box, box)	Returns a box object that is the intersection of the given boxes.
center(object)	Returns a point object representing the center of a given shape (box, circle, polygon).
diameter(circle)	Returns a float8 representing the diameter of the given circle.
height(box)	Returns a float8 representing the height of the given box.
isclosed(path)	Returns boolean true if the given path is closed (a path created with outer parentheses, ' ( ) ').
isopen(path)	Returns boolean true if the given path is open (a path created with outer brackets, ' [ ] ').
length(object)	Returns a float8 representing the length of a given shape
pclose(path)	Returns a closed path created from the given path
npoint(path)	Returns an int4 representing the number of points in a path
popen(path)	Returns an open path created from the given path
radius(circle)	Returns a float8 representing the radius of the given circle
width(box)	Returns a float8 representing the width of the box

The line data type had not been implemented at the time this book was written. The database allows you to create a column with a line type but doesn't allow points to be entered. PostgreSQL throws a *Line not yet implemented* error.

Now, populate the table:

```
insert into "geotest" ("point1","point2","box1","box2","circle1","circle2","lseg1",
"lseg2","path1","path2","polygon1","polygon2") values ('(1,1)','(2,2)',
'((3,3)(10,10))','((4,4)(11,11))','((4,4),3)','((5,5),1.5)','((3,3),(8,8))','((4,5),(7,3))',
'((1,2),(3,4),(4,5))','[(1,2),(3,4),(5,6)]','((1,2),(3,4),(5,6))','((7,8),(9,10),(11,12))')
```

I added a second row of data for the `box1` column. Find the area of the boxes described in the `box1` column:

```
perkins=# select box1 from geotest;
     box1
--------------
 (10,10),(3,3)
 (10,20),(3,8)
(2 rows)
perkins=# select area(box1) from geotest;
 area
------
   49
   84
(2 rows)
```

Now, see whether these boxes intersect:

```
perkins=# select box1, box2 from geotest;
     box1      |     box2
---------------+--------------
 (10,10),(3,3) | (11,11),(4,4)
 (10,20),(3,8) | (11,15),(6,4)
(2 rows)
perkins=# select box(box1,box2);
ERROR:  Attribute 'box1' not found
perkins=# select box(box1,box2) from geotest;
        box
--------------------
 (7.5,7.5),(6.5,6.5)
 (8.5,14),(6.5,9.5)
(2 rows)
```

If you pulled out the graph paper and plotted out the boxes, you would see that PostgreSQL got the intersection right. Now, work with some circles:

```
perkins=# select circle1 from geotest
perkins-# ;
  circle1
-----------
 <(4,4),3>
 <(14,45),3>
```

```
(2 rows)


perkins=# select radius(circle1) radius, diameter(circle1) diameter from geotest
;
ERROR:  parser: parse error at or near "radius"
perkins=# select radius(circle1) as radius, diameter(circle1) as diameter from g
eotest;
 radius | diameter
--------+----------
      3 |        6
      3 |        6
(2 rows)
```

I do map-related projects from time to time, and these PostgreSQL functions are a great timesaver for many common map-related programming problems.

IP Types and Functions

PostgreSQL offers two data types dedicated to TCP/IP address storage.

- **cdir.** Stores an IP address description of an entire network as with from one to four groups of numbers, with or without a netmask. For example, both 192 and 192/8 represent all the IP addresses possible that start with *192*.
- **inet.** Stores a specific host name and netmask information. For example, 192.168.0.1/24 stores the IP address 192.168.0.1 and also stores the netmask of 255.255.255.0. If no netmask is indicated, a netmask of 255.255.255.255 is assumed.

IP data type functions are

- **broadcast(object).** Returns a text object representing the broadcast address of the given cidr or inet object.
- **host(inet).** Returns a text object representing the host address derived from the inet object.
- **masklen(object).** Returns an `int4` representing the length of the given cidr or inet object.
- **netmask(inet).** Returns a text representation of the netmask for the given intet object.

Create a table, with two of each data type:

```
create table "iptest" ("inet1" inet,"inet2" inet,"cidr1" cidr,"cidr2" cidr)
```

Put another way, the table looks like this:

```
perkins=# \d iptest
        Table "iptest"
 Attribute | Type | Modifier
-----------+------+----------
 inet1     | inet |
 inet2     | inet |
 cidr1     | cidr |
 cidr2     | cidr |
```

Now, populate the table:

```
insert into "iptest" ("inet1","inet2","cidr1","cidr2") values ('10.11.12.13/
16','192.168.247.0/24','10.11','192.168.247')
```

Start by making some broadcast addresses for each IP type:

```
perkins=# select inet1, cidr1 from iptest;
     inet1       |  cidr1
-----------------+----------
 10.11.12.13/16  | 10.11/16
(1 row)
perkins=# select broadcast(inet1), broadcast(cidr1) from iptest;
   broadcast   |   broadcast
---------------+---------------
 10.11.255.255 | 10.11.255.255
(1 row)
```

Notice how you wind up with the same result from the different notations. Now, get a netmask:

```
perkins=# select inet2 from iptest;
      inet2
------------------
 192.168.247.0/24
(1 row)
perkins=# select netmask(inet2) from iptest;
    netmask
---------------
 255.255.255.0
(1 row)
```

Finally, find a host address from one of the inet columns:

```
perkins=# select host(inet1) from iptest;
    host
------------
 10.11.12.13
(1 row)
```

Remember, if your table has more than one row, you will get multiple results.

Summary

These data types are good examples of what can be done with an open source data type. Using the C language to create timesaving extensions to the database to solve networking, geometric, and time-related problems is much harder in a proprietary database. If you don't wind up using these data types and functions directly, use them as templates to mold PostgreSQL into the best possible tool for solving your problems.

Chapter 18: Inheritance and Advanced Arrays

tructured Query Language (SQL) is the foundation of all modern databases, including PostgreSQL. SQL provides the industry standard that allows databases and programming languages to interoperate. Because of its basic structure, SQL is easy for most programmers to learn. However, this basic structure can also be a drawback, forcing a programmer to work around SQL's limitations to solve complex problems. The PostgreSQL database has extended standard SQL to include both the object-oriented concept of inheritance and the advanced programming function of arrays.

In this chapter, you will see how these two concepts work in PostgreSQL. I will also discuss some of the pro's and cons of using these extensions to SQL.

Tables, the Object-Oriented Way

The object-oriented approach to programming mimics the real world by assigning values and methods to objects. Objects can be used to break up the complexity of a task into small, easily understandable units. Object-oriented programming can also be used to create incredibly complex and impossible-to-maintain code, but that's a topic for another time.

A common object-oriented example is the *dog* object. In general, a dog has four legs and a tail and barks. All dogs can be generalized into a single object that has four legs and a tail and barks. If you were going to make dogs, it would be more efficient to use a general dog template to handle all the basic dog attributes and spend most of your time working out the specific behavior of an individual dog.

Object-oriented programming is just like making dogs, only you use code. You create an object that contains a general approach to a problem, such as sorting values in a table, and use it as a template to host your specific type of sort. The end result is that you spend more time programming the difficult parts of your system and less time cutting and pasting the same function-oriented code again and again.

The object-oriented principle that separates a language such as Java from a language such as Fortran is *inheritance*. Using inheritance, you design a general problem solution and then inherit from it to solve a specific problem.

Here is a PostgreSQL example that illustrates inheritance: In your database career, you will build many Address tables. Everybody, every business, and every item you track with your database has an address. Rather than write three Address tables, you can use PostgreSQL to design one Address table template. Here is an Address template:

```
create table "baseaddress" ("address" text,"city" text,"zip" varchar(5),"zip4" varchar(4))
```

Looks just like any of the dozens of tables you have created during the course of this book. The magic part is the *inherits* keyword. Create a table that uses `baseaddress` as a template:

```
create table "employees" ("fname" text,"lname" text,"position" text) inherits
("baseaddress")
```

Now put some data into `employees`:

```
insert into "employees" ("address","city","zip","zip4","fname","lname","position")
values ('1234 AnyWhere Pl','Fair Oaks','95628','1000','Tice','Jeff','Director')
insert into "employees" ("address","city","zip","zip4","fname","lname","position")
values ('1567 Orange Crate
Dr','Fargo','59234','9000','Robert','Zman','Entertainment Chairman')
```

Note how the fields from `baseaddress` "inherited" and then used, just like any other field in the Employees table. Let's see what is in the table:

```
perkins=# select * from baseaddress;
 address | city | zip | zip4
---------+------+-----+------
(0 rows)
perkins=# select * from employees;
      address        |   city    | zip  | zip4 | fname  | lname |    position
---------------------+-----------+------+------+--------+-------+--------------

 1234 AnyWhere Pl    | Fair Oaks | 95628 | 1000 | Tice   | Jeff  | Director
 1567 Orange Crate Dr | Fargo    | 59230 | 9000 | Robert| Zman  |EntertainmentChairman
(2 rows)
```

Nothing shows up in the base table, which is good because you didn't put anything there. All the data is stored and related in `employees`. You could put data into the `baseaddress` table, but it wouldn't be related to the `employees` table. If you use the inheritance feature of PostgreSQL, I suggest that you use your templates (*parent classes* in object-oriented speak) as templates instead of storage. This keeps your data in one table, making the relationships in your database easier to understand and maintain.

PostgreSQL allows inheritance from multiple tables. In the following example, a new parent table is created and combined with `baseaddress`:

```
create table "extendaddress" ("state" text,"county" text)
create table "schools" ("name" text,"principal" text) inherits
("baseaddress","extendaddress")
```

Add some data:

```
insert into "schools"
("address","city","zip","zip4","state","county","name","principal") values ('2434
Memory Ln','Carmichel','78888','4000','CA','Yolo','John Holst','Mr Hart')
insert into "schools" ("address","city","zip","zip4","state","county","name",
"principal") values ('3200 Dewey Dr','Sacramento','98887','5000','CA','Yolo','Del
campo', 'Mr Brodie')
```

Finally, see where everything went:

```
perkins=# select * from extendaddress;
 state | county
-------+--------
(0 rows)


perkins=# select * from schools;
    address     |    city     |  zip  | zip4 | state | county |   name    | principal
----------------+-------------+-------+------+-------+--------+-----------+------
 2434 Memory Ln | Carmichel   | 78888 | 4000 | CA    | Yolo   | John Holst| Mr Hart
 3200 Dewey Dr  | Sacramento  | 98887 | 5000 | CA    | Yolo   | Del campo | Mr Brodie
(2 rows)
```

At this point, you might be wondering what happens when one of the parent tables changes. If you look at the syntax for ALTER TABLE, you will notice that there is no way to remove a column or change an existing data type. Adding fields is okay:

```
alter table "extendaddress" add column "country" text
```

Dropping a parent table is a different story. Try deleting the parent class:

```
perkins=# DROP TABLE baseaddress;
ERROR:  Relation '19052' inherits 'baseaddress'
```

PosgreSQL makes you drop all the children before the parent table can be dropped:

```
perkins=# DROP TABLE employees;
DROP
perkins=# DROP TABLE baseaddress;
DROP
```

Recall from Chapter 7, "Basic Relational Database Design," the concept of *normalization*—minimizing the number of times a single piece of data is stored in the database. Inheritance seems to violate normalization by having the same data in different tables—until you remember that all you are inheriting is the structure, not the data (assuming that you don't put any data into your base class).

PostgreSQL doesn't have the SQL extension to exploit the concept of inheritance fully. For example, in an object-oriented language, such as Java, you could create a parent class for a group of forms, containing the background color and any company graphics used on each form. You would then inherit from this parent form to make all the forms in your program. If you wanted to change the background color or graphic on all your forms, you would need to make the change only to your parent form. As you have seen, PostgreSQL's extensions to SQL don't yet include the capability to modify the columns or data types in the parent class.

Arrays in PostgreSQL

Most of the programming languages covered in this book, except standard SQL, have arrays. PostgreSQL adds this concept to your SQL toolkit. To create a table that uses arrays, you do something like this:

```
create table "tasks" ("name" text,"duedate" date,"resources" text [ ])
```

This creates the column resources as an array of text. You don't have to provide a size for the array. PostgreSQL takes care of the required memory allocation as you add elements to the array. Inserting elements into the array is done with the aid of braces, as shown in the following:

```
insert into "tasks"("name","duedate","resources"} values {'Project Plan','15 May
2001,'{"Project Manager", "Technical Writer"}'}
insert into "tasks" ("name","duedate","resources") values ('Requirements','21 May
2001','{"Project Manager", "Customer", "Technical Writer"}')
```

Notice how the various members of the team are added to the resources array. Use a select statement to see how all of it is stored:

```
perkins=# select * from tasks;
    name      |  duedate   |                     resources
--------------+------------+----------------------------------------------------
 Project Plan | 2001-05-15 | {"Project Manager","Techical Writer"}
 Requirements | 2001-05-21 | {"Project Manager","Customer","Technical Writer"}
(2 rows)
```

Now select just one element of resources, using the bracket notation common to many languages:

```
perkins=# select resources[1] from tasks;
    resources
-----------------
 Project Manager
```

```
    Project Manager

(2 rows)

perkins=# select resources[2] from tasks;

    resources

----------------

 Techical Writer

 Customer

(2 rows)
```

Finally, to update data in an array, use

```
update "tasks"  set "resources"='{"Project Manager", "Customer", "Technical
Writer", "Programmer"}' where name='Requirements'
```

This kind of related data is normally handled using a separate table with a key, as shown in Chapter 7.

Summary

The PostgreSQL extensions to SQL, implementing inheritance and arrays, provide you with new ways of constructing and accessing your data. If you use inheritance, keep it straightforward and use it as a template. Keep watching the progress of PostgreSQL to see whether further extensions to SQL are developed, improving the current implementation of inheritance.

Beginners might want to stay away from arrays and use the traditional SQL table and key method outline in Chapter 7. On the other hand, if you are primarily a programmer and want to commit your application to a PostgreSQL only database solution, this is a feature you can use.

In general, inheritance and arrays might be just what you are looking for to solve your application problems. On the other hand, those of you new to databases should probably steer clear of these unique features until you are comfortable with the database basics common to most database products.

Chapter 19: Commercial PostgreSQL

The final question to tackle in this book is how to make and save money using PostgreSQL. Database programming is normally the boundary between recreational programmers and professional programmers, so it is very likely that you are interested in how PostgreSQL can improve your cash flow. This brief chapter will explain how PostgreSQL can save you money and be an important part of almost any commercial application.

PostgreSQL is *Open Source* software, an application built by full-time and part-time programmers and placed in the Public Domain. The Open Source family of software includes the various flavors of operating systems built on the Linux framework and the world's most widely used Web server, Apache. In Eric Steven Raymond's widely read discussion of the Open Source software movement, *The Cathedral and The Bazaar*, he shows how Open Source software fits into the commercial world. The full text of this groundbreaking work is available on-line at http://www.tuxedo.org/~esr/writings/cathedral-bazaar/cathedral-bazaar/. If you have any connection to the commercial software business, you need to read this.

Another, often overlooked, effect of Open Source software is the ease of starting a project by using no-cost and low-cost, commercial-grade software. Often, the difference between doing a project and not doing a project is the start-up cost. You can't sell or be paid for a project you don't start. With Open Source software, you can minimize both the time and money required to get started. Start your projects by visiting http://www.sourceforge.org. This site is the home to hundreds of Open Source projects.

One of the hurdles you might have to overcome in selling Open Source solutions is your customer's reliance on brand names. Most software-savvy customers know that support and maintenance often cost more than the original software and that lack of support and maintenance can render any software investment worthless. For example, Red Hat, at http://www.redhat.com, sells and supports an operating system based on Linux. In return for a small price, you get both a very capable operating system and access to support from a dedicated, commercial organization. Red Hat also sells more upscale versions of Linux, tailored to hosting video streaming or the Oracle Database.

PostgreSQL has also spawned companies dedicated to selling and supporting commercial versions of PostgreSQL. The most prominent of these companies is GreatBridge, http://www.greatbridge.com. GreatBridge wants to do for PostgreSQL what Red Hat has done for Linux. Success for these companies will depend in part on how well software developers learn and utilize their products. I don't expect PostgreSQL to take significant market share from the proprietary databases, but I do think that it will power applications where the proprietary databases are too expensive. The power of PostgreSQL, coupled with its low-to-no cost will also create new, data-driven applications in places such as small businesses, churches, schools, universities, and homes.

Using PostgreSQL, you should also be able to compete with the proprietary databases in legacy applications where a proprietary database is overkill. For example, many small local, state, and federal government organizations have paid for proprietary databases to house very small database requirements. By emphasizing PostgreSQL's foundation in industry standards such as SQL, its supportability through organizations such as GreatBridge, and its capabilities, you should be able to compete on a level playing field with many of the large, proprietary database vendors.

Another trend to watch is the increasing number of "black box" solutions being built with Open Source software. Several companies build small office file servers and Internet connection–sharing devices based on Linux. The next wave of black boxes will include financial and time-tracking software using Open Source software to power a plug-and-play solution. For example, you could deliver a complete small office time-sheet program, using PostgreSQL as the database, in a box that users would plug into their network and access via Web browsers. You have seen enough in this book to write most of the software for this kind of system.

Summary

Well, at least it wasn't boring (I hope). You now know where to get PostgreSQL and how to install it. You are also conversant in how to secure and administrate your database. You can spend all day managing data with SQL queries via pgsql or pgaccess. You have working examples of database programming in eight languages and can put your finger on pages that describe how to design and normalize a database. You have seen command-line systems, graphical user interface programs, and Web applications. In this chapter, you see a commercial framework for your future database and programming work. In short, you have seen, and have working examples of, more than a little of everything. Learn the basics, and do lots of examples! Take advantage of a database you can learn on your home computer and then turn around and sell in your application.

A PostgreSQL Resources

B C/C++ Trigger Functions

C More about Tcl

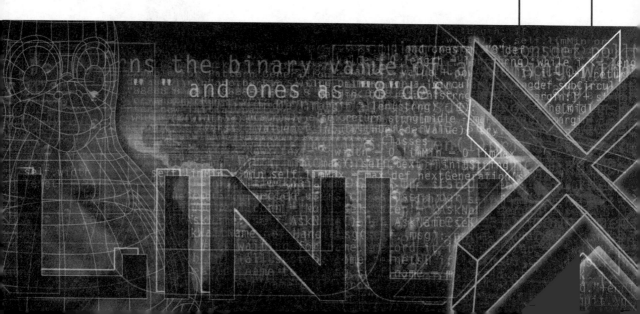

Appendix A: PostgreSQL Resources

Thank these dozen or so sites are the essential starting points for expanding the skills you have learned in this book. Each one of them represents an important technology related to the PostgreSQL system. Each site will also enable you to leverage the skills you learned in this book to other databases and programming languages.

http://www.postgresql.org

This is the site where you can download the latest version or keep up with current developments and trends. If you are (or when you become) an experienced programmer, you might consider becoming part of the team creating PostgreSQL. It's a good way to sharpen your skills, learn new techniques, and meet new friends, all while contributing to an important and useful software project.

http://www.redhat.com

The most popular operating system for the hosting of PostgreSQL is Linux, and at the time of this writing, the most popular commercial Linux venture is Red Hat. Red Hat provides commercial support for the Linux system. The developers at Red Hat work to advance open-source projects full-time while at the same time making money selling support and prepackaged software. (See the paragraph on The Cathedral and The Bazaar in Chapter 20, "Commercial PostgreSQL," for details on this business model.) It's not as tricky as buying eggs for 19 cents and selling them for 5 cents, a la *Catch22*, but Open Source is becoming a viable business model.

http://www.greatbridge.com

Speaking of open-source business models, Greatbridge is doing for PostgreSQL what Red Hat is doing for Linux. GreatBridge sells and supports commercial versions of PostgreSQL, as well as contributing to the PostgreSQL project.

http://www.sourceforge.org

Sourceforge is a good place to start looking for open-source projects.

http://www.freshmeat.com

If you need a piece of software for your Linux system you can usually find it here.

ftp://ftp.gnu.org and http://www.gnu.org

If you need a programming tool, library, or language, you can probably find what you're looking for at one of these sites.

http://www.flex.ro/pgaccesss/

For the graphically inclined or the command line–challenged, there is the pgaccess program, covered in Chapter 5, "Getting Graphical with PostgreSQL, the pgaccess Program." Find it here.

http://www.zeos.dn.ua/eng/

Look here for components compatible with Object-Oriented Pascal.

http://dev.scriptics.com/

A good starting point for all things Tcl. If, after reading Chapter 11, "Programming with Pl/Tcl and Tcl," the Tcl programming language looks like something you can use, set your course for this site.

http://www.php.net/

If you fancy a Web solution, consider PHP, covered in Chapter 14, "Programming with PHP."

http://httpd.apache.org

Visit this site to host your Web application or to use or get involved in many Web-related projects.

http://www.javasoft.com

Many of the Apache programs are Java-oriented. To help understand them and other Java-related technologies, visit this site.

http://www.alphaworks.ibm.com/tech/linuxjdk

This site, along with the Java site listed above, covers or has links to almost every major Java development effort or technology.

http://www.borland.com

Try this site for Java and Object-Oriented Pascal development tools, including JBuilder for Java and Krylix for Object-Oriented Pascal. At the Borland site, you can download a no-cost version of JBuilder—a very capable Java-integrated development environment that runs on Windows and Linux.

Appendix B: C/C++ Trigger Functions

T he trigger functions used in PostgreSQL in C and C++ are dependent on `tg_event`, the seed for all the following. `Tg_event` is passed into the trigger function and can be operated on using the following functions:

- `TRIGGER_FIRED_BEFORE(tg_event)` returns true if the trigger is fired *before* the event takes place.

- `TRIGGER_FIRED_AFTER(tg_event)` returns true if the trigger is fired *after* the event takes place.

- `TRIGGER_FIRED_FOR_ROW(event)` returns true if the trigger is fired for a row event.

- `TRIGGER_FIRED_FOR_STATEMENT(event)` returns true if the trigger is fired for a statement event.

- `TRIGGER_FIRED_BY_INSERT(event)` returns true if the trigger is fired by an insert.

- `TRIGGER_FIRED_BY_DELETE(event)` returns true if the trigger is fired by a delete.

- `TRIGGER_FIRED_BY_UPDATE(event)` returns true if the trigger is fired by an update.

The `tg_relation` variable is a pointer to a structure describing the triggered relation. The file src/include/utils/rel.h contains details about this structure. The interesting bits are `tg_relation->rd_att:`, which describes the relation tuples (*tuples* is an old-school database name for rows), and the pointer `tg_relation->rd_rel->relname`, which returns the relations name. The function `SPI_getrelname(tg_relation)` is used to get a copy of the relations name.

The pointer `tg_trigtuple` points to the tuple(row) where the trigger is fired. If the operation is an insert, this points to the row being inserted. If the operation is a delete, this points to the function being deleted.

When you are in an update operation, the `tg_newtuple` points to the new data for the row. In a delete function, `tg_newtuple` is null.

The `tg_trigger` points to a trigger function, described fully in src/include/utils/rel.h and briefly here for reference:

```
typedef struct Trigger
{
    Oid          tgoid;
    char        *tgname;
    Oid          tgfoid;
    FmgrInfo     tgfunc;
```

```
    int16       tgtype;
    bool        tgenabled;
    bool        tgisconstraint;
    bool        tgdeferrable;
    bool        tginitdeferred;
    int16       tgnargs;
    int16       tgattr[FUNC_MAX_ARGS];
    char     **tgargs;
} Trigger;
```

See Chapter 54 in the PostgreSQL documentation for a complete rundown of the C++ PostgreSQL library, libpq++.

Appendix C: More about Tcl

Tcl is a powerful and full-featured scripting language. It's a very handy tool for manipulating text, but it also does math. Table C.1 lists the TCL math functions.

Table C.1   Tcl Math Functions

Function	Description
abs	Returns the absolute value of a number
acos, asin, and atan	Return arccosin, arcsin, and atan in radians
cos, sin, and tan	return cosine, sin, and tangent in radians
exp	Returns the exponential to the power of e
fmod	Returns a floating-point modulus
int	Converts a value into an integer
log	Returns the natural log
log10	Returns the log base 10 of a number
rand	Returns a random floating-point number between 0 and 1
round	Rounds a number to the next higher number if the decimal portion is greater than or equal to .5
sqrt	Returns the square root of a number

As I said, though, handling text is really Tcl's strong suit. Table C.2 lists the Tcl string functions.

To complement the string functions Tcl has a set of functions to manipulate lists. Table C.3 lists the list functions.

The Tcl chapter covered the basic database functions. Table C.4 provides a list you can use as a reference.

Table C.2   Tcl String Functions

Function	Description
string length	Returns the length of the string
string tolower	Returns a lowercase version of the string
string match pattern string	Returns 1 if the given pattern is in the given string; otherwise, 0
string compare *stringq string2*	Returns -1 if *stringname*1 is less, 1 if it is greater, or 0 if they are equal
string index *stringindex*	Returns the character at position *number* in *stringname*. Zero-based.
string last *string1 string2*	Searches *string2* for a match with *string1*. It returns the index of the last match within *string2* or -1 if there is no match.
string trim *string* [*characters*]	Trims leading or trailing characters from *stringname* that are in [*characters*]. The functions trimleft or trimright trim only the indicated side.

Table C.3   Tcl List Functions

Function	Description
Lsort	Sorts a list
Lsearch	Searches a list
Lindex	Finds the position of a given element in a list
Lreplace	Replaces an element in a list
Lrange	Returns a subset of a list
Llength	Returns the length of a list
List	Returns the elements of a list
Linsert	Inserts elements into a list
Lappend	Appends elements to a list
Join	Joins two lists into one list

Table C.4   Tcl Database Functions

Function	Description
Pg_connect	Opens a connection to the server
Pg_disconnect	Closes the connection to the server
Pg_conndefaults	Returns the available connection options and their defaults
Pg_exec	Sends a query to the database
Pg_result	The object used to manipulate the results of a query
Pg_select	Used to iterate over the results of a SELECT statement
Pg_listen	Used to establish a callback stub for system messages
Pg_lo_creat	Used to create a large object, normally an object containing multimedia data
Pg_lo_open	Used to open a large object, like a file open
Pg_lo_close	Used to terminate contact with a large object, like a file close
Pg_lo_read	Reads a large object, like reading a file stream
Pg_lo_write	Used to write to a large object, like a file stream write
Pg_lo_lseek	Used to establish a particular position on a large object stream
Pg_lo_tell	Returns the current position on a large object
Pg_lo_unlink	Deletes a large object from the database
Pg_lo_import	Imports a large object from an external file
Pg_lo_export	Exports a large object to an external file